Bruce

June 1975

The Witness and I

Consul O. Edmund Clubb
American Consulate General
Shanghai, China, 1940

O. EDMUND CLUBB

The
Witness and I

COLUMBIA UNIVERSITY PRESS
1974 NEW YORK AND LONDON

Library of Congress Cataloging in Publication Data

CLUBB, OLIVER EDMUND, 1901–

THE WITNESS AND I.

AUTOBIOGRAPHICAL.
INCLUDES BIBLIOGRAPHIC REFERENCES.
1. CLUBB, OLIVER EDMUND, 1901–
2. INTERNAL SECURITY—UNITED STATES.
3. LOYALTY-SECURITY PROGRAM, 1947– I. TITLE.
E748.C59A38   353.001'3242'0924 [B]   74-11385
ISBN 0-231-03859-3

To the China Service I Knew

Preface

The fate of Nations is so Precarious and revolutions in
States so often take place at an unexpected moment,
when the hand of power by fraud or flattery, has secured
every Avenue of retreat, and the minds of the Subject
debased to its purpose, that it becomes every well
wisher to his Country, while it had any remains of freedom, to keep an Eagle Eye upon every inovation [*sic*]
and stretch of power, in those that have the rule over us.

SAMUEL ADAMS, "The Rights of the Colinists [*sic*], a
List of Violations of Rights and a letter of Correspondence" (adopted by the town of Boston, Nov. 20, 1772).

The deeper meaning of contemporary events is
sometimes discerned by reference to the past. History
tends to repeat itself, but not exactly; and the variations
may be suggestive of the shape of things to come.

The American nation from its beginnings has shown a
marked ambivalence toward revolution. Although it indeed sanctified its own political upheaval, and has periodically voiced the sentiment that all men might properly
resort to revolution to overturn despotic rule, the United
States has upon occasion denied that professed doctrine by
counterrevolutionary action. Its policies have been both
liberal and illiberal. *liberal = support for revolution?*

It was in line with the illiberal aspect of the national

character that American emotions of fear and hatred, which had been focused during World War I on the foreign foe, were in the postwar period turned, in the light of the Russian Revolution, against those on the domestic scene who might be suspected of thinking to subvert the established political and social order. In prewar grade schools, it had been taught that the early Alien and Sedition Laws were tyrannous and hateful to democratic citizens, but in October 1918 Congress enacted a new sedition law providing that aliens holding objectionable views on economic and political matters might be deported. In 1919–20, by the authority of Attorney General A. Mitchell Palmer, who purported to believe that "a wave of radicalism" was engulfing the country and that extraordinary measures were required for national salvation (read, "the national security"), there occurred the "Palmer raids." They were based upon the concept of guilt by membership (i.e. "association") and were carried out with a general disregard of various basic constitutional safeguards. Several thousand persons were arbitrarily arrested with suspension of the writ of habeas corpus, families were torn apart, and some 700 persons were deported—all in the name of law. World War I had been fought, according to President Woodrow Wilson, "to make the world safe for democracy"; and indeed the dissemination of the doctrine had had a worldwide political impact. But it was easy to see that in the United States itself the meaning of "democracy" was subject to qualification.

The hysteria manifested in the Palmer raids was finally checked, primarily by the efforts of churchmen and a group of courageous lawyers. The artificial domestic "crisis" subsided. The real world crises, brought into being by

failures of Man's governments to accomplish the necessary
tasks of political and economic adjustment of a dislocated
world, continued. In what H. G. Wells called "the Fright-
ening Thirties," the upsurge of the American New Deal
contributed some temporary recovery to a tottering world
economy; but political movements of a type that, though
old, nevertheless seemed to incorporate elements that
were new and powerful took shape in the Japanese invasion of Manchuria, Fascist Italy's conquest of Abyssinia,
and the rise of an exasperated nationalism in Germany. *?*
The democratic millenium had not come; new tyrannies
had appeared.

The totalitarians of Europe reverted to the use of terror
to consolidate their controls, and in organizing their poli-
ties for war discarded certain fundamental human rights
that by the beginning of the twentieth century had won, in *and in*
the Occident, nearly universal acceptance. World War II *the U.S.*
completed the process, begun in World War I, of making *for Blacks*
war total. The humanistic concepts of Christian chivalry *?*
were quite discarded; the standards defined by the Hague
Conventions of 1899 and 1907 were now deemed outmoded. If moral standards were abandoned, the fervor of
religious wars was nevertheless present, fortified by the
sense that democratic civilization was fighting for survival.
From 1941 to 1945, all of our allies were pictured as devoted to a common righteous cause, and good, whereas our
foes were painted as unqualifiedly evil.

Over the coming decades, various shifts of political al-
legiences would prove earlier sentiments of both animos-
ity and friendship to have been more transient than
thought at the time; but the habit of sentimental polariza-
tion persisted. In addition, although the overall concept of

unprincipled total warfare was in due course legally condemned at the Nuremburg Trials, the experience of unbri-
dled brutality continued to wield a baleful influence.
There was the circumstance that the very end of the war
had seen the introduction of atomic warfare; and once it
became possible for Man to annihilate everything, attempts to fix sure limits on the use to which he might put
his new weapons of total annihilation were predestined to
failure.

"Man" — uses it all the time

At that historical moment, the world was in an unusually
unstable condition. World War II effectively marked the
end of empire and political colonialism; but economic in-
equality and domination were left in being and would
come to be aptly defined as neocolonialism. The peoples
of the Third World, released now from *political* colonialism, were bound to aspire to "liberation" from *economic*
colonialism as well. Autocratic domestic rule would promise neither democratic reforms nor—since the autocrats
would be bound to find profit in collaboration with the
neocolonialists—much in the way of economic benefits. It
was nearly inevitable, historically speaking, that revolutionary movements would be mounted against heavily
armed political autocracies with the aim of establishing
one form or another of authoritarian socialism for the purpose of achieving the desired socioeconomic transforma-
tion. And poverty was not readily to be overcome for most
of the concerned peoples of the world's Southern Hemi-
sphere without massive sympathetic assistance from the
richer segments of humanity. The dispossessed would
consequently also develop a demand for a more equitable
distribution of the world's goods *in their entirety.*

The law of human institutions is the law of change; denial of the mutability of those institutions creates a fer-

ment of destructive forces. And the matter was no longer
to be quarantined in some isolated backwoods part of the
globe. The first World War had warned that human organization must change, or humanity would perish; the second advanced that issue to a critical stage. The Reverend
Edmund J. Walsh succinctly described the situation when
he noted that World War II had plunged democracy in
Europe and the United States willy-nilly "into a world
revolution the sequel of which must still be reform,
though late, or disintegration"; but he remarked, in a vein
that showed little optimism, that "man's corruptibility is
every bit as great as his perfectibility." [1]

In sum, the new world situation demanded that the
American national purpose be redefined along humanistic
lines. The challenge facing the United States was to participate in world change and contribute toward giving it intelligent direction, not to thwart revolutions against an an-
achronistic status quo. If history were rejected, and the
problems of a changing nation and a revolutionary world
were delivered over to narrowminded partisans for solution, a dangerous situation was bound to be brought into
being—one of our own making.

Father Walsh's pessimism was justified in the event.
American political fundamentalism, so recently given expression as antifascism, resumed its generic form of an-
tiradicalism. As "Bolshevik Russia" had been regarded as
a revolutionary threat a generation before, now all Communism, and by easy extension revolutionary socialism
too, fell under condemnation as dangerous and inimical to
the proper order of things. "Our" version of political Truth
was threatened; once more, it was deemed that American

[1] Edmund J. Walsh, *Total Power* (New York: Doubleday, 1946), pp. 189,
175.

ideology and military power confronted an irreconcilable antagonist.

In that situation, authoritarian elements succeeded in effecting a deep penetration into the American governmental system. They weakened various basic democratic processes and introduced profound changes into the bureaucratic machinery. Now, in government, given the sweep of the official "anti-Communism" and the frenzies of a partially contrived fear for "the national security," there were instituted new procedures for the close surveillance of government employees; and with the formal identification of a new, ultimate enemy who might totally annihilate us before we might obliterate him there was a progressive militarization of thinking, policies, and processes.

My story is that of one who participated, all too unhappily, in the bleak drama of those times. It recounts an episode in the frenetic hunt for the "disloyal" and for "security risks" in the bureaucracy of the Department of State in particular. The account is limited in main to my own experience, but what happened to me was in basic respects typical of the common pattern, and thus my report can be taken, I feel, as shedding some light on the inner workings of a republican government led to resort to devices of authoritarianism. Given the political and economic state of the world today, and the proven circumstance that authoritarianism feeds upon conditions of "crisis," it is patently not to be taken for granted that there will be full and final recovery in the United States from the aberrations of the past quarter century. All the elements for the eruption of more and larger human crises in the world are present. The new American institutions erected for the nominal— and politically unassailable—purpose of guaranteeing

"loyalty" and providing for "national security" remain in   *yes*
being. The dangerous ideological simplifiers are still at
work in our society. As the nation approaches the perilous
third century of its formal existence, the citizenry are effectively charged with pondering the advice of Samuel
Adams: beware of those rulers who, debasing the minds of
the people to their purpose, would expand their power.
The expansion of oligarchical power can only be at the expense of the citizens' freedom. *Democratic* authority is to
be shared.

———•———

I express my deep appreciation to the many persons
who manifested their understanding and sympathy for me
during my own period of trial; their friendship was a so-
lace and a mainstay. And I acknowledge with profound
feeling the unflagging support given me by my wife
Mariann during that difficult period, and the helpful advice and generous aid she contributed in connection with
the writing of the present volume—which records an experience that was hers as well as mine.

I express my thanks to Random House, Inc., for permission to quote extensively from Whittaker Chambers, *Witness*, copyright©1952 by Whittaker Chambers, Random
House, Inc., and to *Worldview* Magazine for permission to
use elements of my article "Security Risks: National Security and the State Department," as published in its August
1973 issue. I voice appreciation also to William Reuben for
helpful commentary and information on the life and character of Whittaker Chambers.

The extracts from my official dispatches and reports incorporated in this volume are taken from the official dossier of my State Department loyalty-security hearing.

The inconsistencies of usage respecting style and punctuation to be discovered in quotations from the loyalty-security process follow the original text in the official transcript. In a minor surrender to consistency to obviate unnecessary confusion, however, in circumstances where the name of China's ancient metropolis was changed from "Peking" to "Peiping" and then, in 1949, back again, I have used the designation Peking throughout—excepting always where quoted matter may make it Peiping.

O. EDMUND CLUBB
August 1974

Contents

The Witness and I

I

The Cold War and Diplomacy

why open with this quote?

> I believe that it is easier to establish an absolute and despotic government among a people whose social conditions are equal than among any other. I also believe that such a government once established would not only oppress men but would, in the end, strip each man there of several of the chief attributes of humanity.
>
> ALEXIS DE TOCQUEVILLE, *Democracy in America* (ed. by J. P. Mayer and Max Lerner, trans. by George Lawrence)

Before World War II, the United States maintained a well-integrated foreign-affairs establishment, which consisted of the Department of State and the U.S. Foreign Service. We were not a military-minded nation, and there was an unambiguous separation of the military branch from the formulation and implementation of foreign policy. The State Department coexisted with the Departments of War and Navy in a single sedate building on Pennsylvania Avenue, but it retained primary control of the administration of foreign affairs on behalf of the President. There was no thought, in democratic America, that the military might reach out to usurp the civilian foreign-affairs function.

— pre 1945 "democratic" (ref. blacks)

and class
background

The U.S. Foreign Service had prestige, and élan. In 1924 Congress had passed the Rodgers Act, which combined the diplomatic and consular services into a unified Foreign Service; recruitment thereafter was through competitive examinations, and advancement was strictly on the basis of merit. The Foreign Service thus was designed as a "career" branch of government, largely shielded from domestic storms and stresses—and from domestic political influences. In a prizewinning essay of a later date, a Foreign Service officer (FSO) would point up the practical consideration involved:

Without the [permanent] basis as an incentive, the Foreign Service would not often attract men endowed by nature with the ability to succeed in life and therefore able in large measure to choose their own careers. No matter how alluring the opportunities of the Service might be for the achievement of glory and fame, few young men would desire to enter it if their careers might be blasted at any moment by a dismissal having no connection with efficiency and depending merely upon the capricious winds of politics.[1]

In 1924, diplomacy was closely associated in the popular mind with striped pants and formal teas, and the process of selection of U.S. Foreign Service officers was designed to obtain men (and an occasional woman) of high caliber. In my day, if one desired to take the Foreign Service examinations he (or she) had first to present three letters of recommendation from persons of standing in his community. If approved, the applicant was designated to take written examinations, which lasted three days and were of such

[1] George V. Allen, "The Utility of a Trained and Permanent Foreign Service," *American Foreign Service Journal*, XIII, no. 1 (Jan, 1936), 5–7 et seq.

scope and depth that most examinees were regularly eliminated at that stage. Successful candidates were invited to the Department of State in Washington for an oral examination which, delving into both knowledge and personality, further cut down the ranks of aspirants. The few survivors were subject to appointment by the President of the United States, and to confirmation by the Senate, after which one received a commission from the President that, "Reposing special trust and confidence in your Integrity, Prudence and Ability," authorized and empowered the fledgling FSO to have and to hold his office, "and to exercise and enjoy all the rights, privileges and immunities thereunto appertaining, during the pleasure of the President of the United States."

The career Foreign Service, in sum, was made up of men carefully selected and trained as an expert corps—and the American foreign-service establishment ranked high among the professional diplomatic corps of the world powers. In that sense, it was an elite group. ... *in many senses*

There was an exception to be noted: from the beginning of the Republic, American presidents at their pleasure had awarded to amateurs ministerial and ambassadorial posts as political plums, usually in return for services rendered in the domestic arena. Consequently, the men who won the top diplomatic posts were not invariably, or even often, professionals. Yet the career officers were the men who did most of the work. Their duties included dealing with foreign officials, negotiating settlements of issues that might arise in the protection and furtherance of American interests, and keeping the government informed regarding current developments in the foreign areas of their assignment. They provided the raw materials for Washington's formulation of policy, and insofar as their reports and opinions might be given consideration they undoubtedly could *influence* the making of foreign policy, but they exercised no decisive authority in that regard. The field officer's judgment could be ignored—and often was. The final decision-making authority resided with the State Department, and the President.

Within the Foreign Service, there were area specialists—officers who had opted to learn such esoteric languages as Arabic, Turkish, Russian, Japanese, or Chinese. After having acquired the unusual language skill as the result of a special two-year training course, the specialist tended to spend much of his career in the region of his choice. The farther his area of specialization was from the North Atlantic cultural sphere, the more "foreign" was the political atmosphere in which he lived and worked, and the more important were his reports for Washington's understanding of the situation. The easier it was, too, for Washington to greet unpopular estimates with disbelief.

Besides the area specialists, there were the general-service officers, the men concerned with such matters as administration, passports and visas, shipping and seamen. They had their own specialized knowledge, but it was not related to a difficult language or a particular geographic region. They might easily serve in Shanghai for a term, and then go on to Liverpool, Sydney, Buenos Aires, or an African post. In practice, they served worldwide, where needed. Quite naturally, not being concerned with political and economic reporting, they would ordinarily have less understanding of the situation in the country of assignment than did the officer charged with such work. This was especially true in countries distant from the North Atlantic cultural area—China or the Soviet Union,

— why this section on history of foreign service, here?

for example. The general officer often looked on such countries and their peoples with different eyes from the area specialist.

The officer in charge of a diplomatic or consular establishment made annual efficiency reports on his subordinates, and it was largely on the basis of those reports that a man was or was not promoted. Coupled with a system of selection that included recommendation, written and oral examinations, and finally Presidential appointment, that careful annual appraisal provided an adequate guarantee against not only gross incompetence but also the presence of disloyal officers or "security risks." Disloyalty was actually not a practical administrative consideration. It was taken for granted that Moscow could hardly maintain political orthodoxy without periodical purges of its bureaucracy; and the contemporary Japanese campaign against "dangerous thoughts" was viewed as a strange Oriental aberration perhaps not unrelated to an expansive imperialism; but there was no thought, in those halcyon days, that U.S. Foreign Service officers might have to be monitored for signs of heterodox ideology or "un-American" activities.

World War II brought a major expansion of the War and Navy Departments. The State Department, on the other hand, continued in time of war as it had in peace, with little structural change. A variety of autonomous emergency wartime agencies devoted to propaganda, economic warfare, and intelligence sprang into being alongside the three Departments. Those wartime agencies, and the military establishment, came quite naturally to stand in the forefront of relations with our adversaries. "State" was limited to dealing with friends, allies, and neutrals.

In 1944, a development that was ultimately to have great

significance for the functioning of State began in the China war theater. There, the United States was capably represented by seasoned military *and* political observers. Lieutenant General Joseph W. Stilwell, in command of U.S. forces in the China-Burma-India (CBI) Theater and concurrently chief of staff to Chinese Generalissimo Chiang Kai-shek, had more than a decade of experience in the country, spoke Chinese, and knew the people—and the politicians. Ambassador Clarence E. Gauss had served in China even longer; although he did not speak the language, he knew Chinese politics and politicians well. The embassy at Chungking was well staffed with expert China Service officers; and one Japan Service and three China Service officers were attached to Stilwell's staff for political work. Experience and competence were the rule, not the exception.

The U.S. objectives were to win the war against Japan and, at that stage of history, to make some provision for East Asian stability in the postwar era. The weakening Chinese Nationalists obviously offered little potential for contribution to the attainment of either objective. Excepting as they might be able to borrow strength from the United States, they commanded no leverage in the international power structure. Having failed to face up to the nation's economic and social problems, and now overtaken by a war that was beyond their powers (not to mention inclination), they confronted a revolutionary situation. The Chinese Communist revolutionaries for the time being were acting in technical collaboration against the common enemy, Japan. Experienced observers of the Chinese political scene, recognizing both political factions for what they were, harbored no illusions with respect to the future: storms threatened.

The consensus of informed American opinion in the field was that, for increased effectiveness and even survival, the Chinese government needed reform at the top and a broadening of the political base as well. The ruling Kuomintang (KMT) had in fact long before promised to relinquish its one-party dictatorship, but it was patently disinclined to undertake any real sharing of power with the Communists in particular. And the Communists commanded not only bitter memories of past collaboration with the Nationalists, but an expanding armed force that could be fielded for the settlement of future political issues. The American experts judged that the United States would be best advised to maintain an essentially neutral position regarding the unfolding Chinese struggle and thus retain its freedom of action in a changing situation. Instead, circumstances conspired to bring about adoption of an American China policy of one-sided intervention, in open support of Chiang Kai-shek's narrowly based dictatorship. A major Japanese drive of 1944 visited disaster upon the Nationalist forces. Large numbers of Chinese, especially intellectuals, had already been alienated by the regime's inefficiency and corruption; now more citizens despaired. And the transfer of political allegiance to the rising Communists was accelerated. Under pressure of the defeats sustained during the summer, Chiang had agreed in principle to President Franklin D. Roosevelt's proposal that field command of the Chinese forces should be given to General Stilwell.

It was in those circumstances that Major General Patrick J. Hurley in September 1944 arrived in Chungking as President Roosevelt's special envoy. Hurley was charged with promoting "harmonious relations" between Chiang and Stilwell, and with facilitating Stilwell's exercise of command over "the Chinese armies placed under his direction." But Generalissimo Chiang, if he could help himself, was not going to tolerate even an implied challenge to his role as *tsung-ts'ai* (Leader). Now, given the Presidential envoy's vast ignorance of China and of Chinese ways, Chiang found in Patrick J. Hurley an invaluable instrumentality for influencing American policy.

Hurley's primary mission was soon aborted. Chiang demanded that Stilwell be replaced, and Hurley actually supported that position. Stilwell was withdrawn in late October, and Lieutenant General Albert C. Wedemeyer took his place. Ambassador Gauss resigned at the beginning of November, and Roosevelt promptly appointed Hurley to the post. In the service of politics, two prominent China experts had been shelved—and replaced by men largely ignorant of China. The Nationalists' victory over American officials who had been critical of Chinese policies and performance emboldened them to undertake even bigger ventures in the American political arena.

The chief task confronting Hurley, as ambassador, was one to which Chiang Kai-shek had given nominal approval—mediation between the National Government and the Communists, to the end that there might be a political settlement of the issues between the two contending Chinese forces. In the light of history, anyone versed in Chinese affairs would have viewed partisan political professions of both the Nationalists and the Communists with a healthy skepticism. Hurley did not. Early in his mission, Hurley had informed President Roosevelt that he was convinced that "Chiang Kai-shek personally is anxious for a settlement with the so-called Communists." [2] In De-

[2] Hurley telegram to President Roosevelt, November 16, 1944, *Foreign Relations of the United States* (hereinafter referred to as *USFR*) *1944*

cember 1944, in a message to the Secretary of State, he offered his estimate that the greatest opposition to the unification of China came from the "imperialist nations" represented in Chungking by the Dutch, French, British, Canadian, and Australian missions; and, Hurley continued, there were in addition some American military and diplomatic officers "who believe that the present Chinese government will eventually collapse." However, he said, "I have not been impressed by any of the arguments made by the imperialists and other opponents of a unified China. . . ." [3]

The simplistic Hurley approach won little agreement from the China Service officers in the field, but Hurley as principal officer was naturally in a position to incorporate *his* interpretation of Chinese developments into the Chungking Embassy's communications to the State Department. Then, in February 1945, Hurley returned to Washington for consultation. In his absence, Chargé d'Affaires George Atcheson sent the State Department a cable incorporating the views of several of the FSOs on military detail to Wedemeyer's staff—views that differed sharply from Hurley's sanguine estimates of the political situation. In Washington, Hurley charged that his staff had been *disloyal* to him. The broader significance of the charge was clear: in Hurley's view, "loyalty" required that subordinates, regardless of the objective realities, should support him in gross error. By this doctrine, honest dissent was viewed as being out of order.

President Roosevelt upheld Hurley's contention that our

(Washington: U.S. Government Printing Office, 1967), Vol. VI, *China*, pp. 698–700.

[3] Hurley message to Secretary of State, December 24, 1944, *ibid.*, p. 749.

cy Kolko's point — hoping the reason will be brought to bear there, if not here, etc.

China policy should center on support of the National Government. Wedemeyer's Foreign Service contingent was dispersed and removed from China; Atcheson was transferred out of Chungking. Once again China experts, far from being commended for perspicacity and competent performance, had been penalized. The Nationalists' chief American critics in the field had now been silenced. Chiang Kai-shek had effectively enlisted Hurley under the Kuomintang banner, and the American China policy soon came to be fixed in the mold described by one State Department official as " 'blank check' support of the Generalissimo and his one-party (Kuomintang) government." [4]

Speaking about the same time, in April 1945, Hurley expressed views that epitomized his naiveté with respect to the Chinese political scene:

. . . it is a matter of common knowledge that the Communist Party of China supports the principles of Dr. Sun Yat-sen. . . . The three principles are government of the people, by the people, and for the people. All the demands that the Communist Party has been making have been on a democratic basis. . . . The Communist Party of China is supporting exactly the same principles as those promulgated by the National Government of China and conceded to be objectives also of the National Government.[5]

He was wrong on all points, and was thus rendered the more vulnerable to manipulation by the side toward which

[4] Memorandum, Deputy Director of Far Eastern Affairs Edwin F. Stanton to Under Secretary of State Holmes, Apr. 28, 1945, *USFR, 1945*, Vol. VII, *The Far East: China* (Washington, 1969), p. 349.

[5] Senator McMahon, in MacArthur Hearings 1951, U.S. Congress. Senate Committee on Armed Services. *Military Situation in the Far East.* Hearings before the Committee on Armed Services and the Committee on Foreign Relations, U.S. Senate, 82nd Cong. 1st Sess. (Washington: U.S. Government Printing Office, 1951), p. 586.

nor Rhee w/ Noble, or Thieu w/ Graham Martin

he had leaned. Chiang Kai-shek was not the man to let slip so golden an opportunity to harness a great power to his political chariot. Nor did he. As Hurley met increasing frustration in his misguided diplomacy, he became the more firmly committed to maintaining the Kuomintang regime in its position of dictatorial power. But the China Problem was one of social revolution, and there was no possibility of solving it through support of the Nationalist rule against the forces of inexorable change. *The American China policy as formulated during Hurley's ambassadorship for the postwar era was based upon faulty first premises—Hurley's premises.* (*rationality is answer*)

Armed clashes between the two Chinese factions began shortly after V-J Day. In negotiations, the two sides in due course reached a measure of agreement on secondary questions, but none on the substantive issue of the distribution of political power. Chiang, enjoying American support, would not consent to any diminution of the Nationalist authority. The Communists, commanding a strong, disciplined military force, were not prepared to abandon the contest and submit to Nationalist rule. Probably neither side expected any other outcome than breakdown of the political negotiations. Both were playing for time and deploying troops, while engaging in political maneuvers.

Mao, addressing Communist cadres on the subject of the negotiations, disclosed his thinking succinctly: "China's problems are complicated, and our minds must also be a little complicated." Hurley never comprehended the complexity of Mao's mind—or, be it said, of Chiang Kai-shek's. He had no better grasp of the tortuous Chinese political situation. He left Chungking for the United States in late

September 1945, about a year after he had first struck an acquaintance with China.

Beginning in November, the tempo of fighting between the Nationalist and Communist forces increased. From Washington, even through the veil of his ignorance, Hurley could see that the policy—his policy—of all-out support of the Nationalists had failed to bring unity and peace to China. In a letter of November 26 to President Truman, he resigned his position as ambassador.

Hurley made no admission that he had been guilty of egregious errors of judgment in his readings of the Chinese political situation. Instead, he sought to shift the blame for his own failures to the U.S. Foreign Service: "The professional foreign service men sided with the Chinese Communist armed party and the imperialist bloc of nations whose policy it was to keep China divided against itself." Once more, Hurley made no issue of the accuracy of the FSOs' political estimates. For him, those estimates indicated political *preferences* entertained by the reporting officers; and he apparently perceived no incongruity in charging that the alleged culprits were at one and the same time pro-Communist and pro-imperialist.

General George C. Marshall, another military man, succeeded to Hurley's mediatory task in China. Marshall actually succeeded in engineering a truce between the two warring factions within a month after his arrival. But the die had already been cast with respect to America's China policy. Owing in good part to Hurley's efforts, a critical error had been incorporated into our strategy: in a country in full flux of revolution, we had taken sides in a civil war. U.S. military and financial aid continued as during wartime to flow to the Nationalists. Proof of the merit of previous warnings against full American commitment to the Nationalist cause was not long in coming: the Marshall mission failed. In January 1947, Marshall returned to Washington to become Secretary of State.

In the meantime, the State Department had undergone a major metamorphosis. With the war's end, the emergency wartime agencies were indeed disbanded, but many of their functions, and personnel, were transferred to existing governmental departments. State took over the Office of War Information; that organ designed for the dissemination of wartime propaganda was transformed into the United States Information Agency. Parts of the Foreign Economic Administration, and of the Office of Strategic Services (the wartime intelligence agency) were also wedded to State. Under the authority of the Manpower Act of 1946, a large number of personnel were transferred into State and the Foreign Service from emergency wartime agencies and the armed services. In that mushrooming growth, the American foreign affairs establishment lost its integral character and became a conglomerate in which there was now found an important military element.

The introduction of military personnel into State exerted a subtle influence for a change of values in the bureaucracy. Departmental personnel, and Foreign Service officers too, were primarily concerned in their professional capacities with the development and maintenance of friendly relations with other peoples. The concern of military men was contrariwise with "adversary" relationships; armed conflict was their very reason for being. And the appointment of military men in State had the natural (and substantial) disadvantage of sometimes bringing to positions of high authority men who were basically unfamiliar

with the operating procedures of the foreign affairs establishment and unacquainted with its veteran personnel.
The military bent toward authoritarianism, with the parallel requirement of unquestioning obedience from men in
subordinate positions, would in time make itself felt.

The demand for military virtues had grown naturally in
the postwar era. The A-bombing of Hiroshima and Nagasaki in August 1945 had disclosed that the United States
had evolved a new, secret weapon. The victor United
States seemed to bestride the world like a colossus. But,
quite apart from the displeasing course of events in China,
there were various developments elsewhere to the disadvantage of the United States; some of them touched on the
very essence of our world power position. On September
7, 1945, Igor Gouzenko, a Soviet Embassy code clerk in
Ottawa, delivered to the Royal Canadian Mounted Police
documents indicating the existence in Canada of a Soviet
spy ring. Among those involved was a Member of Parlia-
ment and Allan Nunn May, an atomic scientist, whose participation had evidently made it possible for the Soviets to
obtain data regarding the Alamogordo atomic bomb test.

Where American political and military leaders had at
first been confident that the secret of the A-bomb was exclusively American, the uneasy suspicion grew that leak-
ages of information threatened this precious monopoly.
American-Soviet relations had already begun to deterio-
rate. Now something in the nature of a spy scare was
added, to increase the growing alarm respecting Soviet intentions—and capabilities. The U.S. Government tended
naturally to rely even more upon its military arm.

The introduction of military elements into our diplomatic machinery, even the designation of the country's top

military man to be Secretary of State, were thus to be viewed as signs of the time. And in 1947, the Cold War with the Soviet Union—our erstwhile ally against Nazi totalitarianism and Japanese imperialism—formally began. The Truman Doctrine, envisaging the containment of "Communism," was proclaimed; and the Marshall Plan was launched to stave off an economic chaos that might have engendered revolutionary processes in Europe. The decision had been made that Communism had to be stopped, by *any* means available—including use of armed force. A major national effort was now bent toward preparation for military confrontation with a new "enemy."

If, with its assumption of the role of guardian angel for "the free world," the United States had found it desirable to expand its foreign-affairs machinery, the military establishment concurrently had taken on a new importance; and the War Department, assuming the more pacific title of Department of Defense, came to embrace army, navy, and air forces. There was a proliferation of functions, in both State and Defense, to serve the purposes of the Cold War. At the same time, there was organized a National Security Council (NSC)—comprising the President, Vice President, Secretaries of State and Defense, and the Director of the Office of Civil and Defense Mobilization (later, Office of Emergency Preparedness). State was indeed represented on that top-level body, but two features of the arrangement were immediately apparent: there had been a new distribution of foreign-policy responsibility, and the chief concern of the NSC would naturally be the military rather than the diplomatic aspect of "national security." At the same time, there was a rapid expansion of the government's intelligence establishment, with an increased concurrent emphasis on the high necessity of maintaining official secrecy—even about nonsecrets. "National security" became a national shibboleth, and an overriding obsession. In 1947 the Truman Administration set up a loyalty-security program to check on the reliability of governmental employees.

The visceral antipathy toward "Communism," the omnipresent concern with "adversary relationships," and the consequent urge toward intervention in the internal affairs of countries threatened by revolution ("Communism") were compounded by what can only be described as a resurgence of the American sense of "manifest destiny." That drive had taken the United States to the West Coast in the mid-nineteenth century, and to the Western Pacific half a century later. In its unadorned form, it was the urge to dominate political developments, and history. The will to power, however, had struck new roots with the victory over Japan: in Asia, as in Europe, the United States saw itself charged by all that was right and holy to see that things evolved in the pattern of its own orthodoxy. This was the imperial urge; but the age of empire had just ended.

It was in the American moralistic spirit that General Douglas A. MacArthur, in his capacity as virtual proconsul of the defeated enemy, strove to establish a new, idealistic order of things in Japan. Under American inspiration, that country by its new constitution, adopted in 1946, renounced forever, where the United States had never entertained the thought for itself, armaments and the waging of war. In direct contradiction to that idealist approach, in China American aid to the Chiang regime became more "committed" still to martial ends. American assistance in terms of both dollars and military equipment continued to flow to the Nationalists as during the war against Japan; and there was established a Joint U.S. Military Advisory Group at Nanking, at the elbow—and service—of the Nationalists. Washington was no longer encumbered by any need to pretend to neutrality in the Chinese civil war. And Generalissimo Chiang Kai-shek bent his energies, and his lobbying apparatus, to maneuvering the United States into confrontation with the Chinese Communists.

The Chinese Nationalists had won their first big wartime victory in the American political scene in November 1941, when they succeeded in pressuring the Roosevelt Administration into abandoning its project for presenting a proposed *modus vivendi* to the Japanese negotiators at Washington, in favor of handing them a virtual ultimatum instead.[6]

Pearl Harbor followed shortly after, and the later judgment of a not-uninterested observer was that "we went to war with Japan to preserve the independence of China's government." [7]

The taste of victory had whetted the Chinese appetite, and the Nationalists lobbied energetically, and with an effectiveness disproportionate to their weight, in Washington during wartime. The lobbyists at that time were for the most part Chinese—officials, bankers, and the indefatigable Mme. Chiang Kai-shek. China had always had its

[6] See Secretary of State Cordell Hull's testimony, 79th Cong. 2nd Sess., Senate Doc. #244, July 20, 1946, "Report of the Joint Committee on the Investigation of the Pearl Harbor Attack," pp. 36–37; and Cordell Hull, *The Memoirs of Cordell Hull*, 2 vols. (New York: Macmillan, 1948) II, 1081–82.

[7] Alfred Kohlberg, "Delivering China to Russia," *Plain Talk*, January 1947, pp. 16–18.

supporters in the United States, but it was only after the
war that an American China Lobby took form as an open
partisan force.

That Lobby found its leadership among, and drew its
strength from, political figures, businessmen, and a section
of the public media. Sometime Ambassador Patrick J. Hurley contributed to the creation of a feverish political climate when, at the end of 1945, he launched a new blast
against the American foreign affairs establishment with the
charge that "The weakness of the American foreign policy
together with the Communist conspiracy within the State
Department are responsible for the evils that are abroad in
the world today." That statement was a reflection of Hurley's ignorance and frustration, and it was the epitome of
irresponsible conduct on the part of a man who had occupied the position of Ambassador to China—political ap-
pointee though he had been. Hurley's effective charge that
things were going "wrong" in the world because there was
treason in the ranks of American foreign affairs personnel
tended naturally to transform what should have been questions of expertise and judgment into issues of loyalty or
disloyalty to the state—even as he had earlier appraised
the Foreign Service officers' report from Chungking not
for its accuracy but for the authors' "loyalty" to him. The
seeds of McCarthyism had been sown; and a bitter harvest
was to be reaped.

Engagement in the Cold War against Communism introduced a new fever—and new poisons—into the American domestic scene. In important respects, the wartime situation was being reenacted: the United States was
committing itself once more to a crusade against "evil."
This time the enemy was Communism—*a Communism*

viewed as being global and monolithic. The Truman Administration's action in instituting a loyalty-security program in 1947 could only suggest that the danger was at the nation's very gates. The adoption of "anti-Communism" as the order of the day in our foreign policy automatically gave implicit sanction to the Nationalist cause in the Chinese civil war.

Various powerful forces early committed themselves to the Nationalist side. Publisher Henry R. Luce, who when the war ended in victory had predicted that this would be the American Century, with the same evangelical conviction held that the United States should fight Communism, and uphold the rule of Chiang Kai-shek in China. The Luce publications *Time* and *Life* became veritable champions of the Nationalists. But one Alfred Kohlberg, a sometime dealer in Chinese lace, turned out to be one of the most vociferous and vengeful of the lobbyists for the Chinese Nationalists, and against the American foreign affairs establishment. In October 1946, as the Chinese civil war was gathering momentum, he launched a propaganda organ entitled *Plain Talk*. The journal was from its inception openly pro-Nationalist, and at the same time anti-State Department.

Kohlberg hewed persistently to that line over the succeeding years. In May 1948 Kohlberg asked "how many Communist spies are there in the U.S. Foreign Service and in the State Department?" [8] A half year later the same prolific author held that, if it were true that the Chinese National Government then faced imminent defeat, "it would represent the ultimate triumph of American foreign policy," which considered the Chinese Communists not to

[8] "Soviet-American Spy Prodigies," *Plain Talk*, May 1948, pp. 17–21.

be Communists at all but liberals and "agrarian reformers." [9] Various China Service officers in due course came
to be harried by the charge that they viewed the Chinese
Communists as "simply agrarian reformers." Kohlberg
would not have denied himself credit for the achievement;
and he would eventually build up such influence for himself among Chiang Kai-shek's American cohorts that, writing in the right-wing *Facts Forum* in May 1955, he felt
qualified to entitle his exposition of the pro-Nationalist
movement "I am the China Lobby."

Then there were the ex-Communists, who directly or indirectly helped the Nationalists' cause—and the forces of
division within the United States. Viewing the evidences
of Soviet conspiracy in a political situation that could only
be described as fluid, conservative American Congressmen who had never studied Marx, Lenin, or Stalin
learned the horrid truth second-hand from people who
pressed forward with the claim that they were ex-Communists and therefore could be depended upon to give
guidance in the labyrinths of subversion. "In the country
of the blind the one-eyed man is king," but it would not
become evident until later that some of the persons selected as guides to Communism had their one eye singularly cocked.

One such Communist turncoat, Whittaker Chambers,
probably contributed more than any other man, excepting
Senator Joseph R. McCarthy, to the confusion of the
"Communist" issue. Jay David Whittaker Chambers purported to have been one of the elite of the American Communist Party—an underground worker, a true subversive.
But where in the early 1930s he had been a member of the

[9] "Our Harvest in China," *ibid.*, December 1948, pp. 1–4.

Communist underground plotting to overthrow the American political system, in 1937 (or 1938, depending upon which of his versions one chose to believe) he broke with the Communist Party. But he retained his basic dogmatism of spirit, apocalyptic thoughts, an odd mixture of fear and fantasy, and a driving urge to be deemed important. And in December 1948, a decade after Chambers had left the Party, Carnegie Endowment President and sometime State Department official Alger Hiss was indicted for perjury—on the basis of his denial of particulars of Chambers' charge that Hiss, while in the State Department, had been a member of a Communist underground cell. Naturally, the State Department connection cloaked the matter with an outstanding importance.

The State Department occupied a position of special vulnerability in the American political arena: it had no domestic constituency, no dedicated protagonists in Congress. The 1949 report of the Hoover Commission on the organization of the Executive branch of the U.S. Government remarked, as regards the matter of cooperation between the Executive and Legislative branches, that "one particular obstacle which should be frankly faced is the traditionally suspicious attitude of the Congress toward foreign affairs and toward the segment of the executive branch concerned with it."

That "traditionally suspicious attitude" had been notably excited by the developments of the troubled postwar period. In the minds of many, thanks especially to the sweeping allegations of partisans like Hurley and Kohlberg, there had already been established a connection between the unfavorable course of events in China and alleged "disloyalty" in the U.S. Foreign Service. In October

1949, sometime State Department official Noel H. Fields disappeared in Europe, and it was surmised that he had gone behind the Iron Curtain, perhaps voluntarily. Just a short month before, the Soviet Union had exploded its first A-bomb. The American monopoly had been broken that quickly, and American military preeminence had come under challenge. Was not this too, even as the almost coincident "loss of China," the result of some worldwide conspiracy that labored in Washington even as in Moscow?

On January 25, as the result of testimony and evidence supplied by Whittaker Chambers, Alger Hiss was convicted in his second trial. The conviction was for perjury, but the burden of the charges against Hiss was that he had delivered documents to Chambers for transmittal to "the Communist conspiracy," and American public opinion suffered a new shock. Attention centered more fiercely on the State Department. Then, on February 4, 1950, it was disclosed that a naturalized British subject, Klaus Fuchs, had delivered atomic secrets to agents of the USSR over a period of years. This evidence seemed to confirm that the American atomic monopoly had indeed been broken by espionage—within the citadel of the "free world."

Conspiracy and espionage had previously been relatively novel ideas for the United States, but public opinion was by now entirely receptive to suspicions of international plotting and domestic subversion. Real fear began to penetrate deeply in American governmental circles as well—fear, and suspicion of the Government's own personnel.

The developing situation favored the activities of the proponents of Chiang Kai-shek's vanquished Nationalists. When the victorious Communists set up their "Central

People's Government" in Peking on October 1, 1949, it was widely anticipated that the United States Government would before long extend diplomatic recognition to it as a matter of regular procedure. But two months passed and shortly after it was reported, at the end of December, that Britain was proceeding to recognize the new regime, Secretary of State Acheson announced that the United States proposed to "let the dust settle." The Communists themselves contributed to the crystallization of the status quo by their "requisitioning" of the office of the American Consulate General at Peking in January 1950. As a result of that action, the United States withdrew its diplomatic and consular personnel from China. The break thus accomplished was definite, and for the time being it was irreparable. And the Chinese Nationalists were incidentally left occupying a tactical position that enabled them still to play on political forces: they were the only "China" the United States had.

American frustration at seeing in the seat of power in China a force that was stridently Communist and pro-Soviet, and so violently anti-American as to refuse in effect to behave in a manner that would permit the United States gracefully to extend recognition, offered a golden opportunity to the beaten Nationalists, and they seized it with ardor. They announced that they were not dead at all, but had only been betrayed. The Republican minority party in Congress (which in British politics would be termed "Her Majesty's Loyal Opposition") began to build upon the charge that the Democratic Administration had "sold Chiang Kai-shek down the river"—*that* was the reason the Nationalists had been overthrown.

Destiny had thus prepared the way for the demagogue.

He was at hand, and a made-to-order target was available. Senator Joseph R. McCarthy evidently perceived the psychological significance, and the political utility, of playing upon popular apprehensions regarding "the Communist menace" as a means of advancing his political fortunes, theretofore meager. On February 9, 1950, "McCarthyism" was born in the Senator's infamous Wheeling speech in which he alleged that there were 205 "members of the Communist Party" in the State Department "still working and shaping policy." This statement not unnaturally brought the Senator into the headlines—which, of course, was where he wanted to be. He continued thereafter along that line, juggling the numbers to read 81, 57, "over 200," and then 26. The Senator wandered occasionally into other areas in searches for deviant Far Eastern scholars or heretic bureaucrats, but he continued to concentrate his attentions primarily upon the State Department.

The basic thesis of McCarthyism was that, since the United States had manifestly experienced foreign-policy failures, those failures must be the fruit of treason and the guilty traitors were logically to be found in the State Department; all one had to do was to list enough names, and he must eventually hit upon a villain. The environment in which the phenomenon known as McCarthyism appeared was American, and the basic tactics were peculiarly fitted for employment in one particular sector of the American scene. Given Congressional suspicion of that governmental organ which dealt with "foreigners," and the absence of any substantial popular support for that organ, from a Machiavellian point of view McCarthy's strategy of attacking the State Department in order to further his political fortunes was in February 1950 basically sound.

Others joined him in the nefarious witchhunt; and the challenging political slogan of the Republican Opposition of the 1950 election year predictably became "Who lost China?"

The professionals of the U.S. Foreign Service knew the answer to that insinuating question: Chiang's Nationalists, by their political and military inefficiency and their corruption, had "lost" China. I was myself a China Service officer, and for practically my entire career had engaged in extensive political and economic reporting of the Asian scene. As it happened, I had not been involved in the Stilwell-Chiang-Hurley embroglio. Caught in Indochina by Pearl Harbor, and interned there for eight months by the Japanese, I had returned to China in 1942 to serve briefly in the wartime capital of Chungking, but then had gone on to open a consulate in Chinese Turkestan; from there, I had returned to the United States to serve briefly in the State Department in 1944, then returned to the field as Consul General at Vladivostok. I had however gone back to China soon after the war was over, and as Consul General successively at Mukden, Changchun, and Peking (Peiping) had viewed the development, and the dénouement, of the civil war.

I was thus one of the officers who had been charged with keeping the State Department informed about the course of events, and with giving my judgments on political developments. To me, with a background of two decades of service in East Asia, it had long been evident that the Nationalists would almost inevitably lose; the Communist victory had therefore come as no surprise. As part of the operation of withdrawal of the last American diplomatic and consular personnel from China in April 1950, I closed the Consulate General at Peking. At that juncture, after months of intense concern with the revolutionary developments in China, I had scant appreciation of how differently Far Eastern developments were currently being viewed in certain quarters in the United States. It was two months after McCarthy had sounded the false tocsin at Wheeling—but I do not recall having even heard of that episode in Peking.

I took up my new post as Director of the State Department's Office of Chinese Affairs in early July. Dean Acheson was then Secretary of State. The upper levels of the departmental organization reflected the influx of military men after the war. Rear Admiral William D. Wright Jr. was chief of the Division of Foreign Service Administration. My immediate superior, in the position of Assistant Secretary of State for Far Eastern Affairs, was Dean Rusk, who had served as a colonel in the China-Burma-India Theater. The setup was typical of the current complexion of the organization.

The outbreak of the Korean War in June had further exacerbated political passions, and partisan attacks on the State Department were building up fiercely. In an atmosphere charged with passion and demagoguery, it was easy for Congress to override Truman's veto in September and pass the Internal Security Act, further institutionalizing the artfully created popular fear of subversion of the Republic. The intervention of Chinese "volunteers" in the Korean War in October, and their infliction of humiliating defeats on American troops shortly thereafter, further exacerbated existing American suspicions and hatreds.

I knew that the State Department's loyalty-security program had hit a number of my colleagues, that all personnel were being "rescreened," and that this process was requiring able officers to appear before the Loyalty-Security Board, to prove their innocence in grueling hearings. But I harbored no fears for myself: my good record—attested to by my assignment to a series of important posts requiring both ability and discretion and my rapid rise in the Foreign Service—in my mind constituted ample assurance that I should not become a target.

The Korean War, and problems centering in China proper, lent unusual excitement to bureaucratic days. At the end of 1950, I looked back at certain accomplishments of my Office as jobs well done. Between Christmas and New Year, I availed myself of a few days more of a vacation I had interrupted in July by reason of the outbreak of the Korean War. Our daughter, Zoë, was living with my wife, Mariann, and me; our son, Oliver, had driven down from the University of Minnesota, and our family was reunited for the holiday season in an atmosphere of unusual liveliness and happiness. The children had their party on New Year's Eve and we had ours, but we greeted the first day of 1951 together. As Oliver left later that New Year's Day to return to his studies in Minnesota, none of us perceived clouds on the horizon. On the contrary, there seemed to be every promise of the "Happy New Year" we had a few short hours before so warmly wished each other. I myself felt fit and expansive in spirit. I figuratively stretched myself, and contemplated the future in pleasurable anticipation of new challenges in my professional career as a U.S. Foreign Service Officer.

On January 2, replete with the holiday spirit of refreshed well-being, I resumed my customary habits and made ready to return to the office. Breakfast was given a bizarre touch by Zoë's recounting to Mariann a "terrible dream" of the night before. She had dreamed that she and I had been walking together down the road, and that some people threw knives at me. The knives missed their mark, but finally a car without lights had suddenly tried to run me down. It too missed, but its driver, "a tall dark man," had stopped the car, jumped out, and stabbed me. "Well," Mariann casually asked, "was Daddy badly hurt?" Zoë reported that I had not been killed, but that the attack left on my back "a mark like a cross."

But we are no believers in dreams, our hearts skipped none of their regular beats, and everything was the essence of normality when I arrived at the State Department. The hours of accustomed desk routine passed. And then, shortly before the day was out, I received a visit from a legal officer of the Department's Loyalty Security Board (LSB). He handed me an interrogatory dated December 28, 1950. The first three questions set the tone:

1. Are you, or have you ever been, a member of, affiliated with, or in sympathetic association with the Communist Party, or any organization which is a front for, or controlled by, the Communist Party? . . .

2. Have you ever believed in, or supported the ideologies and policies of, the Communist Party, or any organization which is a front for, or controlled by, the Communist Party? . . .

3. Have you ever made a contribution of time, talent, or money to any activity known to you to be sponsored by, or closely affiliated with the Communist Party?

There were next listed eight allegations, "by various informants," namely "That you"—

a. Associated with Communists in Hankow, China, 1931–1934.

b. Viewed some aspects of Communism favorably, 1932–1934.

c. Were "favorable" to the Communists, 1933–1934.

d. Had distinct "pink" tendencies at Peiping, China, 1934–1935.

e. Had a marked preference for some Communist principles in the early 1930's.

f. Were friendly toward the U.S.S.R. and Communism, 1935–1937.

g. Were classified as "mildly Red" and espoused doctrines of a "Communist" nature prior to 1940.

h. Were "100% pro-Red" at Shanghai, China, in 1940.

The interrogatory directed: *like thought reform confession*

Comment fully on these allegations, setting forth in detail an explanation of your political philosophy and orientation from 1928 to date, with particular emphasis on any change in such philosophy or orientation.

The interrogatory then asked about my relations with five named persons, in each case desiring to know whether I had been "aware of his alleged pro-Communist sympathies and activities?" And the further question was put: "If you have been aware of such alleged sympathies and activities, what has been your attitude toward them?" Then came a final item, No. 20:

It is alleged that in 1932 you delivered a sealed envelope to the office of the editor of the "New Masses" magazine in New York City for transmittal to one Grace Hutchins, a reported Communist employed by the Labor Research Bureau, an alleged Communist organization.

Comment fully on this allegation, giving your complete knowledge of the circumstances surrounding the episode, *if it happened,* including any former acquaintanceship with the "New Masses" editor, your knowl-

edge of and association with Grace Hutchins, the nature
of the document transmitted, the sender of the document, how it was known to you that Grace Hutchins was
the addressee, and how it was known to you to effect
delivery at the "New Masses" office.

It would have been quite understandable in 1951 if the
State Department, receiving from some dark and possibly
anonymous source information indicating that one of its
officers was a Communist, should have asked that officer
for clarification. But for a senior commissioned officer of
long service to be charged with having "viewed some
aspects of Communism favorably" in the Hoover Administration and having had "'pink' tendencies at Peiping,
China" in the mid-1930s and with having been "friendly"
toward the USSR long before World War II, and then
being asked to set forth his political philosophy from 1928
(the date of my entry into the Foreign Service) to the
present, smacked strongly of political inquisitions of other
times and places. And yet, there was that puzzling allegation about a visit to the *New Masses:* what could that
mean?

I read the letter in the presence of the Board's Legal Officer. It left me with a feeling of incredulity. I knew from
the tribulations of so many Russians, Germans, and Chinese particularly how political purges functioned coldly,
mechanically, and often stupidly. My brain understood the
significance of the words contained in the letter, but I
could not perceive in my heart how an officer with my
record could be summoned by an administrative tribunal
to respond to such picayune questions as those contained
in the interrogatory just handed to me—vague inquiries
into my political attitudes as a young man, and one lone

concrete item that meant absolutely nothing to me. But there the LSB's interrogatory was, on my desk. The Legal Officer left me alone.

My natural desire was to discuss the matter immediately with Mariann. When I returned home, she was preparing for the arrival of dinner guests. I chose not to spoil the evening for her, and held back my news. And then, when the door closed well after midnight behind our last guests, I handed the LSB's interrogatory to my Foreign Service wife, who had experienced jointly with me many of the vicissitudes met in the two decades of work for the State Department. Thus began the hardest year of our lives. Given the variety of Alice-in-Wonderland fantasies and concepts and events met in the course of 1951, Zoë's dream of New Year's Day would at times seem less weird than the reality.

President Calvin Coolidge's Commission to O. Edmund Clubb as U.S. Foreign Service Officer, May 1928

II

Historical Excursion I— Nationalist China — *back to 1928*

The mock trial of the Associated Press correspondent at Prague, Mr. William N. Oatis, has now been brought to a conclusion. The sentencing is but an epilogue to this ludicrous travesty of justice. . . .

The proceedings revealed the flimsiest kind of alleged "evidence," even more insubstantial than the Communists are accustomed to produce in trumped-up trials of this type. . . .

Such an attempted hoax on the intelligence of World opinion will fool no one. While it had all the trappings of legal procedure, it was in fact a kangaroo court staged before the kleig lights of propaganda. . . .

The "confession" of "espionage" was in truth but the admission of an American reporter that in the high traditions of his profession he was attempting under the most unfavorable conditions to report a true picture of the conditions and events in Czechoslovakia as he saw them.

Dept. of State statement of July 4, 1951 on occasion of the sentencing by a Czechoslovak court of AP correspondent Oatis to ten years imprisonment.

I had received my commission as a Foreign Service officer in 1928 over the signature of President Calvin Coolidge. I naturally viewed the event with justifiable

pride, and with broad expectations. The commission
opened up the promise of an interesting career; the State
Department brochure, noting that the monetary rewards
were meager, promised as much. Shortly after entering the
Service, I volunteered to take the Chinese-language training course at Peking. In the 1920s, American Sinologs
were given a high rating, and the China experts of the
Foreign Service constituted a corps of acknowledged ability and high esprit; it was only later that Far Eastern experts would be harried through the thickets of Washington's bureaucracy by political foxhunters bent on winning
a trophy in the chase after those tagged with responsibility
for "the China debacle." The course given at Peking was
comprehensive, covering Chinese history and other subjects as well as the language. The two years of training in
those days probably cost the United States Government a
minimum of $10,000 per officer, a tidy sum in 1920 dollars.
It was presumably thought worth it.

For my part, in 1928 I had thought it a good choice to
qualify as an expert on matters pertaining to China. After
eight months of preliminary training in the Department, I
knew very well what would be expected of me. A departmental brochure of later date gave a good general description of the functions of the Foreign Service Officer:

Broadly speaking, the responsibilities of a Foreign Service
Officer are to carry out the foreign policy of the President as
expressed in the directives of the Secretary of State, to keep the
United States Government informed of developments abroad, to
protect American citizens and interests in foreign countries, and
to cultivate and maintain friendly relations with peoples of other
nations.[1]

[1] "Preparing for a Career in the Foreign Service of the United States,"
Dept. of State publication 3668, Department and Foreign Service Series
9, Jan. 1950.

More specifically, the young Foreign Service officer in China was charged with performing the routine work connected with issuance of passports and visas, registration of American births and deaths and the witnessing of marriages, the handling of ship's papers and the repatriation of destitute seamen, administration of estates of deceased American citizens, and the administration of the office and its property and accounts. On occasion, he might be called upon to rescue a missionary from Communist hands, get an American out of jail, handle a drunk, identify a stray corpse, or perhaps traverse the deserts of Central Asia. And always, he was expected to report on political and economic developments as he saw them. Those things, and others more onerous, I was to do in the service of the State Department.

The only doctrine of vicarious responsibility that I had heard of at the time was that formerly practiced by the Manchu rulers of China—and condemned by the Occidental powers as a relic of barbarism. At the end of the 1920s, there were no prohibitions in effect in the Foreign Service against association with persons of particular political conviction, and no blacklist of American citizens and others supplied for our guidance; we budding "China experts" were even encouraged to "make contacts" in order to enhance our usefulness as reporting officers. But that was when Hoover was President, and none of us could have anticipated the advent of "McCarthyism" in 1950, or could have foreseen that suspicion would replace massive evidence in written records as a standard for judgment.

When Mariann and I arrived in Peking in 1929, China was a nation in metamorphosis. The slow, graceful tempo of existence discovered in the former imperial capital might bring the visitor, or the resident, to muse upon the

charms of a vanished era, but placid surface manifestations
in the ancient walled town were belied by the ferment
beneath China's vast surface—an explosive force that
frequently burst forth in violent events to work deep
changes on the face of the disintegrating Chinese society.
The few surviving Manchus still bowed deep on one knee
in salute, and when older Chinese couples walked the
streets the woman trailed submissively some ten feet behind her spouse. But the queues, which had been the male
Chinese badge of servitude to the Manchus, were getting
ever fewer; and most younger women had not bound their
feet, and often bobbed their hair. The upcoming generation of the Republican period was superseding the generation linked to the end of the Manchu Dynasty. Buddhist
temples were still crowded with monks and worshippers;
but within five years the population of resident monks
would fall drastically, reflecting a decline in faith owing to
the early Nationalist drive against religion. Twenty years
later, the last remnants of institutional Buddhism would be
virtually wiped out by the Chinese Communists, complet-
ing the process the Nationalists had began.

   The National Government had been formally established at Nanking in 1928, with American recognition
promptly extended, in disregard of the regime's violent,
revolutionary past; for by 1928 the Nationalists had taken
on a conservative cast as far as domestic economic and
social matters were concerned. But Nanking's writ did not
by any manner of means extend unchallenged over all the
country, and force and violence, rather than law, were
more often than not the order of the day. Natural forces
joined with the man-made ones to foster disorder. The imperial concept had been discarded in 1912 prior to the dis-

covery of a new doctrine of political legitimacy adequate for the times, and for China's problems. The Buddhist-Confucian culture was decadent and dying, and for the whole two years of my assignment to Peking the forces of revolutionary change rumbled underground. The significance of current social and political phenomena was entirely apparent to those with a sense of history and a knowledge of social dynamics; but there were those too who found any change in the status quo to be unthinkable. "There is none so blind as they that won't see."

The spring of 1929, my first year in China, was the time of the brief but jarring Sino-Soviet conflict in Manchuria; the Soviets emerged easy victors from the affair the over-confident Chinese Nationalists had started. In 1930, I spent a month's leave on an irrigation project in Inner Mongolia, and saw at first hand what an area, and a population, looked like at the end of several years of drought and famine. I extended my studies farther than dictated by the scope of the examinations confronting me, and on the completion of my two-year course in Peking, in April 1931, I submitted to the Legation a memorandum offering certain observations under the title "Disruptive Elements in China." Significantly enough, my first official political report from the field was thus on the subject of the Chinese revolution. I there pointed up the near inevitability that the process of disruption of the aged civilization would continue. It required no extended research to reach that conclusion.

Leaving that offering behind me, I journeyed to my new post, Hankow, where I had been assigned as Vice Consul. I went alone, for Zoë had just been born, and Mariann was still unable to travel. This family separation was to last for half a year, for soon after my arrival in the Yangtze port the great river burst out of its banks. The swirling flood waters spread over all of the river's middle valley, took some two million human lives, and caused hundreds of millions of dollars worth of property damage. The streets of Hankow itself were under water for nearly two months. By carrying my surveys as a consular officer into the camps where refugees who had escaped the floodwaters were dying of starvation, cholera, and dysentery, I learned much more than books had told me of the miseries that oppressed the Chinese people. They were truly *les misérables* of the twentieth century.

In a fundamental sense, the flood was an integral part of the whole lugubrious national picture. The 1927 split of the Nationalist-Communist coalition into Right and Left had brought about the destruction of Communist power in China's towns, but the leadership maintained itself largely intact, and the causes of revolution were still in being. In 1931, political unrest was epidemic in different parts of the countryside in a form officially termed "Red banditry." Two military campaigns launched in the preceding six months for the avowed purpose of annihilating the "bandits" had left the task admittedly uncompleted. A new campaign began in June 1931, and it was at Hankow, when the Reds drove to the outskirts of the town, that I heard my first—but not my last—hostile machinegun fire in China. The Communists, however, were not the only dissidents of the period. In the southwest, a coalition force headed by two prominent generals threatened to march against the central Government at Nanking. In all of west and northwest China, a variety of warlords held out against Nanking, and spent their spare time fighting each other. In the north three other leaders in 1930 had taken a stand in opposition to what they termed the "dictatorship" of the National Government, and two of the triumvirate still maintained their independent attitude. Domestic squabbles were dwarfed in that same 1931, however, by an event that shook Asia and disturbed the world. Having learned well the lessons of the Sino-Soviet brawl of 1929, Japan invaded Manchuria.

Those events foreshadowed the pattern of turbulence for the decade ahead. They were the backdrop for my introduction to work in the Consulate General at Hankow. My various duties consisted of office drudgery as well as tasks that required me to use my newly acquired language. In due course, regular reporting on political and economic developments became my chief assignment. This function was of course essentially similar to that performed by the numerous Occidental news correspondents, writers, and scholars then residing in the country. I was initiated into that work under the able guidance of two experienced senior consular officers, first Frank P. Lockhart and then Walter A. Adams, with my training completed later at other posts by hard-headed Clarence E. Gauss. They presented me with no political mold for my reporting, and with no rules for political conformity (which in 1931 would have had to be Hooverian Republicanism, with a shift in the political line, presumably, to New Deal Democracy in 1933). I was called upon to report with accuracy, objectivity, and timeliness. I was expected to gather facts where they might be found, with commonsense discretion the rule.

So, even as at Peking I associated with a wide variety of people of all nationalities, including politicians and businessmen, naval officers from the gunboats that lay anchored in the river, Sinologs, missionaries of every sect, and journalists of all political complexions. If one were to compute a man to be the sum total of his associations, I should have been a strange mélange indeed. But associations were not at that time a major concern, and we Foreign Service officers took it for granted, as we worked to get glimpses of the future through the political murk of the time, that the government had confidence in our integrity—as the President's commission said.

While I was still in Washington, a scholar of wide experience, Tyler Dennett, had advised me to begin my career by becoming a specialist in some one field. I had taken his advice to heart, and my volunteering for the Chinese-language course had been in line with that idea. At Peking, I had delved into the subject of social change in China, with emphasis on the period since the mid-nineteenth century. Later, at Hankow, I found rich opportunities to develop specialized knowledge of two contemporary Chinese phenomena—the flourishing opium traffic and the social revolution that had earlier caught my attention. I was never charged, either at the time or 20 years after, with having been corrupted by opium through my study of it. My inquiry into the Chinese revolution, however, evidently led a bare handful of my more conservative colleagues to conclude that my own political sympathies must reflect the color of the phenomena I observed.

There was an early example of that facile illogic. In a long report of September 1931 from Hankow, I surveyed the devastating impact of the aforementioned Yangtze flood on the peasant economy of Central China and observed in conclusion:

Napoleon remarked at Helena that "the sword settles nothing." Assuredly, in the solution of the tremendous problems involved in the knitting together of the Chinese people into a nation with unity of political direction, and the establishment of that nation on a firm economic basis which guarantees the social well-being of the people, militarism is not enough. If the regional leaders cannot compose their differences and effect a unified program of economic construction, it will be the Communist Party, with its definite orientation, that will finally inherit their power in south and central China. This flood makes more poignant the need that is the economic basis for the widespread movement of revolt that now exists.

In addition, I noted that there was possibly corruption in the administration of the flood-relief funds. I qualified my suggestion: "There is no intent to imply that more than a minority of Chinese officials are corrupt, but with government, as with apples, the rotten part characterizes the whole."

Reading this report, a fellow consular officer in Shanghai said that it indicated to him that I was a "Red." It was only when I was passing through Shanghai about a year later that I learned of this characterization of me, which was repeated by another Shanghai officer when deep in his cups one evening. But had I obtained this knowledge at once in Hankow, it would have made no difference to my reporting. I had early acknowledged the right of other citizens to disagree with me, and at that very time there were being exchanged between Republicans and Democrats in the United States epithets that made the uncongenial description of me seem but a pallid reflection of native political emotions.

In 1931, that incident claimed from me no more than casual, passing attention. I worked on as usual, and in April 1932 submitted a 124-page memorandum on "Com-

munism in China," related to my earlier essay "Disruptive
Elements in China." The memorandum was in main a survey of the contemporary growth of Communist organization and activity, but I briefly offered certain evaluations
of my own in conclusion:

> Only one thing will stop the growing wave of social revolution
> in China—the bettering of the economic conditions of the popu-
> lation. It is impossible to halt the flow of ideas that is impinging
> upon the consciousness of the people, and it is apparent that the
> solution of the problems of China will be a catastrophic one. (p.
> 104)
>
> A social revolution, such as China is now going through, is
> frustrated unless it has its roots in the great body of the people.
> The development that suffered a break in 1927 has now, five
> years later, evidently reached another nodule in the progression
> from an Imperial feudalism to democratic institutions more con-
> sonant with the time. The development will apparently be slowly
> toward a form of State socialism, with the San Min Chu I and the
> Kuomintang and its ghostly adviser all to be dropped. It is to be
> expected that the actual pressure of economic circumstances will
> make requisite an attitude on the part of the new Chinese nation
> that will not be characterized generally by open hostility toward
> other countries. But that may not be said certainly. (p. 112)

The monograph was very favorably received by our
Foreign Service offices in China, including the Legation
itself. The thesis ran counter to the thinking of some who,
in accord with the official Chinese Government "line,"
wished to believe that the rebellious peasants were only
"Red bandits." However, the course of events over the
coming years would bear out my analysis.

The State Department, which did not comment on my
monograph until 1933, differed from all of the China offices and, although nominally concerned in main with
questions of grammar used and sources tapped, indicated

disbelief in the validity of that survey. The reason for this
adverse reaction was not clear to me at the time; it was
only long years afterward that I learned that the Department's critique was based upon a memorandum written by
a member of the *Russia* Service, who had never been in
China. Although my critic's acquired prejudices proved in
the long run less reliable than the conclusions I had
reached on the basis of close-range observation, this official criticism nevertheless tended to strengthen the impression I had discovered in some quarters that the study
of Chinese Communism could perhaps be classified as a
"hazardous occupation."

A year later, in early 1934, in the light of a British
scholar's high evaluation of the monograph, I asked the
Department's permission to publish it. The Department
refused my request, but changed its position to commend
the work as "a useful contribution to the Department's
records on the subject of Communism," and expressed the
hope that I would continue my interest in that subject,
"reporting to the Department from time to time as occasion might arise." [2]

In China, in the meantime, armed conflict continued to
engage the major attention and energies of the National
Government, and economic misery and social unrest
spread. The conflict between the Nationalists and the
Communists expanded, and the guerrilla warfare in the
countryside very obviously was assuming graver, more
revolutionary aspects.

From 1931 on, wrathful demands were being heard in

[2] The memorandum was eventually published under the title *Communism in China, As Reported from Hankow in 1932* (New York/London:
Columbia University Press, 1968).

all parts of the country that the Nationalist regime resist
further Japanese encroachments. Far from acceding to the
popular will, the government bowed to Japanese pressure
in North China. Chiang Kai-shek, speaking April 7, 1933,
to some of his high-ranking generals on the subject "Consideration of Most Recent Bandit-Suppression Strategy,"
set forth the obiter dictum that "The enemy of our revolution is not the dwarf robbers [the Japanese], but the bandits [Chinese Communists]." Open revolts against Nanking's authority by outraged military men were successfully
put down by force of arms. The old revolutionary leader
Hu Han-min, in Canton, warned that "unification of China
by armed force and suppression is bound to fail." [3]

In August 1933, Nanking launched its *fifth* "bandit-
suppression campaign," and the drive was pushed all
through 1934 under the expert counseling of German generals Hans von Seeckt and Alexander von Falkenhausen.
In a memorandum forwarded from Hankow July 6, 1934, I
commented on the situation:

. . . it is not believed that the present politico-economic situation warrants any sanguine belief that the 5th Anti-Red Campaign will accomplish its purpose within this latest time-limit. It
seems more probably [probable?] that the roots of revolt will
strike deeper in west China especially if the onslaught on the
Fukien-Kiangsi area continues and results in the dislodgment of
the Reds.

In a dispatch of August 22, I reinforced my forecast:

[3] Cf. the comment by Lt. Gen. Albert C. Wedemeyer on August 24, 1947,
on the conclusion of his survey mission in China in behalf of President
Truman: "It should be accepted that military force in itself will not eliminate Communism." —U.S. Department of State, *United States Relations
with China* (Washington: U.S. Government Printing Office, 1949), p. 764.

In the solid Soviet region overlying the Fukien-Kiangsi border, the other Red armies may be trusted to defend the Red area until the cause seems quite hopeless, in which case they would presumably break away also for a foray across the countryside that would probably land them in west China. *a prediction of Long March*

In a report of September 1, 1934, entitled "The Crisis in Chiang Kai-shek's Power," I analyzed the internal weaknesses of the dictator's rule. Those weaknesses, aggravated as they were by China's international difficulties, were shortly to become increasingly evident. In October 1934, the Communists began the withdrawal of their main force from their base in southeast China, and broke out of the Nationalist encirclement. The capital town of the Red "Provisional Soviet Government of China" was occupied by the Nationalists in November. But the hard core of the retreating Communist forces arrived one year later, at the end of their "Long March," in northwest China. It was from there that they were ultimately to drive to power over the whole country.

That fall, I was transferred back to Peking. My new chief, Clarence E. Gauss, outstanding for his direct honesty and courage, would before long defend my reporting of the political situation against the contention of the Military Attaché, Lieutenant Colonel Walter Drysdale, that his reports were more accurate and should suffice—since he had access to Generalissimo and Mme. Chiang Kai-shek. Said Gauss in effect: Clubb will continue reporting. At Peking; I had even greater opportunity than before to follow political developments, including those bearing on the Chinese revolution, and the record shows that I was generous in my offerings of estimates and prognostications of the probable shape of things to come in China.

Washington, London, and Moscow alike watched the development of Japan's imperialistic drive on the Asia mainland with growing trepidation. The 7th COMINTERN Congress, at Moscow in 1935, adopted the "united front" policy, which called upon Communist parties everywhere to join ranks with all groups that would oppose the common enemy. The Chinese Communist Party had "declared war" on Japan in 1932 and ever since had been inviting support for its struggle against both the National Government and Japan. Beginning in January 1936, it expanded its call for allies against the Japanese to include the National Government itself. On March 27, 1936, when Communist military action was being expanded outward from their new base in Northwest China, I observed:

> If any move by the Communists northward from Shansi or Shensi were to develop, or perhaps if it were only that General Chiang Kai-shek's power in Shansi gave the appearance of offering a threat to the Japanese . . . , the Japanese militarists would become immediately concerned. . . . It may be said . . . that the present situation in Shansi holds several important possibilities, chief among which are 1) the extension of General Chiang Kai-shek's control to include Shansi and 2) the precipitation of a forward movement by the Japanese.

The Communist drive into Shansi was defeated by the intervention of Chiang Kai-shek's own forces. On August 7, 1936, I reported that the results of recent maneuvers had been:

> 1) the defeat of the new Communist policy insofar as it was based on an expectation of popular response to an appeal to nationalistic sentiments; 2) the establishment in Shansi of the nucleus of General Chiang Kai-shek's power; 3) the providing of the Japanese militarists with a significant talking-point in their negotiations with the Chinese; and 4) the worsening of economic con-

ditions in Shansi. It is to be concluded that Chiang Kai-shek's military power, with alike the checking of the Communists in Shansi and the crushing of Ch'en Chi-t'ang's power in Kwangtung, has been considerably strengthened. Nevertheless, deleterious economic and political factors continue in operation, and it may properly be expected that the next turn of the wheel might easily discover new dangers for the Nanking regime.

The "Southwest Political Council," of which Ch'en Chi-t'ang was a member, had demanded in June that the National Government mobilize the nation against Japan. Despite the Government's efforts to keep attention focused on the "bandit-suppression campaigns," the nationalistic fervor rose ever higher during the year. The popular sentiment had turned decisively against continued civil war, and against further concessions to Japan. On December 12, 1936, Generalissimo Chiang Kai-shek was kidnapped at Sian by a warlord combination which demanded that the Government fight the Japanese instead of the Chinese Reds. The issue was civil war or an aggravation of the strife between China and Japan. The Chinese Communists intervened to bring about agreement between the Generalissimo and his captors, and Chiang Kai-shek was released on Christmas Day, his life evidently saved through the intercession of the "Red bandits" he had fought so long. In the face of a clear warning from Japan that it would brook no Nationalist compromise with the "pro-Communist" elements who had captured Chiang, a united front was established between the National Government and dissident Chinese elements. The die was cast. A major clash between the advancing Japanese dynasts and the Chinese, who had determined to retreat no farther, had now become highly probable.

In a dispatch of January 14, 1937, I analyzed the consequences of the so-called "Sian Incident," and observed:

> Reports persist to the effect that the Kwantung-Army–inspired
> military establishment in Chahar is being strengthened. If on the
> other side of Suiyuan Province there is to be put into motion an
> anti-Japanese force calling for the expulsion of Japanese forces
> from Chahar and East Hopei, a clash in the not distant future
> would seem entirely possible, with Northwest China the theatre
> of operations.

Shortly afterward, with nearly five years' field service
behind me since our last home leave, my family and I
made another visit to the United States, reporting to the
Department and visiting relatives and friends as usual. In
China, the forces set in motion by Chiang Kai-shek's Sian
agreement with the dissident generals and the Chinese
Communists were at work. On July 7, 1937—almost immediately after our return to Peking—there occurred the
"Marco Polo Bridge Incident," which began the Sino-
Japanese War. The anticipated Japanese advance had
taken place in the most violent form.

We of the Embassy Office undertook our function of
protecting American lives and property under war conditions. While artillery fire drummed in the suburbs and the
Japanese warplanes divebombed troop concentrations in
full sight of observers inside the old capital's walls, and
the wounded poured into town, we evacuated into the
Embassy compounds, for protection, all Americans willing
to leave their residences. (Some chose to remain in their
homes to guard against looting.) Each official householder
put up as many of the evacuees as he could, and others
were housed in tents on the Embassy lawn.

It was at this juncture that there was shed the only blood

that flowed inside the walls—American blood. The Chinese garrison forces had dug trenches across the streets for one of their oft-advertised "last-ditch stands." I was at a barrier helping Americans through when there approached, *from the rear,* a mounted detachment of the American Marine Guard. The Chinese in charge at the entrenchment called out a command to halt, in the direction of the advancing troops—to whom all Chinese would have been less intelligible than Greek even if they could have heard the man's voice at that distance. (The Chinese commander subsequently explained that he thought they were being attacked by the *Japanese* legation guard.) And then, even as I was shouting that the troops were American, a machine-gun turned loose. The gunner luckily shot high, and the Marines gained the refuge of a side blind alley; the only casualty was one wounded man. I loaded him into my car, took him to the Marine dispensary, and reported to the Marine command the whereabouts of the mounted detachment. Our own American rescue operation was completed with dispatch.

The battle of Peking was also soon over. The Japanese Army, having wiped out the defenders around the massive walls, shortly entered the town, and its poor internal defenses were never opposed to the enemy.

One of the first directives received from the Department after the beginning of the war "advised" Foreign Service personnel to ship their dependents out of embattled China, either to the United States or to nearby areas such as Japan or the Philippines. In family council, I decided that Mariann and the children should wait until it was seen whether the Chinese forces would make a stand at Paoting (some 100 miles south of Peking), for it was my estimate that unless the Chinese fought there they could not be expected to fight in North China. All other families evacuated; mine waited. The National Government sent neither planes nor troops to support the North China commanders, and the Chinese lost Paoting (after putting up a fight, to be sure), and continued their retreat. The war had passed us by. My family remained in Peking with me, while the other official dependents stayed in exile in the hills of Baguio and Japan for upward of two years before the State Department would authorize their return. That was *one* separation we missed.

The developments of the Sino-Japanese War naturally left their impression on our work and our lives. The formation of the Nationalist-Communist "united front" and the exigencies of the war against the invader pushed revolution into the background for the time being. The Chinese strength was insufficient even in coalition, however, and the defenders were rolled up before the well-oiled Japanese military machine. The National Government fled from Nanking to Hankow, then on to Chungking—over a thousand miles from the coast. The American Embassy accompanied it, and I was detailed at the beginning of 1939 to administer the Embassy office in Japanese-occupied Nanking. Conditions in the former capital were then such that officers were detailed there for only limited periods, and in October I was transferred to Shanghai; my family took up residence there with me. With hundreds of thousands of destitute Chinese refugees crowded into the foreign concessions for safety's sake, conditions in Shanghai were in some respects even worse than in Nanking.

The Occidental Powers were confronted with what was in truth the beginning of the end of an era in China.

Whereas the Chinese themselves had fought for years against the "unequal treaties" which gave the foreigner special rights, it was finally the Japanese who won a position that enabled them effectively to vitiate those rights. "Asia for the Asians" was the political slogan of the day; the handwriting on the wall was plain to see, and the message was emphasized by indignities deliberately heaped upon Occidentals by the Japanese conquerors. In a dispatch from Shanghai on February 21, 1940—shortly after the outbreak of the European War—I did some speculation on "Possible Trends toward Revival of Asian Nationalism":

It is conceivable . . . that Sino-Japanese "cooperation" in China Proper may take a form which has in it more real substance than its prototype in Manchuria. It is not without logic to believe, for instance, that the aforementioned factors now operating in the international field, may cause Japan to emphasize in its relationships with the proposed new central Government of China those elements which will forward directly "pan-Asianism" as such. If that policy were to be chosen . . . the attack on existing foreign rights and interests in China would be stronger than at any time subsequent to 1927. . . .

It is obvious that if, by hypothesis, there were to develop, for the purpose of furthering the Machiavellian ends of power politics, a four-Power front comprising Germany, the Soviet Union, Italy and Japan, the attack on the Far East interests of the so-called "democratic" Powers would probably be accelerated.

The pressure on British and American positions in Asia in fact increased. Foreign Service personnel in China and Japan were again authorized to evacuate their dependents, this time to the United States. My family stayed on with me until mid-1940, when once more we journeyed together to the United States for home leave. The war clouds were perceptibly lowering in Asia. We discreetly availed ourselves of the Department's pressing "authorization" for my family to remain at home, and I went back to China alone. The duties of my office had caused me to be separated from my family for the third time.

This separation was to last longer than those occasioned by the Hankow flood and my Nanking detail. In 1941, I spent another brief period in Nanking, and then was sent to Hanoi to relieve my colleague Charles S. Reed, who was going home on leave. Reed and I got down immediately to the work of turning over the office and making the necessary official calls. Two days later I formally assumed charge of the office and Reed left. As a representation-observation post functioning as a branch of the Saigon consulate, that office comprised only a room in the Metropole Hotel, and a secretary. I administered my new post a day and a half, and got acquainted with the files. I sent out, on December 5, one telegram, addressed to Cavite for repetition to the Department of State, the Embassy at Chungking, Peking, Hongkong, Shanghai, Tokyo, Bangkok:

> There have been recent rumors of the presence of a Japanese transport convoy off the northern coast of Borneo and on December 2 (?) what appeared to be a blacked-out convoy traveling under destroyer escort was encountered fifty miles south of Hainan proceeding northward. It is now reported by a reputedly reliable source that thirty Japanese transports carrying an estimated division of troops have arrived at Camranh Bay, point of embarkation unknown; that disembarkation has however not commenced and it seems possible that the convoy may proceed elsewhere; and that "a large (?) number" of Japanese planes is expected to arrive at Camranh Bay.

(The question marks indicate garbles in the message as decoded in Washington.) That telegram, bearing its clear warning to a reputedly alerted Government of a possible impending move directed toward the Philippines, I ultimately found in the Department's files. It bore the record of receipt at 5:21 A.M. and was stamped "Division of Far Eastern Affairs," December 6, 1941. The next day, December 7, the disaster of Pearl Harbor occurred. War had come to the Pacific. At 3 A.M. of that same day (that is, an hour before the official declaration of war by Tokyo), I was roused from bed in my hotel room in Hanoi by Japanese gendarmes and made a prisoner.

III

Historical Excursion II—
War and Civil War

It has been a dominant characteristic of modern totalitarian dictatorships, as it was in Japan's feudalistic past, to establish and maintain a strongly centralized police bureaucracy headed by a chief executive officer beyond the reach of popular control. Indeed, the strongest weapon of the military clique in Japan in the decade prior to the war was the absolute authority exercised by the national government over the thought police and the Kempei Tai, extending down to prefectural levels of government. Through these media, the military were enabled to spread a network of political espionage, suppress freedom of speech, of assembly, and even of thought, and by means of tyrannical oppression to degrade the dignity of the individual. Japan was thus in the fullest sense a police state. . . . It should never again be possible for anti-democratic elements, either of the extreme right or the extreme left, to enmesh the freedom of the people in a web of police terrorism.

GENERAL DOUGLAS A. MAC ARTHUR, letter to Japanese Prime Minister, Sept. 16, 1947, "A Brief Progress Report on the Political Reorientation of Japan."

The enemy's internment of me was hard and unusual throughout. By December 1941 France was of course out of the war, and Indochina was nominally under the administration of the Vichy government. I addressed a series of letters to the commanding general of the Japanese forces, and to the French governor-general, protesting my detention and requesting variously that I be permitted to resume my functions as U.S. Consul at Hanoi, that I be transferred to the custody of the French, that various private papers taken from my room at the Metropole Hotel be returned to me, et cetera. Those protests were ignored. On December 19, a Japanese gendarme and a French officer removed me to a new, comfortably furnished house on Rue Daurelle, and I was indeed put under the light guard of a single French sentry; but that very evening a squad of Japanese soldiers appeared and, after a brief altercation, ousted the French sentry and took over. I thereafter was watched over by a Japanese guard force, which comprised a full squad of troops stationed in a garage in the courtyard. I was not permitted to leave the house to go out into the spacious courtyard, and two soldiers from the squad kept constant surveillance over me inside the house, following me wherever I went—excepting only the bathroom.

The American office at Hanoi, because its chief function was obviously observation of the Japanese encroachment on Vichy Indochina, had been viewed with patent suspicion by the Japanese. My letters of protest also undoubtedly irritated the Japanese command. Besides this, I early refused, under a combination of blandishments and threats, to surrender the keys to the consular safe. And although the Japanese could have taken the keys forcibly from me, this seemingly was outside their orders.

But I was caused to pay for my persistent resort to legal-isms, and for my obduracy with respect to the keys, by spending two months in solitary confinement. In the spacious house that had been provided by the French Governor-General, I was left in wintertime without either heat or hot water. In early January, I was removed from Hanoi to Haiphong, where I was installed in an abandoned Socony oil installation about a mile from town, with the most primitive of accommodations: my bed consisted of bare boards and straw matting, and a rickety chair and table made up the rest of my furniture. However, now only one sentry was stationed at my door, I was permitted access to the premises' small courtyard, and I was able to take a daily hot bath—in a tub that had been placed in the courtyard.

On my birthday, February 16, I was removed from the Socony compound and put with an Englishman, the Reuters man Brian Connell, in the midst of a Japanese military camp on the other side of town, Camp de la Digue. Connell and I were naturally kept under constant guard, but we were permitted to walk down the main street of the camp, and to cross a moat to exercise on a small parade ground. This was a substantial advance over the conditions under which I had lived since Pearl Harbor Day.

The Swiss consul, Robert Blattner, had been able to visit me for the first time in mid-January, although the Japanese expressly limited the conversation to the matter of his providing me with funds for my use (including the purchase of food from l'Hotel de l'Europe). However, I was permitted to see Blattner on a later occasion, and the conditions of internment were further regularized. In April 1942, I received the two trunksful of books and other personal possessions I had been forced to leave behind in l'Hotel

Metropole in Hanoi when arrested on December 8. In May, I finally handed to Blattner, against his receipt, the keys to the consular safe.

I was permitted to receive the local French newspaper, but I was otherwise cut off from the outside world, except for several letters sent me by friends in Shanghai. (The State Department informed my family that it was unable to get mail to me.) In mid-May 1942, Connell and I were at last moved into new quarters, in Haiphong proper; then, a little over a month later, I was separated from my fellow-internee and sent to Saigon for repatriation via an exchange of American and Japanese diplomatic personnel at Lourenço Marques. The issue of my personal belongings came up again upon my departure: I was informed that I might take along as baggage only what a man could carry. I disposed of my larger trunk to Swiss Consul Blattner; the other, a steamer trunk, I personally carried across the street and loaded into the waiting van—rather ostentatiously, I grant, to prove that it could be done.

In Haiphong, I enjoyed a week in the company of American and British consular colleagues who had been held there under far easier conditions, but a final trial was reserved for me: on the eve of our ship's departure the Japanese authorities demanded that I either broadcast, record for broadcast, or sign a statement to the effect that I had been well treated in internment. I refused. The session was long and stormy, but I stood firm. And although the last words of the irate Japanese officer directing the interview were to the effect that I had been deprived of my status as diplomat, I was loaded with the others aboard the *Asama Maru* for exchange at Lourenço Marques, Mozambique. (I had occasion to muse on the vicissitudes of time

and circumstance some eight years later when I received
from the Japanese Vice Minister for Foreign Affairs a letter
expressing the "sincere thanks" of the Japanese nation,
and especially of those Japanese "who were direct benefi-
ciaries of your kindness," for aid and facilities extended to
Japanese nationals in Manchuria and North China at the
time of their own onerous return to their homeland in
1946–47.)

Aboard the *Asama Maru,* I wrote up my reports to the
State Department (not omitting to locate the Camp de la
Digue for the benefit of our bombers) and thus completed
the Hanoi tour—eight months of internment. The State
Department, short of experienced men for its Near Eastern
and Asian posts, radioed to the repatriates aboard the
Asama Maru a call for volunteers. My family was anxiously awaiting me in the United States, I had just experienced some rough going, and the decision was hard; but I
put my name down to return to field service immediately
instead of going home aboard the S.S. *Gripsholm.* Some
thirty of us officers and clerks stood on the Lourenço Marques dock and saw the repatriation ship sail. Another
officer and I, as seniors of the group, took informal command, and we went on to Johannesburg to board the special plane that would take us back to work.

The next months brought kaleidoscopic changes for me.
Our plane took the India and China personnel as far as
Karachi. There, twelve of us, because we lacked yellow-
fever certificates, were held in quarantine for a period of
tedious days. Released, we went on, and a heavily loaded
military plane flew four of us over the "Hump" of the
Himalayas into war-torn China. For four months, as Second Secretary of Embassy, I remained in the grimy, bomb-

shattered capital of Chungking, with its shops well stocked with goods from Japanese-occupied Shanghai and with its travelers to and from Japan's puppet Government in Nanking. It was interesting but far from inspiring to live and work in the unhealthy atmosphere of corruption, political intrigue, and domestic tensions found in the vicinity of the National Government. It was with pleasure that I left for Lanchow, Kansu Province, with the mission of proceeding later to Sinkiang, in Central Asia, to open an office there. The air seemed fresher over the mountains.

At Lanchow, the terminus of truck caravans bringing in Soviet goods and taking back return cargoes of tungsten and tea, I performed my solitary tasks for two months. Then, in March, I was told by the Embassy that a plane of the old "Eurasia" line was flying to Tihwa (Urumchi), that they had reserved a seat for me aboard, and that I should proceed to my new post at once. The plane came in, but left without me: my place had been preempted by extra poundage for a cargo of Nationalist banknotes. The Chungking government was at that juncture absorbing political power from the Sinkiang warlord, who had recently shifted his sympathies from Moscow to Chungking, and it was not neglecting the profitable economic potentials of the operation. Another plane might not be along for months (Eurasia, a Sino-German undertaking, naturally no longer functioned as a regular transcontinental airline), and the next plane too might not have room for me. Rather than wait, a couple of days later I took passage on a ten-truck caravan leaving for Hsinghsinghsia (Ape Pass) on the Kansu-Sinkiang border, and left at once, informing the Embassy that I was off. Fifteen days and two changes of vehicle later, I was across the Taklamakan Desert and over the T'ien Shan range, in Tihwa. I informed the Embassy that the new Consulate had opened for business.

At Lanchow, I had been a one-man office. At Tihwa, with the 700,000 square miles of Sinkiang my district (and no other American in it), my staff comprised three aliens— a messenger, a watchman, and a cook. The only other foreign mission there was a powerfully staffed Soviet Consulate General, headed by Georgi M. Pushkin (who became well known later for his role in postwar Germany). At Kashgar was an old friend, British Consul General Michael Gillett, but hundreds of miles of desert lay between us. After some four months, bluff and likeable Geoffrey Turrell arrived to represent the United Kingdom, and set up his consular office alongside my own. In that Asian society of native Turki peoples, minority Chinese rulers, and Soviet and refugee Russians, my duty was again observation, under circumstances where the United States was interested in doing everything possible to keep China in the war, even if this meant transshipment of supplies across Central Asia—if *that* were found possible. In working on the mission my government had given me, I ranged as far as Kashgar, and Kuldja in the rich Ili Valley.

The Nationalists had worked not only at easing warlord Sheng Shih-ts'ai from power (they eventually succeeded), but also at eliminating Soviet influence from the province. In a dispatch of November 1, 1943, at which time the Soviets had completed the withdrawal of both troops and advisers from Sinkiang, I commented upon a report by the Nationalist Special Commissioner that the local authorities were experiencing much "trouble" of late with the Soviets. Against a thumbnail sketch of the history of the relationship between the Soviets and Sheng, I said that

It appears to me that two things must be kept in mind in judging contemporary developments in Sinkiang: 1) some future developments will be unfavorable for the Chinese, because of the deterioration which has occurred in the economic and political situation, and the Chinese authorities, desirous of placing blame on other shoulders than their own, might well find it convenient to charge events up to international plots instead of their own actions; and 2) logically, in view of past Chinese diplomatic practice, the Chinese would desire under present conditions to bring to bear against the Soviet Union, to cause it to be more "reasonable" in its policies vis-à-vis China, pressure from third Powers—and one way to enlist that aid, the Chinese might consider, would be to indicate in the first instance that the Soviet Union is at present acting in the wrong. . . . That the Chinese authorities in Sinkiang have heretofore endeavored to play against the Soviets, in their dealings with them, the fact of the establishment in Tihwa of American and British Consulates, appears to me highly probable. That the Chinese will where possible endeavor to play the Americans and British against each other as well seems also probable. The basic Chinese assumption, that all Occidental Powers are so desirous of the political favors and mythical "trade possibilities" of China that they would severally be led to disregard their other intimate associations of war or peace, however, would appear to have little reference to the tremendous tasks facing the United Nations in 1943.

In December 1943, suffering from dysentery, I was replaced, under orders to return to the United States. It took me only two days to cover by plane the distance between Tihwa and Lanchow I had taken an arduous fortnight to traverse by truck eight months before. In the interim, I had written 75 dispatches and many more telegrams for the information of the Embassy at Chungking and the Department at Washington. By an instruction of April 25, 1944, the Department of State commended me for "the energetic and competent manner" in which I had performed my mission at Tihwa, stating that my reports from that post "have been valuable to the Department not only for their timeliness with respect to important current developments in Sinkiang, but also for the useful background information which they have provided in regard to that area." The Department's communication singled out my above-mentioned dispatch of November 1, and another of December 3, 1943, on the topic "U.S.S.R.–Sinkiang Relationships," both graded "Excellent," for special mention.

It was more than three years since I had seen my family, and I hoped to be home for Christmas. But my roundabout wartime air route from Tihwa measured about 18,000 miles, and travel by military planes with their erratic schedules was not speedy enough. I was not reunited with my family in St. Paul until early in January. My son, Oliver, who had been a little boy of 11 when I last saw him, was now taller that I, and Zoë was a young lady entering her teens. Mariann showed no change, but my mother was notably grayer, and I knew poignantly that I had missed rich years with them. But their hearts were the same, and they had waited to share Christmas with me—the first Christmas my family had ever had together on American soil. The needles on the tree had dried from waiting and were beginning to fall, but it was a gay party that gathered around it.

After undergoing necessary medical treatment, I took up my next assignment, Washington; but I had hardly arrived when I was asked to replace Angus I. Ward at Vladivostok. This would mean another family separation after the long one just ended, when the children were growing and needed both their parents. Still, it was wartime, and I spoke both Chinese and Russian. Early in July I left to become Consul General at Vladivostok, again limited to the personal possessions I could get into that carefully weighed dufflebag of wartime travelers. Mariann remained with the children through the summer vacation, then put them in school, and in October set out with her own duf-flebag on the long road after me. I arrived at my new post in August, Mariann in December. The home to which I welcomed her was not in the pattern of "lush living" that some believe is customarily enjoyed by American diplo-mats. The dilapidated government furniture (the Wards had shipped out their own by Soviet vessel) was enough for the bare needs of eating and sleeping, but no more. Cracked brown linoleum covered the floors, and greenish-black blackout curtains were the draperies. Vladivostok was without house-furnishing shops, but Mariann made paper shades for the lamps, decorated the walls with pic-tures taken from *Life*, and concentrated the meager pieces of furniture at one end of the large living-room. At the other end we improvised a deck-tennis court. We were again "settled down." A half-year later, the promised gov-ernment furniture arrived.

The Maritime Province in which Vladivostok was lo-cated had been designated a military zone by the Soviet authorities, and local restrictions and prohibitions re-flected this condition. No American newsmen, or indeed any foreigners other than a handful of American, Chinese, and Japanese on official business, were permitted to travel to wartime Vladivostok. The only foreigners resident in town were those in the three small consular offices—the American, Chinese, and Japanese. Our office counted (in-cluding Mariann) seven Americans. Assistant Naval Attaché George D. Roullard kept an eye on Lend-Lease shipments brought in by Soviet shipping, and I watched everything that was visible. My staff was able and willing, and under my administration the Vladivostok office prepared more economic and political reports than ever before.

But at last the A-bombs fell on Hiroshima and Nagasaki, the USSR declared war, and V-J Day came. Vladivostok was immediately shorn of its wartime importance. In neighboring Manchuria, on the other hand, the Soviet troops that had entered to fight the Japanese planted their feet down—solidly. The end of the war marked, in the field of international affairs, the beginning of developments that had long been suppressed in service of the more urgent matter of national survival.

Viewing the Far Eastern situation from Vladivostok, and perceiving the development of a new imbalance in East Asia, promptly after V-J Day I forecast for the benefit of the Department the development of instability in Manchuria and the possible growth there of Soviet influence. In a long telegram on October 31, I analyzed the existing situation. I remarked that the Soviets probably did not anticipate that the restoration of international peace would introduce an era of domestic reconciliation and orderly reconstruction in China. I held that Moscow would assuredly view with deep sympathy any rise of the revolutionary tide in China, and observed that the Soviet Union was in a physical position to extend assistance to the Chinese Communists should it wish to do so. I also offered the opinion that most of such assistance would consist of material aid rather than personnel. Noting that the basic conflict between the Nationalists and Communists was evidently about to be put to the issue in China, I said that for the Soviets the desideratum would probably be the establishment of control over Manchuria and North China of a pro-Soviet regime under Communist leadership.

The Department had actually ordered me shortly after V-J Day to proceed by rail directly to Manchuria and ascertain the condition of our official property and interests in Harbin, Mukden, and Dairen. However, the Soviets made no reply to any of the requests made at Vladivostok and Moscow for approval of the projected travel. American weather stations had been set up in the summer of 1945 at Khabarovsk and Petropavlovsk, of course by agreement with Moscow, for facilitating the anticipated joint prosecution of the Pacific War. About the beginning of December the Soviets requested prompt closure of those stations and withdrawal of personnel, and at the end of December an American warship arrived in port for the outbound transport of men and equipment from the Khabarovsk station. In my own case, although I had in the meantime been assigned Consul General to Harbin, and it had been nearly three months since I had applied for my exit visa, my efforts to proceed to my new post by the direct, overland route had clearly failed. But the first American merchantman to call since the outbreak of the Pacific War, the S.S. *Edwin J. Berwind,* was due to arrive i a few days with a cargo of Red Cross supplies for the USSR. The Department approved my proposal that I should try to take up the Harbin assignment by traveling via Shanghai. Given this change of plan, Soviet exit visas for Mariann and me were forthcoming within a few days.

The *Berwind*'s master, Captain Hansen, made himself unforgettable by giving to us Americans, who had not seen the like for so long a time, a basket of luscious fruit. With that taste of the pleasures of the outside world, we prepared to depart. Ward had been the first Consul General of the office upon its reopening in the Soviet era. I was the second, and the last. Worsening American-Soviet relations were soon reflected at Vladivostok, and were marked by the arrest and disappearance of an American stenographer, Irene Matusis. Within the year, the office would be closed. It was with a feeling of the changed nature of things that we looked out from the deck of the *Berwind* on "Vladi" for the last time as the ship made its way out of the Zolotoi Rog (Golden Horn), through the ice, in early January 1946. Four days later we steamed into the Yangtze River. We were back in China.

Hospitalization required by both Mariann and myself kept us in Shanghai a full month. The Department shifted assignments. An old-time China colleague, A. Sabin Chase, was given the Harbin assignment, and when ready to travel I was charged with reopening the Consulate General at Mukden. From my hospital bed, I enviously saw Chase depart, and after him Major Robert B. Rigg, detailed to Manchuria by the U.S. Army. At the end of February, Mariann and I started northward. The Soviet forces were still in Manchuria, and although little enough was known about what was happening there, it was quite evident that conditions were badly unsettled. I left Mariann behind me, once more, in Peking. Then, passing Chase in Tientsin (where he himself had been hospitalized), I arrived in Mukden in early March, a few days after the Soviet troops had withdrawn north.

"Bob" Rigg was ahead of me, and with friendly energy had secured rooms for the two of us in the sometime Yamato Hotel—now "Intourist" and Soviet-operated. Even with the biggest open-pit coal mine in the world located a mere thirty miles away, in Manchuria's frigid late winter the hotel was without heat except for an hour in the evening. Hot water was practically unknown, and the cold water came only intermittently. Sometimes we had electric light, but more often we had to use only the dimmest of thin, guttering candles for lighting. The cuisine was an abomination, no less. But this was the best temporary accommodation available in Mukden after a hard war, and we made it our base.

The former Consulate General had been gutted, and I never discovered its archives or equipment. Ex-Japanese buildings were being grabbed right and left by Chinese organizations and politicians, for this was the day of The Great Inheritance. Chinese officialdom expressed every wish to be helpful to Americans, but for some reason it seemed difficult to come by any suitable piece of loose real estate. The former Japanese Consulate General was reserved for the exclusive use of Generalissimo and Madame Chiang Kai-shek should they ever come to Mukden—as they did, once. I was able to save the British-registered Moukden Club from going the way of other unattached real estate by running up the American flag when it was threatened and getting expeditious approval from the British Embassy in Chungking for taking it into custody. But I was unable to get effective Chinese aid in the search for suitable official quarters. It was entirely through American efforts that new premises were found and the Consulate General reopened. Mariann came from Peking and went to work in the office pending the arrival of regular Civil Service stenographers, for Mukden surged with activity and there was much for our office to do. In the beginning, we regularly worked late into the night getting the office established and functioning.

Nominally, the primary task confronting the Chinese nation was reconstruction, and UNRRA (the United Nations Relief and Rehabilitation Administration) did in fact promptly go into action. The Nationalists, for their part, forcibly recovered from Soviet hands certain real property acquired during the military occupation. The displacement and repatriation of the Japanese was in progress. The Pauley Reparations Mission came, surveyed the ravages of the wartime and postwar periods, and departed. The U.S. War Department increased its representation. And all the time, Nationalist and Communist troops were pouring into the vast power vacuum of some 400,000 square miles. Manchuria was predestined to be an arena for postwar struggle between the Kuomintang dictatorship and the Chinese Communist revolutionaries.

Thanks to the mediation of General George C. Marshall, a military truce had been signed on January 10 and an Executive Headquarters had been set up in Peking for the consolidation of peace in China through a tripartite effort by the Nationalists, the Communists, and the "neutral" United States. Clashes had already occurred at various points in Manchuria. After some difficulty and delay in obtaining Chiang Kai-shek's agreement, Headquarters branches were established in Mukden, Changchun, Harbin, and other Manchurian points in early April. The conflict of purposes nevertheless led inevitably to aggravation of the situation, and the truce agreement was patently being strained to the breaking point. It was now reported that the Soviet Union was withdrawing its military forces from Manchuria by April 30. In a telegram of April 11 to the Department I commented that such action, which was in accord with the Nationalist desire, would bring matters to an open issue between the Nationalists and the Communists. The Nationalists, I pointed out, faced a difficult problem of logistics; and I remarked that there probably existed more opposition strength in the countryside than the limited probings of the government armies had thus far uncovered. Taking note of Chiang Kai-shek's stated position that the only issue was China's recovery of sovereignty, I said that on such a basis the Communists had little choice but to fight, if they desired influence in Manchuria.

The Soviet forces withdrew by early May, and the struggle for power between the Nationalists and Communists was stepped up. On June 6, Chiang Kai-shek issued new orders nominally aimed at stopping hostilities. But the Nationalist commander in chief in Manchuria, General Tu Yu-ming, issued an interpretation of the order that betrayed an absence of bona fides, and in a dispatch of June 12 I commented on that interpretation:

> . . . the spirit of General Tu Yu-ming's statement . . . is not such as would give sound basis for belief that the Communists would accept the "truce" as thus arbitrarily offered them, unless it can be assumed that they already feel themselves defeated in Manchuria. It is my estimate that they do not feel that their position has become untenable.

The truce ran out at the end of June, and the Chinese Communists take July 1946 as marking the resumption of the civil war.

Chase had also failed to reach Harbin, and I was again assigned that task. Oliver and Zoë had now rejoined us, and we started out northward together in October. We reached Changchun, which (as Hsinking) had been the capital of Japan's Manchoukuo. We were about halfway to our official destination. A skeleton staff set up by Chase before me awaited our arrival, Bob Rigg was stationed there as Assistant Military Attaché, UNRRA personnel were also present, and so too was British Consul General designate to Harbin, Colonel Eric Jacobs-Larkcom. The Executive Headquarters branch dominated the scene with its equipment. Their planes (all American, of course) regularly flew between Changchun and Harbin with Nationalist, Communist, and American Headquarters officials; and they freely carried between those points, over the battle lines dividing Manchuria, a variety of news correspondents. The journalists included Frenchmen and British subjects, Soviet TASS correspondents, and pro-Soviet Anna Louise Strong. But I could not myself obtain passage, to be dropped off unannounced in the Communist-controlled city of Harbin. The Colonel in command held that if this were done without Communist consent (which admittedly could not be obtained) it would possibly interfere with the accomplishment of the mission of bringing peace to China.

That mission was not to succeed, and my chances for reaching Harbin were rapidly disappearing over the horizon as the tide of an angry civil war surged higher. I proposed, and the Department approved, the formal establishment of an office in Changchun, and in October 1946 I opened a new Consulate General in what was effectively the Nationalists' northernmost major outpost. On October 15, within days of my arrival, I reported in my tenth telegram from the new office that the period ahead promised to be one of unusual political and economic difficulties for the Nationalists; and I pointed up salient factors in the situation operating to the Nationalist disadvantage: (1) vulnerability to aggressive Communist action, of the limited area of Manchuria controlled by the Nationalist armies; (2) the little promise that existed for economic renaissance in the visible future, given the destruction of material plant that had occurred; (3) the possibility that the Soviets would take fresh action to influence events in the period ahead.

In January 1947, when the Nationalist high command was warming its heart with the comforting self-assurance that "It is too cold in wintertime in Manchuria for the Communists to fight," the Communists launched the first of a series of drives that rolled the Nationalists back into their fortified towns. A second drive came in February. On March 1, while out on an inspection trip, Rigg and his assistant, Captain Jack Collins, were captured by an unperceived Communist column near Changchun. They were imprisoned in the Harbin we had tried so hard to reach. We finally succeeded in negotiating their release, some forty days later, and one spring day Colonel Edward T. Cowen and I crossed the Sungari River into Communist territory under a white flag of truce and received custody of the two officers. It was also at Changchun that I rescued 38 White Russians, who had fled from Communist territory, from being returned to the hands of the Communists by the Nationalist authorities.

But there was no saving the Nationalists from themselves. A third Communist drive came in April, and lapped closer still around the jerry-built Changchun fortifications; the railroad was cut, the airfield was endangered. At the Embassy's urging, I evacuated women and children, ex-

cept two stenographers who were willing to stay on—and
Oliver, who was enjoying the excitement. This was our
sixth family separation caused by the existence of hazardous conditions at my post of duty. At a juncture when I had
been nineteen years in the Foreign Service, those breaks
totalled roughly six and one-half years. Three years more
of separation from the children, who would duly return to
school in the United States, were to be added to the already unpalatable total.

But the Communist military threat had visibly grown. In
a dispatch of June 12, 1947, I outlined the situation as I
saw it:

. . . the Nationalist military strategy in face of the present Communist drive has been essentially defensive, with all initiative in
the field left to the Communists. . . . The Nationalists at every
point have either pulled back in belated attempts to consolidate
their over-extended forces, or have dug in where they stood in
accordance with the dictates of a passive strategy of waiting inside Nationalist strong points for the Communists to attack or,
preferably from the Nationalist point of view, to go away.

In those circumstances, even allowing for some salvage of broken units, it is fairly obvious that the Nationalist position in Manchuria cannot be restored without the dispatch of large numbers
of reinforcements here from China Proper. . . .

It may be that, having their eye on the probable effect of withdrawal on any possibilities that may remain of the National Government's obtaining the desired US$500,000,000 loan, the Na-
tional political leaders will choose a middle-of-the-road course
and encourage the local military leaders to hold out as long as
possible for political reasons. In that awkward position, they
would fall between two stools, losing both Manchuria and the
remainder of the good armies stationed there. It is moreover
hardly probable that, in those circumstances where they faced
heavy odds, the Nationalist forces in Manchuria would put up the
utmost determined resistance: it appears more probable that

many of them would surrender to the Communists, with resultant profit to the latter. Failure to withdraw if reinforcement is infeasible, in short, would indirectly contribute to the further strengthening of the Communist armies and thus advance the day when North China itself would be threatened with Communist conquest.

In August of the same year, I participated in the briefing of the Wedemeyer Mission at Peking. I discussed the relationship of Koreans and Mongols to the Communist movement in Manchuria, the relationship of Japanese holdout troops (for some Japanese had refused to surrender) in that area to Communist actions, Soviet policies and actions vis-à-vis Manchuria, and the thorny problem of our own interest in, and policies toward, China. One of the four memoranda I submitted on August 3, 1947, offered summary conclusions that seemed a distant, final echo of my original 1932 report on Chinese Communism:

In sum, the Communist conquest of Manchuria would seem to herald the beginning of the end of Kuomintang rule, and the introduction of a new stage in Chinese revolutionary history. Unless the National Government embarks upon such measures of radical political reform as would counteract the Communist program and effect a commensurate strengthening of the Nationalist hold on the loyalties of the Chinese people (and particularly on the people of Manchuria), and unless in the immediate future the military position of the Nationalists in Manchuria is strengthened by the dispatch of a large number of reinforcements, it is to be anticipated that, as shown by the developments of the past year when the Nationalists became weaker in Manchuria and the Communists continued to grow in strength, the Communists will achieve their ultimate aim of establishing their power over all of that strategic area. Whether or not the National Government will embark upon major political reforms depends upon the influences which can be brought to bear by other non-Kuomintang and non-Communist political groups in China. Whether the National Government can afford to reinforce Manchuria with troops which may now be in the line or on guard inside the Wall is problematical. That there exists in China a revolutionary situation which can be met effectively only by political and military means of fundamental nature, designed to go to the roots of maladjustments which have troubled China since the Revolution of 1911, is however apparently beyond controversy.

In October 1947, I left the Changchun office in the hands of Vice Consul Allen C. Siebens. Siebens had been part of the Harbin skeleton staff set up by Chase, and had worked with me at Changchun for the past year. He was intelligent and energetic, knew the area, and would ably administer the office until it, like Vladivostok, was also closed. Without ever having reached the post of my original assignment in postwar China, Harbin, I went back south to take charge of the Peking office.

By this time, the situation in North China itself was being threatened by events in Manchuria. I repeated some of my previous warnings in a dispatch of February 11, 1948:

(1) the leadership of Generalissimo Chiang Kai-shek, who fully displayed the dogmatic and even medieval character of his mind in his book *China's Destiny,* will probably prove inadequate to lift the nation from the political and economic mire in which it finds itself, for all of the belief held by some of the Generalissimo's "indispensability"; (2) the Chinese Communist Party—if Communist policies as proven time and again have any value as precedent—are assuredly bent on ultimate conquest of China as a whole; (3) both Nationalist and Communist elements at the present time, with foreign aid tapered off and the Japanese wealth which was found in this country on V-J Day largely consumed, are cognizant of approaching exhaustion and increasing difficulties and are alike desirous of at least a temporary cessation

in the fighting; and (4) it would seem apparent that it is too late (if there has been a time) to save Manchuria for the Nationalists, given the existing political situation. Most of North China also is already in Communist hands, and the remaining points and lines can hardly be held for long in the event of Communist victory in Manchuria. The successful withdrawal to North China of those Nationalist forces now in Manchuria would of course contribute some military stability—valuable even if only temporary—to the former area. Present developments, where it is already so late, however, would seem to indicate that the withdrawal intact of the Nationalist Manchurian garrison over a line of retreat where the rail communications have been destroyed all the way from Taling River to the outskirts of Sinmin, would be an extremely difficult and hazardous undertaking.

By November of that year, after the surrender of some 300,000 Nationalist troops and the loss of vast stores of American military supplies, all Manchuria would be in Communist hands.

In a dispatch of February 19, 1948, I speculated on what the immediate aim of the Communists might be:

> Their aim truly seems to be at this time to effect an interim "coalition government" from which the leading Kuomintang figures of the present day shall have been eliminated and in which they, the Communists, will play an important role.

The "Central People's Government" established at Peking on October 1, 1949—over a year and a half later—was, as anticipated, nominally a "coalition" arrangement, with the Communists of course dominant.

With the fall of Mukden on November 1, 1948, North China's days were numbered. On our official advice, most of the American community left. The Communist "People's Liberation Army" (PLA) surrounded Peking and Tientsin, and cut communications between them, in mid-

December 1948. As in 1937, when the Japanese military forces struck, the National Government at Nanking was generous with advice to field commanders in North China, but niggardly of material support. Tientsin was selected by the Communist strategists as their first target, and fell on January 15, 1949, after a harsh bombardment. Consul General Robert L. Smyth, an old friend of the China Corps, in the accepted high tradition of the Foreign Service with calm and savoir faire brought his staff and his office safely through the danger and disorder.

Peking was bombarded in a more desultory, quasi-ritualistic fashion, evidently designed to prod the Nationalist garrison in the direction of surrender while preserving intact the architectural monuments located inside the Ming Dynasty walls. The defending general, Fu Tso-yi, without hope of getting effective aid from Nanking, actually began negotiations with the Communist side several days before the fall of Tientsin. He held out, however, until Generalissimo Chiang Kai-shek, who had twice before at critical junctures in history been forced to renounce leadership, on January 21 "retired" in favor of Vice President Li Tsung-jen. Peking's surrender was announced the following day. The besieging Communist forces, almost completely fitted out with American equipment they had captured from the Nationalists, on January 31 marched into town through the swirling dust of a cold, windy winter day. The American arms supply had sufficed for *both* sides. The Communists had taken twenty-eight years to reach Peking. But their aim had never wavered, and they were able to attain their goal at last because the National Government had lost the confidence and support of the Chinese people, who turned to another political force in the desperate hope of finding answers to their oppressive problems.

The denouement came swiftly. In April, the negotiations that had been undertaken at Peking in search of a compromise agreement between the Communists and the National Government broke down. The challengers, with victory in sight, demanded virtual surrender. The PLA armies crossed the Yangtze River on April 20 and occupied Nanking—virtually unopposed—a couple of days later, with the National Government withdrawing to Canton. The end was approaching.

During the "united front" period, the Communists had shown a mild, even genial, countenance to foreigners and uncommitted Chinese groups alike. There were signs, however—particularly in the increasing violence of their anti-American propaganda—that a harder attitude was in the making. And the fate of the Mukden consular personnel, who in November of the previous year had been virtually imprisoned in their consular compound, was a clear warning of the dangers that threatened. After the capture of Nanking and Shanghai, with victory to all intents and purposes won, the Communists showed a markedly grimmer visage to both Chinese and foreigners. At Nanking, some Communist troops invaded the American Ambassador's bedroom. In Shanghai, labor troubles boiled over into the consular office itself. At Tsingtao, the Communists requisitioned the consular premises. In Tientsin, and then Peking, (American) Economic Cooperation Administration (ECA) stocks were taken over forcibly by the new authorities. The Consulate at Tihwa closed, and its personnel escaped before the Communists by crossing Tibet and the Himalayas into India. Seemingly the U.S. Foreign Service (though it was not the only foreign diplomatic and consular establishment to suffer) was viewed by the Communists as an enemy.

In the disjointed circumstances, each consular office was largely on its own. The Communists refused to deal directly with consular officers on the ground that the governments to which those officials belonged had not yet recognized the Communist regime—even though until October 1, 1949, the Communists had no national government that *could* be recognized. At Peking, the various consular and diplomatic officials (excepting the Soviets, who dissociated themselves from the consular corps) consulted and coordinated to a remarkable degree. At Tientsin and Peking alike, tight restrictions were early placed on personal movement. At Peking, this meant the placing of guards at the gate to the official compound, and the stopping, interrogation, and general intimidation of visitors—and sometimes of our own personnel. For months we and other foreigners could not pass through the city gates even to go into the suburbs. Finally, we were allowed to get travel passes to go to Tientsin, but the Tientsin Consulate General was unable to obtain permission for its personnel to travel to Peking. The Peking Consulate General kept its radio installation functioning—the only one of the four North China consular offices successful in so doing. This was a matter of prime importance, since foreign consular offices in China, pending the establishment of regular diplomatic relations with the new regime, no longer enjoyed confidential diplomatic pouch facilities, nor would the Communist authorities permit them to send telegrams in code to their respective governments by Chinese facilities. Peking's radio station was thus our only means of communication with Washington. But the Peking and Tientsin offices stood before the storm together, and our station served Tientsin.

One of the main difficulties faced by foreign organizations of whatever nature in China (Soviet enterprises always excepted) was labor disputes. American consular offices had been authorized to make such settlements as they might find necessary. I at Peking was the only principal officer to take my labor disputes through formal arbitration process before the Labor Bureau, and through the Communist court, to reach settlements in accordance with the wage scale provided by the regulations—and nothing more. The arbitration and court procedures required my sitting long hours in unheated administrative offices and submitting to the tirades of hostile Communist officials, without benefit of legal counsel (lawyers were proscribed). But I succeeded in getting decisions which were at least held within the bounds of local regulations.

Bigger things than labor disputes were afoot. On January 4, 1949, when Peking was already under Communist siege, I had reported to the Department on a conversation I'd had with an ECA representative in which I set forth my attitude respecting ECA North China policy for a (still hypothetical) post-Communist occupation period:

I said that it was better, in my opinion, to put the matter on a "24 hour", "watchful waiting" basis, with the present relief program to stop upon its legal termination and with nothing else offered to the Communists at the present time. I gave it as my opinion that we had better terminate for the present, with the termination of ECA, the policy of charitable relief that we had continued in China since V-J Day and let our American merchants in China bear the standard for a while and see how they got along. . . . if some fine day the Communists wanted to "talk turkey" about relief or credits, the United States would be well advised to undertake such matters only on a good horse-trading basis; that is, we should indicate that we would do business only in so far as it might be profitable for us in either a political or economic sense.

Now, on June 1, I reported an approach made apparently by Communist leader Chou En-lai, through an intermediary, for American aid—presumably economic. In a telegram of June 2 to the Department, I analyzed that *démarche,* remarked that China faced grave economic problems, and set forth my assumption that the move reflected an anticipation of impending food shortages in circumstances where the Soviet Union was unable to meet China's economic needs, rather than evidencing any change of political sympathies. Observing that the Communist regime seemed to wish to continue with its diet of Soviet political bread while supplementing that diet with American economic cake, I opined that both the Chinese Communists and the Soviets would probably be willing to have the United States resurrect something like ECA and beg China to accept American aid. But I said that if this were done while China maintained close political ties with the Soviet Union, China would be strengthened the better to render political and military aid to the Soviet Union against the United States in hypothetical future contingencies, and I proposed that China be required to pay on the barrelhead for goods received, either in economic equivalent or in political concessions.

In actuality, the Communist side refused to accept a proposed direct reply from the Department, and on July 1 Mao Tse-tung made his famous "lean-to-one-side" speech: China was going to depend upon the Soviet Union for aid.

I reported progressively on the apparent hardening of the official Chinese Communist attitude toward the United States, but still had occasion to report other indirect suggestions that the United States extend economic assistance but expect nothing in return, not even a cessation of anti-American propaganda. I advised against any such approach.

The problem of relations with China took on a new and immediate importance with the formal establishment, on October 1, 1949, of the Central People's Government at Peking. In a telegram of October 10, I invited the Department's attention to the shrinking authority of the Nationalist regime, said that the Communists would soon be in effective control of all but the periphery of China; and there, I said, the main conflict was with the Soviet Union, and that conflict could be expected to grow.

Observing that the *least* effective way of influencing the China situation was by divorcing oneself from it, I recommended that the policy of nonintervention on behalf of the dying Nationalist regime be continued, that the United States temporarily maintain a noncommittal position but early show interest in the new regime's policies, let the Communists for their part get a glimpse of the benefits to be obtained through commerce and good relations with non-Communist countries, and then, in circumstances where by hypothesis the Nationalist regime had collapsed and the Communist regime had indicated a readiness to follow accepted standards of international behavior, extend recognition to the new Chinese government. I remarked in that connection that the Communists would have to discover for themselves that political and economic relations with the United States and others on "our

side" would promise more profit to China than depen-
dence upon the Soviet Union, and that in the interim the
United States could only view with the best grace possible
the growing Soviet influence, with an appreciation that
that development by itself might help bring schisms in
Chinese politics favoring independence from the Soviet
Union.

With the New Year, as the first anniversary of the Communist occupation of Peking drew near, a crowning difficulty loomed up. On January 6, 1950, the Military Control Commission plastered on the gates of the British,
French, Dutch, and American consular and diplomatic establishments in Peking an announcement that within six
days it would requisition the former military barracks of
the several offices. London extended its formal recognition
to the Peking regime that same day (an action the Communist authorities had known was scheduled), and the no-
tification was removed from the gate of the British compound that evening; but the three other foreign rep-
resentations were left confronted with the issue. In the
American case, the former barracks had been converted
into offices for the Consulate General, with attached language school and U.S. Information Agency, as was of
course well known to the Chinese. In sum, the new
regime proposed to confiscate the premises housing official U.S. Government organs.

The Chinese side made no direct contact with the principal officers of the concerned consular offices. We con-
ferred with each other, reported to our respective governments, tried fruitlessly to contact the municipal authorities
(nominally responsible for the actions of the Military Control Commission), and sent notes to the Foreign Ministry—

without eliciting a response. The U.S. Consulate General took no action in the direction of removal, knowing that any sign of acquiescence would be interpreted as surrender. We stood pat, hoping that a State Department ultimatum, delivered by me, that American representation in China would be withdrawn if the Communists persisted in the move, might prove effective. It did not.

The Communists came in on the stipulated date, and said that I was guilty of bad faith in failing to cause removal of our effects and would have to take the consequences. They fixed a midnight deadline (it was already 10 A.M.) for such removal. We were in constant radio contact with the Department, and under instructions began to move. Every man and woman of the consular staff and their dependents turned out and set about removing all the office equipment in a three-story barracks, our commissary stores and office supplies, some 300 tons of coal, the contents of storerooms in which we kept both Army and Navy property left behind, and the households of the half-dozen residences in the compound in question. The personnel, alien as well as American, frail Chinese stenographers as well as husky workmen, responded magnificently. Excellent headway was made during the first day, and in the early evening I was called over to the Alien Affairs Office. After a long session in which it was again drilled into me that I was personally responsible for any delay in schedule, a 24-hour extension (through Sunday) was granted. I returned to my staff, we worked all through the night—with Mariann providing hot coffee and food for the staff—and then all day Sunday.

At five minutes to midnight on Sunday night we finished the job. There was nothing movable left in the immense

compound except enough coal to keep the fires burning in
the furnaces so that the pipes would not burst from the
frost. On the next day the Communists entered a deserted
compound where the doors were open and keys were in
the locks, where the flag was off the staff, and where no
one was present but a watchman who kept the gates until
the arrival of the occupying party. The radio station of the
Consulate General had been transferred into the new compound without break of contact with Washington, and on
Tuesday morning the Consulate General itself again
opened for business in our old office, the former chancery
of the American Legation. It was a well-nigh herculean
achievement. The United States Government could well
have been proud of such a loyal staff.

But the U.S. Government's ultimatum had been given,
and the breach was irreparable. We now gave notice to the
Peking authorities of the impending withdrawal of all official personnel from China. Some posts, as indicated
above, had already been abandoned because of prevailing
difficulties. The several remaining offices bent their main
efforts to the winding up of outstanding affairs and the liq-
uidation of our large establishments. In Peking, personnel
began to depart in January, commensurate with the reduc-
tion of our official activities. The office nevertheless continued to fulfill its basic reporting functions, and on February 20 and 21 I sent the Department two long telegrams
offering an analysis of the significance of the Sino-Soviet
agreements of February 14, 1950. In the first communication, I gave my estimate that the agreements
clearly fell short of Chinese aspirations, and said that scat-
tered Chinese reactions were thus far unfavorable, the alliance being viewed as a crystallization of the situation to

China's disadvantage. I suggested that, on the basis of past experience, the Chinese would probably regard the agreements as being more imperialistic than anticipated, and that, given China's staggering political and economic burdens, Chinese discontents and resentments would pile up. I further expressed the conviction that, besides the published documents, the two sides had reached certain secret agreements at Moscow; and in my followup telegram of the next day, in which I speculated on the potential significance of the agreements, I said that those agreements seemed to increase the possibility of war, and that the essential American task was to consolidate its strength in areas of prime importance, against possible contingencies.

One day near the end of March, the Chinese Communists came in and shut down our radio station; the action cut in half another long telegram of political observation in the process of transmittal. Then, on April 10, I saw the last of my staff off on the train, and closed the office officially at the end of business that day. All confidential records and codes had been destroyed. On April 12 we took down from the compound gate the official seal and then performed the saddest service of all: we lowered the American flag for the last time in the Peking consular compound. Those attending the ceremony were Mariann and I and several faithful alien personnel of the once imposing American Consulate General of Peking. On the same day Mariann and I took our own departure from the ancient capital we had loved so much. The Shanghai and Tientsin personnel also left before the month was out. For the first time in a century the United States was without official representation in China. That was evidently the way the Communists had wanted it.

At the port of Tientsin, before we were permitted to embark, the Communist Customs authorities went through all
of our luggage, and even through our pockets. We had
been forewarned by the experience of other travelers, and
I had therefore destroyed all personal correspondence and
papers of possible interest, but I brought along with me all
of the office accounts for the past year (when we could not
trust the mails), and confidential documents attesting to
destruction of codes, currency, et cetera. I succeeded in
running the gauntlet without detection of the confidential
material. Then we sailed on a British vessel for Japan. We
were safely out of China. But behind us the Chinese Communists rifled our cargo of personal effects of 50 of the
choicest treasures we had collected in our two decades in
China, and of 25 Chinese-language works (some of them
running into many volumes). That was my "reward" from
the Chinese Communists. We could, and did, feel pangs at
the loss of the things of beauty we had gathered over the
years; however we were not surprised. Yet we were not,
after all, fully sophisticated: we should at that time have
thought anyone quite mad who might have charged that I
had been engaged through my years in the Far East in
furthering the Communist cause.

We remained three weeks in Japan. I was "debriefed"
in one session with General MacArthur, and gave some six
to eight talks on the China situation to officers and men of
the American occupation forces. In the last of those talks,
at Yokohama, I warned of impending difficulties in the Far
East, but expressed the conviction that the United States
possessed adequate strength to handle any emergency that
might develop. We made our way to Washington with the
knowledge in our hearts that we had a solid record of able
performance. On June 16, at a high-level State Department

conference, I warned of a threat to South Korea. We went on leave immediately thereafter—only to hear shortly of the North Korean aggression of June 25. We cut short our vacation and returned to Washington, and on July 6, 1950, I took up my new post as Director of the Office of Chinese Affairs.

So my record of accomplishment was a solid one. The Department had never manifested lack of confidence in either my ability, energy, or my probity and discretion. The contrary was the case. The various commendations I had received, and the regular and rapid promotions that had brought me in April 1949 to Class I, at the top of the Foreign Service list, constituted concrete evidence that my performance of a wide and arduous variety of functions over two decades had given satisfaction. I was in fact informed that in 1949, while I was in Communist-occupied Peking, it was only because of the possible political implications with respect to Sino-American relations that the Department had refrained from nominating me for the position of Career Minister.

The later testimony of a high Department official set forth a rationale for my assignment to the post of Director of the Office of Chinese Affairs. The witness had just stated "I think it was generally accepted in the [Nanking] Embassy that Mr. Clubb was not only the most prolific but the soundest reporting officer in China." This exchange between the witness and my representative followed:

Q How, in your opinion, does Mr. Clubb rank concerning his knowledge of Chinese Communism both in terms of knowledge and of judgment?

A I remember a good many talks that Mr. Butterworth, who was then Assistant Secretary of State for Far Eastern Affairs, and I had when the question came up of filling the post of director of the

Office of Chinese Affairs. We went over, I think, with considerable care, all of the senior officers with experience in China, and we were both of the opinion that Mr. Clubb's knowledge of China, his extended and recent experience there, in particular his dealing during the last year or year and a half of his stay in Peiping with the Communist regime, as he was forced to, and living under their rule in Peiping, made him the best qualified, logical choice for that position in the Department. I think—it has been my impression certainly from both talks and study of memoranda prepared in the past year by Mr. Clubb that he has had a deep and effective grasp, not only of Chinese history and Chinese psychology, but of the nature and the character of the Communist regime which has come into power in China.

Seemingly, that was how I came to be appointed to the post of Director of the Office of Chinese Affairs.

The succeeding six months in the State Department were filled with activity and interest. The warfare in Korea naturally constituted a major concern for the Far Eastern Division (of which the Office of Chinese Affairs was an integral part). It was part of my job to concern myself with China's relationship to the developing situation on the peninsula, and on July 14, a scant nine days after assuming my new post, I submitted a memorandum on "Relationship of Chinese Communists to Korean Affair" in which I set forth four possible alternative developments deriving from that relationship, as follows:

(1) Direct intervention by Chinese Communist military units in support of North Korea;
(2) Indirect assistance, by Chinese Communist "volunteers" in Korean uniform;
(3) Chinese Communist attack on Formosa, adjusted to Korean developments;
(4) Like attacks against Hong Kong and/or Indochina.

I stated that "the theoretical alternative of the Chinese Communists remaining passive may be arbitrarily ruled out."

At that time, the South Korean defense had been shattered, and the UN–U.S. forces were being pressed into the Pusan perimeter, and I suggested that in the circumstances there were reasons to believe that the Chinese might choose to attack Formosa. As regards Indochina, I said that:

. . . the present logic of the situation . . . seems to indicate that Chinese Communist intervention in the Indochinese conflict could . . . best be fostered by the use of indirect methods only, that is, by the support of Ho Chi Minh with materiel and possibly "volunteers" instead of by direct intervention of Chinese Communist military units in a struggle for "national liberation." Likewise, Hong Kong would hardly be attacked before everything was ready for the launching of a general war.

In another memorandum, of October 4, referring to Chinese Premier Chou En-lai's warning just after midnight of October 2–3 to Indian Ambassador K. M. Panikkar that China would intervene in the Korean War if *American* armed forces were to cross the 38th Parallel, I stated that "The Chou En-lai démarche cannot safely be regarded as mere bluff. . . . His démarche must be regarded as having been made with foreknowledge and support of USSR. The political and military stakes are considerable, and Moscow and Peiping may be prepared to take considerable risks."

At the Wake Island conference with President Truman in mid-October, however, General MacArthur held that there was "very little" chance of Chinese intervention, and said that "If the Chinese tried to get down to Pyongyang there would be the greatest slaughter." He expressed the belief that enemy resistance would have ended throughout Korea by Thanksgiving, and envisaged the withdrawal of the bulk of the U.S. forces back to Japan by Christmas.

In actuality, U.S. forces crossed the 38th Parallel, and Chinese "volunteers" intervened in the Korean War in late October (although not in Korean uniforms). In a new memorandum of November 4, 1950, I treated the matter of "Chinese Communist Intervention in Korea: Estimate of Objectives," in which I held that "The minimum Chinese Communist objective must be considered to be either the restoration of the status quo ante June 25 in North Korea or the expulsion of UN forces from the entire Korean peninsula." My recommendation was that the united UN front be maintained at all costs.

On December 7 I submitted a long analysis of the developing situation, then threatening grave danger for the UN forces, under the title "Chinese Intervention in Korea—Current Intentions." I set forth various benefits which could be expected to accrue to the UN allies through continuation of the military action under the seemingly unfavorable circumstances, including:

5. The very successes which have attended the Chinese drive will tend to increase their self-confidence, even their arrogance. This might possibly be true to a certain degree even vis-à-vis Moscow. . . . This situation will be aggravated perhaps by the circumstance that the Chinese Communists will be in occupation of an area long considered by the Soviet Union (and before the USSR, by Tsarist Russia) to be of considerable strategic and political importance to Russia rather than to China. There does exist in the present situation, in short, the seeds of some possible dissension between the Moscow-Peiping alliance.

6. For so long as the Chinese Communists are engaged in

Korea they will presumably be correspondingly braked as regards other ventures directed, by hypothesis, toward Indochina, Formosa, or other areas on their periphery. This would constitute a net gain.

And I rounded out my first half-year as Director of the Office of Chinese Affairs by submitting a memorandum of December 18, 1950, entitled "Estimates of Moscow-Peiping Time-Table for War," in which I speculated, in several different "scenarios," on possible war plans of the Sino-Soviet allies.

This, then, was the kind of record—my record—that had come under the challenge of the State Department's Loyalty-Security Board. I thought it good.

IV

The Witness and I

WHEREAS disregard and contempt for human rights have resulted in barbarous acts which have outraged the conscience of mankind, and the advent of a world in which human beings shall enjoy freedom of speech and belief and freedom from fear and want has been proclaimed as the highest aspiration of the common people,

WHEREAS it is essential, if man is not to be compelled to have recourse, as a last resort, to rebellion against tyranny and oppression, that human rights should be protected by the rule of law,

WHEREAS it is essential to promote the development of friendly relations between nations, . . .

Preamble to the Universal Declaration of Human Rights.

As Mariann and I pored over the LSB's interrogatory, we wondered as to the origin of the various allegations, and the significance of this move. We were not so innocent in the ways of bureaucracy as to assume that no unfriendly colleague would ever seize an opportunity to trip me up. We thought of the few men who might have harbored enmity toward me. An officer with whom I had served first at Hankow and later at Shanghai was one whose image early found a prominent place in our speculative search. I was a political reporting officer, B—— was an administrative officer; and our political viewpoints were far apart—especially regarding my area of specialization, China. And at Shanghai there had been a clash between us. Mariann and I concluded that B—— was probably to be found somewhere in the picture.

There were other, impersonal partisan forces that stood ready to destroy those who might seem to stand in their political road. Given the rich opportunities for profit by exploitation of the "China Question," a China bloc had grown up in Congress; and, outside Congress, a supporting pressure group that came to be known as the China Lobby was taking form. The loyalty-security system offered facilities for planting venomous allegations of wrongdoing against those thrust into the category of "enemy"—of whomsoever. We could with logic suspect that some inspiration for the present inquiry might have had its ultimate origin in that quarter. General Stilwell had been felled by the convoluted efforts of Chiang Kai-shek's cohorts, essentially because he had not shown himself sufficiently pro-Nationalist and had thought of employing the Chinese Communists in the war against Japan. Ambassador Patrick J. Hurley in 1944 had himself begun the ill-fated American mediation between the Kuomintang regime and the Communists; however, the action that had won him high favor in Chiang Kai-shek's camp was his shift to a position of all-out support for the Nationalists. He had moreover made a substantial contribution to the creation of an atmosphere of suspicion with regard to the loyalty of State Department personnel. The National Government itself had on two occasions, over long years, maintained closer relations with the Communists than was possible for any American diplomat, but there was obviously no exemption offered to American FSOs who had

served in China during its "controversial" period. Some of
my Far Eastern colleagues had in fact come under attack
for various "associations" with the Chinese Communists—even though, in undertaking those relationships,
they had been acting in accord with the policies and instructions of the U.S. Government. And the hard fact was
that one of the allegations with which the LSB had confronted me was that I had "associated with Communists in
Hankow, China, 1931–1934."

And then there were the other allegations, attributed to
anonymous "informants" and extracted from unknown
contexts. What was meant when it was said that I had
"Viewed some aspects of Communism favorably," was
" 'favorable' to the Communists" (and *which* Communists?), had "distinct 'pink' tendencies," was "friendly toward the U.S.S.R. and Communism," and "espoused doctrines of a 'Communist' nature"? The LSB's interrogatory
related the allegations to no specific writings, statements
or acts—not even to a particular part of the world—
although the dates used left the easy inference that the
scene of my alleged ideological deviations was China.

The interrogatory thus presented little solid substance
for one to work on. Mariann and I could only attack the
problems it posed with due regard for all possible angles.
We went forward with our analysis of the strange document, probing its inner meaning and remaining alert to the
possible presence of inimical forces. From the practical
standpoint, of course, we had to address ourselves to the
specific allegations as such, and not to some elusive
shadows in the background. The Department's LSB evidently proposed, through a probe of my subjective attitudes, to determine whether my loyalty and security were

flawless beyond its capacity for doubt. It was useless to argue against the system. The task at hand was to convince the LSB that I, with more than two decades of service with the State Department to my credit, and with that service voluminously documented in the Department's records, was both loyal and "safe"—by the unknown pliant standards of a new era of suspicion.

The only specific allegation, and clearly that most heavily loaded with potential danger, was the final one: that in 1932 I had "delivered a sealed envelope to the office of the editor of the 'New Masses' magazine in New York City for transmittal to one Grace Hutchins, a reported Communist employed by the Labor Research Bureau. . . ." The LSB asked for my complete knowledge of the episode, *"if it happened,"* including "the nature of the document transmitted," previous acquaintanceship with the *New Masses* editor, and association with Grace Hutchins.

That allegation puzzled us the most. The crux of the matter surely lay hidden in the words "sealed envelope," "document," and "Grace Hutchins": it was being charged, in essence, that I had been the instrument for delivery of a presumably confidential—possibly State Department— document to a suspected conspirator. I knew that I would have done no such thing; but we lacked even primary elements that might have had a bearing on the charge. We could remember going home to Minnesota when on leave from Hankow in 1932 easily enough, but after eighteen years we couldn't accurately reconstruct our other movements in the United States from memory; we weren't even certain that we had visited New York on that occasion. And I, who had been in so many strange places of the world, didn't remember ever having gone to the *New*

Masses. Moreover, probe my memory as I would, I could resurrect no recollection of ever having heard the name "Grace Hutchins," to say nothing of having had any "association" with her. We started on this item with a complete blank.

In a letter of January 4 the Board stated that it was "by no means arbitrary in enforcing the ten-day limitation if the nature of your reply requires additional time for preparation or if the pressure of your duties will not permit you to submit your reply within the ten days." I was still performing my regular duties, and was to continue to carry on with those not unimportant functions for the whole period of the interrogatory process. I applied for, and received, an extension of ten days.

In a letter of January 22, I made my first response to the LSB interrogatory. I gave a categorical answer to the questions about my relationship to the Communist Party: I had never been "a member of, affiliated with, or in sympathetic association with the Communist Party, or any organization which is a front for, or controlled by, the Communist Party." Next came the allegations that I had viewed "some aspects" of Communism "favorably," had "pink tendencies," possessed "a marked preference" for, and been "friendly toward" Communism. The mystics who had pretended to knowledge of my inner attitudes and convictions had offered nothing tangible to grapple with; and the LSB, which was in the comfortable position of having to prove nothing, had not told me its interpretation of the data it had seen fit to use against me. I only knew that the LSB was charged with fearing, suspecting, and looking for the worst.

In my responses, I therefore set forth some measure of

definition of my own in order to provide a solid foundation. Responding to the allegation that I had "Viewed some aspects of Communism favorably, 1934–1935," I observed:

It is difficult to understand what is meant by the term "some aspects of Communism". For example, the general principle of land reform would be supported variously by the Kuomintang, the Chinese Communist Party, and SCAP [Supreme Commander for the Allied Powers—MacArthur]; and, the resistance of the USSR to Nazism from 1941–[sic] to 1945 might, by logical interpretation, be regarded as an "aspect" of Communism. "Some aspects of Communism" might, in short, upon occasion be found identical with American aims.

And then there was the charge that I had been "friendly toward the U.S.S.R. and Communism, 1935–1937." Here I endeavored to provide a somewhat fuller context for allegation and response, observing:

The United States Government recognized the Soviet Union in 1933, in accordance with an agreement which presumed that relations between the two countries would thenceforth be on a regular and friendly basis. Official pronouncements emanating from the Department [of State] at that time reflected that assumption. The first American Ambassador to the Soviet Union, Mr. William C. Bullitt, by common repute was a man who had a deep sympathy for the Russian people, as well as a thorough understanding of Russian Communist motivations. There was between the two countries neither state of war nor—so far as could be observed—covert hostility in that 1935–37 period when Italy had invaded Abyssinia, Japan Manchuria, and Nazi Germany had begun its drive to power in Europe. There was no charge on Foreign Service Officers to manifest open antipathy towards the Soviet Union—nor was there in the later period 1941–45. I was in fact interested in learning more about the Soviet Union, for it seemed to be a growing power (this concept, be it noted, was not in favor in certain American circles at the time). I had begun the study of the Russian language in 1930, and pursued my studies of both the language and Russian history in various sparetime hours subsequently. It was because of my k own qualifications in this regard, it has always been my assumption, that I was in 1944 selected to take up the post [of Consul General] at Vladivostok. For some critics, however, interest—even if attended by other, countervailing interests—is commonly confused with "friendliness", "preference" or "favor". It is here submitted that my political reporting from Vladivostok and other posts where I have had the opportunity to observe the Soviets at first hand (as, also, in Tihua, Mukden, Changchun) will demonstrate clearly that 1) I strove for honest understanding of the political phenomena with which I was confronted, 2) my understanding was critical, and 3) my loyalties were solely to the United States.

The challenges to my political beliefs took extreme form in the charge that I was " '100% pro-Red' at Shanghai, China, in 1940." I went to some length to deal with that allegation, citing my 124-page study of Chinese Communism (taking the occasion to express the doubt, in passing, that there could be found anywhere in my writings a characterization of the Chinese Communists as mere agrarian reformers), and expressing the opinion that this was the basic material that caused a small number of my Foreign Service colleagues to discover differences in thinking between them and me, "and to conclude that the differences indicated that I was out of political step." I said that "The occasionally somewhat reckless bandying about of comments along those lines contributed substantially to keep alive in the 1930's the recurring rumor that I was perhaps 'pro-Communist' in my orientation—although substantial evidence was never offered to show that my thinking was so radically to the left." Then I offered an example:

One of the FSO's who evidently harbored suspicions of my ideology was Mr. B——, with whom I had served for a time in Hankow. After my assignment in 1939 to Shanghai, by which time I believe the "pro-Communist" legend had little life left in it in the posts where I had served, Mr. B—— would occasionally take the opportunity to dig at me for my political beliefs. One day, whether in 1939 or 1940 I am now unable to say, he badgered me for a time in the open office before others of the American staff, and finally called me a "Communist". I called him "a liar" in return, and a number of hot words (now in main forgotten) were passed. Subsequently, when we were alone, he indicated that he had not made the charge seriously and that I had erred in wrangling with him in the presence of the staff. I replied that the fault was his, for he was acting in a manner which might be damaging to me and my career, by pinning on me a label which, as he well knew, carried social odium and once applied, rightly or wrongly, could only with difficulty be shaken off.

In treating the first seven specific allegations with respect to my political attitudes—together with my added interpretation that the purported attitudes would implicitly have had me guilty of disloyalty or of being a security risk or both—I had rejected them successively as "false." As regards the eighth allegation:

The charge that I was "100% pro-Red" in 1940 is, then, false. More, since it is connected in time with a date when the USSR had signed a non-aggression pact with Germany, when war was in progress between Germany and France and the United Kingdom, and the United States had already gone a long way in support of the allies against Nazi aggression, the while the USSR had taken an anti-France [sic]–British stance and was grinding out propaganda to the effect that Russo-German relations were in fine shape and the allies were at fault in the pursuit of what was "an imperialist war", that charge would purport in essence that I took an attitude in support of the USSR directly antipodal to the policies of my own Government. Because of the seriousness of

this charge, the person making it, if an FSO, should of course
have brought it at earliest opportunity to the attention of the
Department—assuming that he himself believed it. Because it
lacks any foundation in or semblance of truth, I can only conclude that this charge was made by one motivated by some personal malice, or else is simply a calloused, unquestioning repetition of the original statement given by Mr. B——, in semi-public
utterance.

And, as directed, I set forth a statement of my "political
philosophy and orientation" in which I tried to meet the
Board's presumed questings for assurance as to my political orthodoxy:

Specifically, I believe that the wisdom of the people instead of
the "inspiration" of a dictator of whatever type or period is the
best guide to the establishment of political measures which
would bring to humankind an adequate measure of happiness, or-
derliness, and the requisite amounts of material good. That this
philosophy has necessarily to be interpreted pragmatically, for effectiveness in the present age of humanity when our social organization is becoming ever more complex and crowded and we
frequently have to face both economic and political dangers, is
believed by me to be supported by the history of recent years in
both the domestic and international spheres. This of course need
not be an occasion for my arguing the virtues of such democratic
pragmatism: there will be those that adhere still to the school of
laisser-faire and those again who would support a Byzantine regi-
mentation, but I would only report that I belong to neither of
those extreme schools, adhering instead to that philosophy which
derived in direct line from the Greeks whom I consider to have
been the greatest inspirers of the philosophy which purposes the
greatest measure of political liberty consonant with that degree of
economic order and economic well-being necessary for decent
livelihood. . . .

[As to whether there had been any progression or change in my
political philosophy from 1928 to date] I have been strengthened
in the conviction particularly that periodic and realistic reference

to the needs and desires of the people as a whole is the very essence of a working democracy, and that the means adopted for satisfaction of the expressed needs of the people should be related to practical results and not to preconceived dogmatic concepts whose content is mainly emotion—that is to "isms" which purport to give in advance all of the answers required by a dynamic society. I have also become increasingly aware, with the years, of the great complexity of society, the tremendous difficulty of effecting suitable and just balances in that society, and have discovered new values to be given many aspects of that varied human society: life has, in short, taken on a less simple aspect. . . .

[As regards the moot questions of Russian and Chinese Communism] It will be noted that the opinions of Governments as well as of individuals respecting the power motivations, bona fides and even permanency of the Soviet Union, have differed greatly through the years. The attitude of the United States Government itself, be it noted, has changed at various times during the period from 1917 to 1951 as regards the perennial subject of Soviet Russia. The conflicting opinions of Presidents Hoover and Roosevelt might be cited as typical of the changes that time and circumstance—and personalities—have wrought with estimates. Likewise, the estimates of both military and political observers respecting the character, strength, capabilities, intentions, and direction of the Chinese Communists have differed greatly during the period of progress along the road to power. . . . I have never pretended to infallibility respecting current interpretations of communism despite my long study of it, but my experience in both China and the Soviet Union has led, I believe, to a steady increase in my understanding of the aims and tactics of the international Communist movement. . . .

It would in due course become clear that this exercise in self-revelation quite failed in its sober purpose of satisfying the Board's questioning. I had tendered no "confession," and did not even deny liberalism, but instead—in a commentary prefaced by reference to Thomas Jefferson and names like Ralph Waldo Emerson, Thorstein Veblen, and Henry George—had spoken of the good of humanity and the needs and desires of the people as a whole. I had also remarked differences of opinion with respect to both the Soviet Union and the Chinese Communists in terms that could readily be interpreted as meaning that I thought there might be more than one simple answer to problems in those areas of our foreign affairs. And in the climate of the time, the LSB probably found it unusual that, in responding to their political inquisitiveness, an FSO should put reliance upon the philosophy of the ancient Greeks.

In my response, I went on to cite relevant reports and memoranda from the field and in the Department, as present in the official files. And I remarked in summation:

All of my political reporting was in accord with my assigned functions. Any questions should be related, therefore, only to the question of general accuracy. It is believed that the record will show that I strove for objectivity in reporting, that I was prepared to give fully to the Department my best energies and best estimates in the reporting and interpretation of current events, and that my estimates of the importance of the revolutionary movement in China have been borne out in main by events. I am prepared to stand on the record of my reports as contained in the files of the Department, and have that record judged for accuracy.

I also responded to the LSB's inquiry regarding my acquaintanceship with the five named persons, and the related questions: "To what extent, if any, have you been aware of his alleged pro-Communist sympathies and activities? If you have been aware of such alleged sympathies and activities, what has been your attitude toward them?" I had in fact known four of the five—but I had known none as a Communist. The LSB did not explain the reasons for the blacklisting of the four, three of whom were Americans (one of them a Foreign Service colleague) and one French, or of the fifth, who bore a Russian name. I was therefore groping in the dark without a guide when I gave a sketch of my relationships with those individuals who had inferentially been adjudged unfit associates for a U.S. Foreign Service officer.

I believed that my responses adequately met any legitimate purpose of the Board. However, there was one question that I left unanswered on January 22—the last, with its allegation of a "document" in a "sealed envelope" left at the *New Masses* for delivery to "Grace Hutchins, a reported Communist." I said that I was without present recollection of "any occurrence such as alleged," and that I was not then in a position "to establish what the facts of this incident in which I was allegedly concerned, might have been in actuality." I reported that I had taken a number of steps (which I listed) in an effort to determine the facts, and I requested that the Board grant a further extension of time to enable me to exhaust the various existing possibilities for the collection of relevant data. But I gave an assurance: "I can say now with certitude that I would never in any event have visited the *New Masses* office or any other place with disloyal intent."

The steps I had taken in the effort to solve the LSB's riddle had centered primarily in efforts to obtain from the Department's files the facts establishing my 1932 schedule and itinerary. I had been in New York at various times in my life, and Mariann and I had thought that we had gone to Washington every time we came home on leave. But the Division of Foreign Service Personnel at first informed me orally that the personnel file showed no record of my hav-

ing been ordered to the Department in 1932 in connection
with my leave, and it seemed to Mariann and me that,
given our financial condition in that year, we should
hardly have proceeded to Washington (and then on to New
York) unless our way had been paid to the capital. I had
therefore requested the Department's Division of Finance
to obtain my original travel account from the General Ac-
counting Office's archival vaults in Virginia. I asked my
mother in Minnesota to check her memory regarding our
movements that year, and I requested the British Chargé
d'Affaires at Peking to forward my 1932 diary from storage.
Those things I told to the LSB.

I had done more. As was my very limited privilege, I
had approached one of the legal officers of the Board with
the request that he give me what additional information he
could in regard to the point in question, to help me in
dealing with the problem. He told me that, in the course of
the alleged visit to the *New Masses,* I was reported to have
asked in the first instance for a Walt Carmon. After this
conversation, I checked the masthead of the *New Masses*
for 1932 at the Library of Congress, and discovered that
Walt Carmon was listed in the June number as Managing
Editor, but that his name had been dropped in the July
issue. First among the six persons listed as constituting the
editorial board in the July 1932 *New Masses*, however, was
Whittaker Chambers. And it was about July that I should
probably have made any 1932 trip to Washington and New
York. Given the new eminence of Whittaker Chambers as
a source of startling testimony regarding "Communists in
government," this new factor clearly multiplied the threat
inherent in the allegation. But I was still without any clue
as to the nature of the "document" that I was alleged to

have delivered to Grace Hutchins, or anything indicative of the details of the story that had come to the LSB.

In a new development, one of the Department's personnel officers now informed me that his records showed that I had been on consultation in Washington July 5–6 and July 11, 1932, and had made a visit to New York in the interim. I informed the LSB accordingly, and then visited New York to interview the principal of the allegation. On February 27, I found Grace Hutchins at the office of the Labor Research Association (not "Bureau," as termed by the LSB) by the simple process of looking up the organization's address in the telephone book and dropping by.

Miss Hutchins was a woman in her 60s, quite unferocious in appearance. I would learn later that this person of colonial ancestry and good education (she was a graduate of Bryn Mawr) had spent her lifetime working with peace and labor movements. She was unabashedly leftist in political complexion. In the early 1920s, she had been secretary of the Fellowship of Reconciliation, had next acted for a couple of years as investigator for the New York State Bureau of Labor's Bureau of Women and Children, and in 1927, in collaboration with Anna Rochester, had organized the Labor Research Association, which prepared economic analyses for trade unions. In the 1930s, she several times ran for state offices on the Communist Party ticket.

I identified myself to Grace Hutchins, and frankly explained my errand. Miss Hutchins expressed puzzlement. She said that she had been a missionary schoolteacher connected with the Episcopal Mission in China from 1912 to 1916. She had not returned to China after that tour except for a brief visit in 1926 or 1927—that is, before my

own arrival in the country. She said that she had no recollection of ever having met me, and that she could think of
nothing either she or the Labor Research Association
might have received from China by hand in 1932. We concluded after casting about that the only person in China
whom we might both have then known was Episcopal
Bishop Logan H. Roots.

But Miss Hutchins had not been in communication with
Bishop Roots at that time. Furthermore, she asked logically, why would anybody carrying something for her
leave it at the *New Masses,* instead of delivering it to her
personally at the Association premises only a few blocks
away? She remarked that she had had no connection with
the *New Masses* at the time. When I informed Miss Hutchins that the source of the report seemed possibly to be
Whittaker Chambers, she told me that she knew Chambers
and had been present at his wedding, but that after his
apostasy Chambers had testified that she had once threatened to kill him.[1] She went on to express a pungent doubt
regarding the presumed informant's veracity. I departed
no closer than before to the solution of the mystery of the
"sealed envelope." But it was now evident that, if
Chambers were in fact the informant, it would have been
no spirit of benevolence that led him to introduce Grace
Hutchins into his story.

Before leaving, I had asked Miss Hutchins whether she
knew the whereabouts of Walt Carmon. She gave me the
name of Carmon's wife. And, again by simply using the
phone book, I found a number, called it, and got Carmon
himself. I arranged to go right over. Once more I told the

[1] See in this connection Whittaker Chambers, *Witness* (New York: Random House, 1952), pp. 48–50.

tale of my quest for the solution of a mystery, and asked whether he could shed any light on the matter. Carmon professed likewise to be entirely without information bearing on the allegation. He too said that he had no recollection of ever having met me before. He pondered on the dates, and said that he had left the *New Masses* sometime in the summer of 1932, and prior to his departure had been ill and absent from the office. He struck on the same question as Grace Hutchins: why deliver to the *New Masses* office anything intended for Miss Hutchins, who would have been available at the Labor Research Association so close by? I had no explanation. After all, it was the LSB's question, not mine. I had the task of finding the answer.

On March 2, I submitted my first response to the Board's question about the mysterious delivery of a document, "completed to the best of my ability." I noted that I had been unable to obtain any pertinent information from the other reputed principal in the case, Grace Hutchins, and expressed regret that, "given only the present characterization of the alleged incident," it would appear impossible for me to provide any further information of value to the Board respecting the matter in point. But, I said, I was naturally desirous of contributing to the best of my ability to a definite clarification of the matter "and should the Board be able to obtain further information from its informant identifying the material which I am alleged to have left at the office of the NEW MASSES for transmittal to Miss Hutchins, or otherwise shedding light on the motives and particulars of the alleged incident, I should of course welcome the opportunity to assist in every possible way to achieve that definitive resolving of the allegation."

It appeared to me that, as far as the record showed, the

LSB had failed to ask its informant some very obvious questions. On the day after forwarding my second letter to the Board, therefore, I handed the Board Chairman a set of pertinent questions which I suggested be put to the LSB's informant. Three paragraphs had to do with the informant's identification of the caller, and the contact he might have had with Walt Carmon respecting the call and the envelope. A fourth paragraph went to the heart of the matter:

How did you know that the sealed envelope was for Grace Hutchins? Was it so addressed, and if not, how? Did you deliver it to Miss Hutchins, or what disposition did you make of it? If other disposition, what and why? How did the caller explain his proceeding to the NEW MASSES to deliver an envelope intended for Grace Hutchins, who was located, apparently, only a few blocks away? Did you direct the caller to Miss Hutchins' office, and if not why not? Did the caller indicate from whom the envelope came, or its contents? Was the envelope large, as if containing bulky material, or small such as might have contained only a letter?

I am unaware whether any of those questions was ever asked of Whittaker Chambers. Within a matter of days, however, I was faced with a new development. In circumstances in which the State Department's loyalty-security proceedings were supposed to be kept confidential, and no word of the LSB's interrogation of me had leaked to the press or been given general circulation in the Department, the House Un-American Activities Committee (the "Wood Committee") subpoenaed me to appear before it, in executive session, on March 14. Someone high in that section of State's administrative apparatus concerned with loyalty-security proceedings had obviously tipped off the House committee; here was another action in which benevolent motive had to be presumed absent.

On March 14 I duly presented myself to the Wood Committee, and by the conventional routine was called upon to set forth my educational background, and to list my assignments in the Foreign Service. Then the Committee interrogators got down to business. The first name they confronted me with was that of Grace Hutchins. I told them of the LSB's interrogatory. They asked me about other persons—Walt Carmon, Owen Lattimore, and the Inner Mongolian leader Teh Wang. For some unknown reason, the Committee seemed to think Teh Wang (Prince Teh) was a Communist. He was not. In fact, while first standing for Inner Mongolian autonomy, Prince Teh had finally joined the Japanese camp.

The inquiry next led among names the majority of which were unknown to me and then the Committee worked back to the general area of the LSB's concern: did I know Agnes Smedley? Anna Louise Stong? Richard Sorge (Soviet spy in Japan)? Gerhard Eisler? David Whittaker Chambers? Anyone who "used the single name 'Carl'?" Of these, I said that I had known Agnes Smedley, and had met Anna Louise Strong once or possibly twice when she passed through my post of assignment at Changchun. I was asked: "did you ever deliver a message or envelope or anything of that nature which had been given you in China to anyone in the United States other than some official of the State Department?" I admitted to carrying and delivering a number of letters of introduction to persons in the United States.

The Committee confronted me with additional names, some of persons with whom I was acquainted, some of individuals who had recently won a measure of notoriety, some names again that were quite unknown to me. Once more my questioners returned to the matter of my alleged

visit to the *New Masses*. I reported what I had already told
to the responsible agency of my own Department, but I
was unable to contribute more. The Committee offered
this much: "The person that you actually called upon has
related that there was a conversation between you and he
[*sic*] with respect to China, a detailed conversation." But
the Comittee, like the LSB, conveyed to me nothing more
of what "the person" had informed them. And so the session ended. I was left no wiser than before about the nature of that ominous allegation that in 1932 I had carried a
mysterious "sealed envelope" for Miss Grace Hutchins.
The Committee had at least collected some miscellaneous
bits and pieces to fit into the complex picture of my "associations"—and perhaps now had a better appreciation of
the political attitudes of Prince Teh of Inner Mongolia.

My 1932 diary arrived from Peking on May 29. I opened
it skeptically but hopefully, for this seemed the only
chance that the mystery could ever be cleared up. And
there I discovered entries covering a three-day weekend
visit to New York, including one of July 9, 1932, which
read as follows:

The most interesting meeting thus far was that with the New
Masses. Their so-called "revolutionary organ" is a horrible rag,
but Agnes had given me a letter of introduction to Walt Carmon
and so I went to see.

It was a ramshackle place to which one went by a rambling
rickety staircase. There were many Masses cartoons on the walls,
a charming Jewess, typing, who acted as Secretary. She introduced me to Michael Gold as "Comrade Clubb", and I talked
to him a while while waiting. He spoke of revolution, but had no
"hopes" of it for the United States at the present, bemoaning the
lack of organizers when the field is prepared and the crop so ripe
for the harvest.

He asked of China. And then there was the successor to Walt Carmon, one Whittaker-Chambers, a shifty-eyed unkempt creature who nevertheless showed considerable force and direction in asking me about the Red movement in China. In turn, I asked him of conditions in the United States, but we didn't talk smoothly. I was, after all, out of my bailiwick, masquerading somewhat under false pretenses, so that I felt too much like a stranger to show the proper "revolutionary enthusiasm".

It was thus I had met the man who was to become known as "The Witness."

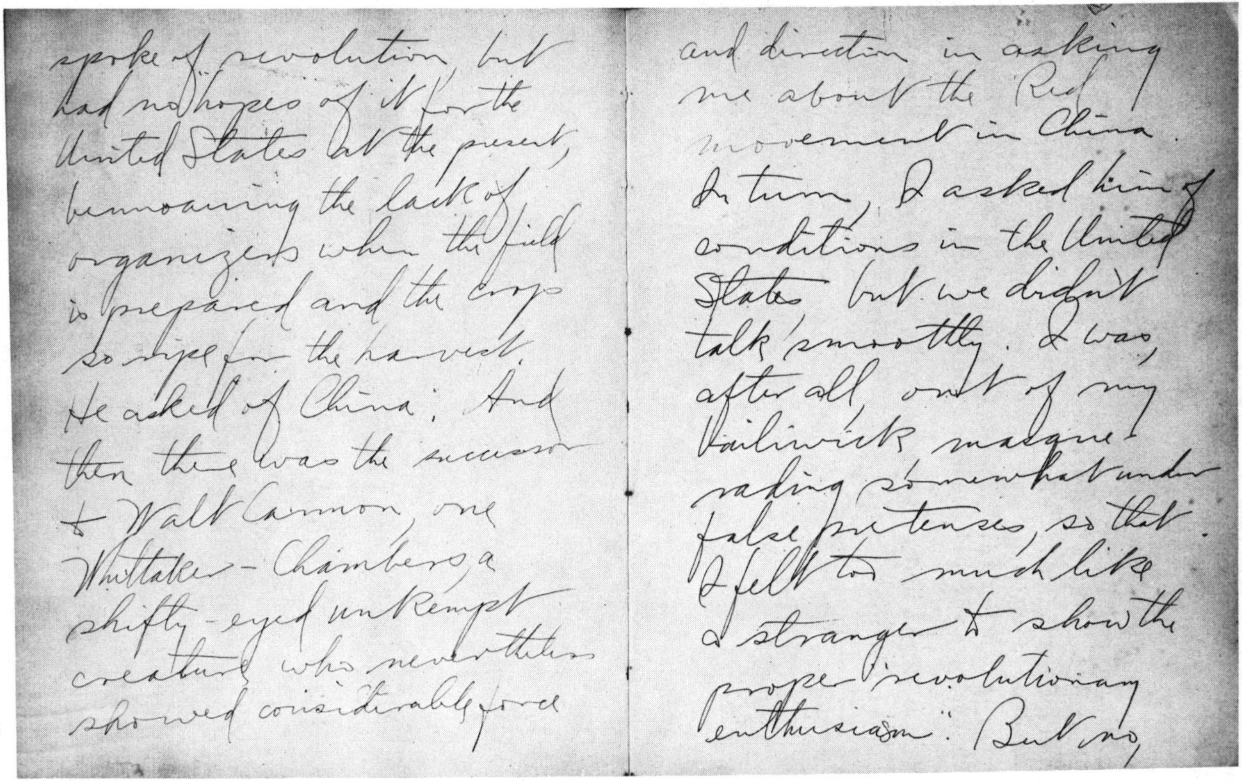

Extract of Clubb diary entry of July 9, 1932

V

"The Gods Are Athirst"

"Full discussion can take place only in an atmosphere
of freedom—an atmosphere in which a different, or even
an unpopular idea does not render the motives and patriotism of its proponent suspect, as would be the case
in a totalitarian country. This national asset must be pre-
served. . . . there appears to be a growing confusion as
to what are wise and appropriate security measures and
what are measures that have little or no merit in terms of
security, but which may and often do inflict irreparable
harm upon innocent individuals and at the same time
gravely injure real national security by enforcing conformity of political expression and thought."

PRESIDENT HARRY S. TRUMAN, letter to Criminal
Law Section of the American Bar Association,
Sept. 1, 1951.

It was a troubled, changing world in 1932, when I
had casually dropped in at the *New Masses*. Great tensions
were everywhere. There have been remarked above some
of the grave problems then besetting China; but at that
time Occidentals were most concerned with their own
troubles. In 1929, the economies of both Europe and the
United States had begun to slip badly down the slope to
depression. By the American Presidential election year
1932, cries of impending doom were heard from many
sides. There had developed a crisis that terrified many to

the point of paralysis. In Europe, weakened by economic distress, democratic elements staggered under the attack of the totalitarian forces. We who had seen those developments from China "as through a glass, darkly," had seized with avidity upon the opportunity offered by home leave to refresh our knowledge of the United States and get American assessments of the significance of current world events.

The atmosphere in the United States was one of crisis. The stock market had crashed, with the Dow-Jones index falling from 381 to 41 in the summer of 1932—a drop of nearly 90 percent. Many who had deemed themselves well-to-do were impoverished. The economy was faltering. There was widespread unemployment, with consequent human distress. Veterans of World War I staged a "Bonus March" on Washington, only to be dispersed in late July by troops commanded by General Douglas A. MacArthur. There were those—including people as unradical as bankers—who thought that the American politico-economic system might finally have failed.

A few brief quotations give the temper of the times. That was the year when New York Governor Franklin D. Roosevelt observed that "Not since the dark days of the '60s have the people faced problems as grave, situations as difficult, suffering as severe. . . ." John W. Davis expressed the opinion that "at this particular moment the instinct of the people has not misled them, and that a large part, far the larger part, of the ills from which the world is suffering is due to the folly and unwisdom of the rulers and their inability to face the inexorable facts."

Justice Brandeis, in one of his famous dissenting opinions, observed that "The people of the United States are now confronted with an emergency more serious than war. . . . Some people believe that the existing conditions threaten even the stability of the capitalistic system." President Hoover himself, addressing the Senate on May 31, 1932, regarding the "emergency" that had developed, remarked upon "the continued downward movement in the economic life of the country" and warned: "In your hands at this moment is the answer to the question whether democracy has the capacity to act speedily enough to save itself in emergency."

Dr. Nicholas Murray Butler observed: "We are living in a wholly new kind of world, and most of the grievous troubles which beset us and cause so much anxiety and distress are due to the fact that we do not recognize or understand this new kind of world. . . ." But, he said, there would be little help to be had from the politician in facing the stern realities of the situation, for "He is too fearful, too timorous and too lacking in courage even when he understands. . . . Would to God we could exchange a thousand politicians for even one statesman."

And then, on June 30 at Chicago, Franklin D. Roosevelt, in accepting the nomination to the Presidency, warned his hearers not to misunderstand the patience of the American people, not to try to meet the danger of radicalism in the existing conditions by reaction, but instead to offer a workable program of reconstruction. He said: "I pledge you—I pledge myself—to a new deal for the American people. Let us all here assembled constitute ourselves prophets of a new order of competence and courage. This is more than a political campaign; it is a call to arms."

The American political atmosphere for my homecoming in June 1932 was thus one of economic crisis attended by violent political contention. The "Bonus Marchers" were already gathering in Washington. It was the most natural thing in the world that I, who had been charged with following and reporting upon important developments in China, should be deeply interested in discovering, during my short home leave after an absence of three years, what was happening during that critical time in the United States. It never occurred to me *not* to endeavor to do so; I was politically minded by nature.

My diary sketched the story. Trying to get as clear a picture as possible of the various aspects of the kaleidoscopic scene, I had talked to friends, and to officials in the State Department; and while at Washington for consultation I had made that three-day visit to New York. I carried a number of letters of introduction given to me by acquaintances in China. On that hot July weekend, I found few of the addressees in town. As I went down the list, I came in due course to a letter of introduction addressed to Walt Carmon, Managing Editor of the *New Masses*. In those days, that organ was avowedly Leftist, but was not officially Communist in character, and among its contributors were a number of American writers who have since gained no little fame in the literary world. It was then fifteen years before the initiation of the Government's loyalty program, and the most prescient of men could hardly have imagined that a casual visit to the magazine in question might years later be taken as prima facie evidence of wrongdoing.

So in all innocence I had made that visit, and as a casual diarist had duly recorded my impressions. And then, sometime in the hectic, busy nineteen years that followed, the brief call at the office of the *New Masses* and the ac-

cidental meeting there with an unkempt individual named
Whittaker Chambers had been erased from my memory.

The State Department's files, however, contained the
text of a speech I had delivered in Hankow in the spring of
1933, after my return to post from home leave. I there set
forth my ideas on "Liberalism in the Present World Crisis." The conclusion to the speech gave its essence (which
would have offered an interesting contrast to the thought
of Whittaker Chambers as reflected in the columns of the
New Masses for the same general period):

Liberalism is, then, an open flexible system, not a closed system
of dogma assuming certain a priori principles to be applicable in
all circumstances. The form Liberalism takes depends upon time
and environment, but it is always progressive with an essentially
humanitarian outlook—not a material one. Anticipating unending
change, even though it be but in the form determined by "the inevitability of gradualness", but uncommitted to any dogma concerning the unknown future, the Liberal proceeds along nonsec-
tarian lines toward the solution of the problems confronting
society, by discussion (with every group and all interests) and
agreement (of the whole or great majority). It is his contention
that it is not inevitable that violent revolution must be used to effect necessary changes in a society but rather that the clear expression of the will of the people will suffice unless thwarted by
undemocratic forces. This will of the people is the expression of
public opinion, formed and unified by the educational force of intelligence. It is the Liberal belief that it is not "radicalism" any
more than "conservatism" that is the danger, but that *ignorant
radicalism* and *ignorant conservatism* alike are detrimental to
the health of our civilization. The liberal is prepared to be conservative where there is good to be conserved, and to be radical
when fundamental changes are required for the social good. He
is definitely opposed to social and political ignorance, philosophical dogmatism, and injustice. He is a humanitarian seeking
the good of mankind—and at this time he is surer than ever that

such general good should be sought if only for selfish reasons, for
an enlightened selfishness recognizes that there cannot in this
day and age be particular good without general good. It is, finally, the understanding of the Liberal that if revolution would
be avoided it is necessary to attack the causes that make for revolution and eliminate them—institutions must be kept abreast of
the times if they are not to collapse in ruin.

Noting the crisis in our civilization, I said that it was incumbent upon us to search for a way out instead of twid-
dling our thumbs placidly in the belief that "economic
law" would assume responsibility for getting us out of the
fix into which we had gotten ourselves. And I drew a dis-
tinction:

> Marxians are prepared to admit the truth of my last statement,
> but they contend that, whatever the desirability, the change *can-
> not* be accomplished except by the sword. . . .
> The Liberal, oppositely, believes in the efficacy of the method
> of "discussion and agreement" for the accomplishment of neces-
> sary social change, holding steadfast to that method as preferable
> to that of the sword.

The date of my speech was February 14, 1933, and
Franklin D. Roosevelt would not be inaugurated as President until March 4. In my speech I had defined two points
of view, and two kinds of politically minded men. I spoke
as a liberal working in the service of the United States
Government. At that same date one Whittaker Chambers
by his own testimony was, as a Communist, acting as a
functionary in the Soviet underground, and hard at work in
the effort to foment violent revolution *against* the U.S.
Government.

The windfall discovered in the diary greatly elated
Mariann and me, for now we had the answer in hand. It

was established that I had indeed gone to the *New Masses*, but simply to present a letter of introduction to Editor Walt Carmon, not a "document" for a "Grace Hutchins." I had told the Wood Committee on March 14 that I recalled having carried a number of letters of introduction to persons in the United States in either 1932 or 1937. My diary showed this to have occurred in 1932. The motivation for the actions of the LSB and the Congressional committee now had been brought to light: by accident, I had met Whittaker Chambers nearly twenty years before, Chambers had produced the musty datum, and the Government of the United States suspected that where Chambers was involved high treason might be found. But the diary entry had given the answer—and the diary was hand-bound in Hankow and the entries hand-written. It seemed evidence enough to satisfy any reasonable man.

Over the weekend I composed what I assumed would be my final, definitive response to the LSB regarding its presumed primary concern; and on June 4, with no little satisfaction, I sent it in. I sketched the history of my efforts to obtain the diary, and quoted the diary extract for the information of the Board. I observed that my initial inability to recollect the incident derived naturally from the circumstance that the visit 19 years before was patently not a major event in my life, and I remarked that "the actual circumstances of the visit differed in important respects from the version set forth in the allegation and the implications thereof." In conclusion I stated that, to the best of my recollection and belief:

I had no previous acquaintanceship with any one of the NEW MASSES editors, including Messrs. Carmon, Gold and Chambers, and, in fact, prior to viewing my diary entry I had no recollection of having met Gold and Chambers; I had not prior to receipt of the LSB's reference interrogatory had knowledge of or association with Miss Hutchins, and that I met her for the first time on February 27, 1951 in search of evidence having a bearing on the LSB's interrogatory; the "document" delivered to the office of the NEW MASSES was a simple letter of introduction; the writer of that letter (or, "sender of the document") was Agnes Smedley; and addressee was not Miss Hutchins, but Mr. Carmon; and, the address given me by the sender, and perhaps enscribed on the envelope, was presumably the office of the NEW MASSES where Mr. Carmon had been employed as Managing Editor, but in his absence, I met instead Michael Gold and Whittaker Chambers (the "successor" to Mr. Carmon).

I was certain in my own mind, I said, that this new evidence gave "the correct record and definitive explanation of that visit." Like my previous responses, this was submitted in the form of a sworn statement.

After this, Mariann and I felt that we could afford to relax. We treated ourselves to a short trip to Minneapolis, and with parental pride saw our son Oliver graduate cum laude. We had but little time at our disposal, and drove back to Washington a few days later. Oliver followed us shortly, bringing with him my mother, aged 84. This was to be a brief family reunion, for Oliver would soon join the armed forces, and we could look forward to having Zoë with us only for the time remaining before she finished college. My mother was the only one of our four parents alive, and I had enjoyed only brief visits with her since my marriage and entry into the Foreign Service in 1928. We felt happy to have the rare opportunity to savor once more the warm, pleasurable family associations of which "the exigencies of the Service" had so largely deprived us, and hoped to cram into the month before us a maximum amount of family happiness, to make up for years apart. We looked forward to full realization of that aspiration, for had I not been able to provide solid answers to all of the LSB's questions?

I had planned from the beginning not to stop with simple answers to the LSB's questions, for the Board regularly contended that it was "not an investigating agency," and this controlling conviction kept it from checking the actual work an employee had done in the service, though not from giving the gravest consideration to any report, no matter how scurrilous or fantastic, that might be turned up about the employee. The LSB, in short, merely took data available in the officer's efficiency reports, and those coming from the Federal Bureau of Investigation and other agencies (anonymous and unevaluated and "raw" though the reports might be), and threw them at the officer to disprove. Shortly after receipt of the LSB's interrogatory, therefore, I had begun a survey of my pertinent reports as contained in the Department's files, from 1931 to date.

The file room patiently produced reams of reports; an administrative secretary generously helped me with the work of extracting and recording elements pertinent to the subject. I had been concerned for practically all of my career with political and economic reporting, even when acting as principal officer (in a total of eight posts), and prominent among the wide-flung subjects of my work was that in which the LSB was so fervidly interested—Communism. I had, by common repute, done more reporting on the Chinese Communist movement than any other officer in the Foreign Service. I had reported factually, and moreover frequently forecast for the Depart-

ment of State the shape of things to come, without regard
for the bureaucratic danger of "sticking my neck out." I
compiled 100 solid pages of extracts of analysis and forecasts from the many dispatches and telegrams that I had
written through the years on developments regarding
Chinese Communism and Sino-Soviet relations. The record digested in those pages was, I believed, remarkable
as a picture of work faithfully and well done by a Foreign
Service Officer charged "to keep the United States Government informed of developments abroad." I was confident that it would stand any test, and resolve any doubts.
On June 22, I forwarded that survey to the LSB.

There was one further item of outstanding business. To
bring the House Un-American Activities Committee up to
date, and complete the record there, I took my diary volume and, in the company of Deputy Under Secretary for
Administration Carlisle H. Humelsine, visited the office of
Congressman Francis E. Walter. Having reference to
my testimony before the Committee on March 14, I
showed the Congressman the diary entry in the original.
Congressman Walter read it, handed it back to me, and
said that there remained no further interest in my case. I
had brought a typed copy of the entry, and offered to leave
it with him for the Committee's records. Walter did not
want the item, and I returned it to my briefcase. During
the interview the Congressman manifested calm and comprehension, and seemed entirely satisfied with both the
evidence and my bona fides. Humelsine, contrariwise,
wore a serious mien for the whole occasion, and seemed
inclined to consider my position still exposed to attack. He
remained with Congressman Walter when I departed. At a
later date, primed with more doubt respecting the political

ways of Washington, I should probably have viewed Humelsine's behavior as ominous. At the time, however, I went my way feeling that, even as I must have satisfied the curiosity of the LSB, so now I could count on having finished with the Congressional committee that had interested itself in my 1932 trip.

In the meantime, over the preceding six months, domestic strife regarding our Asia policy had intensified. Although the Congressional elections were now out of the way, partisan fighting in the domestic arena continued with respect to "the loss of China" and, of course, the Korean War. The divisions between the opposing camps were substantially aggravated when five-star General Douglas MacArthur was removed from his command by President Truman for insubordination and arrived home in April 1951 to take the spotlight of a Congressional investigation that took a full 42 days of the crowded hours of the concerned Senators. In millions of words, the pros and cons of America's Far Eastern policies and plans were surveyed. There was a parade of witnesses, who added their thoughts and comments to those of the General. Military and political estimates regarding present and future were dragged from secret hiding places and "declassification" made it possible to show the bulk of such material to a goggling world. And then, when the hue and cry was over, it was as if those words had all canceled each other out. The proceedings were over, but the mighty labor gave birth to no conclusions. There were no lessons pointed up, and no new policies laid down in resolutions expressing "the intent of Congress" for future guidance. The fighting in the Far East went on, and so did the strife at home.

It might have appeared, in fact, that for certain Congressmen domestic quarrels took precedence over war abroad. Secretary of State Dean Acheson was a favorite target for Senator McCarthy and some others. Few Democratic Congressmen defended either the Secretary or his policies. The State Department continued to be buffeted about, the unloved orphan of the Government family. A ruthless demagoguery spewed venom at all who failed to agree with the new, belligerent dogma regarding what was good for the Far East, and who would not employ American forces for the effecting of our will.

Senator McCarthy in a speech at Fort Atkinson, Wisconsin on April 7, 1951, said: "It is high treason to refuse MacArthur permission to use Chinese Nationalist troops." Shortly afterward, on April 20, there occurred a scuffle between Senators Capehart, Humphrey, and Lehman in a recording studio of the Senate Office Building when Senator Capehart charged that, if his two colleagues did not favor using Chinese Nationalist troops in Korea, that meant that they were basically sympathetic with the Chinese Communists. President Truman was threatened with impeachment for the manner in which he had exercised his functions as Commander-in-Chief of the United States. Those were signs of the times.

The MacArthur affair, however, monopolized the center of the political stage for much of the spring of 1951, and the furor about "Communists in the State Department" had somewhat subsided. McCarthy would have to make a gigantic effort if he were going to get the spotlight again. He made it. He promised to the Congress of the United States the most important "revelations" of all, and before an audience that dwindled down to five presumably tense Senators, on June 14, he leveled charges of conspiracy against General George C. Marshall. He put direct the question that, in essence, always guides the hunter of scapegoats: "How can we account for our present situation unless we believe that men high in this government are concerting to deliver us to disaster?" The Senator supplied his answer: "The President is not master in his own house. Those who are master there not only have a desire to protect the sappers and miners. They could not do otherwise. They themselves are not free. They belong to a larger conspiracy, the world-wide web of which has been spun from Moscow."

Major General Hurley, testifying that same month before a Congressional hearing on the military situation in the Far East, similarly extended the sweep of his charges of State Department wrongdoing:

American diplomats surrendered the territorial integrity and political independence of China, surrendered the principles of the Atlantic Charter, and wrote the blueprint for Communist conquest of China in secret agreement at Yalta. . . . Your diplomats and mine surrendered in secret every principle for which we said we were fighting.

McCarthy, in posing his rhetorical question, could hardly have hoped for an answer better fitted to his purposes. Statesmanship was being forced to cede ever more ground to domestic politics. Knowledge and experience were under attack by prejudice, and hatred was being mobilized for selfish ends. Such statements by the likes of Hurley and McCarthy were monstrously false, but in 1951 the opposition to demagoguery was perceptibly weakening.

The Government's loyalty-security program, and the mode of its administration, reflected the Truman Administration's embattled position, where defensiveness was the watchword. In the spring of 1951, President Truman changed the standards for the administration of loyalty cases. In his original directive, Executive Order 9835 of March 21, 1947, it had been provided that:

The standard for the refusal of employment or the removal from employment in an executive department or agency on grounds relating to loyalty shall be that, on all the evidence, reasonable grounds exist for the belief that the person involved is disloyal to the Government of the United States.

By this carefully worded order, which was issued at least in part to abate the more frenetic fears of the dangers of subversion from within, it was necessary to establish by positive evidence that the employee was "disloyal." Now, by Executive Order of April 28, 1951, the standard was fixed as being "that, on all the evidence, there is reasonable doubt as to the loyalty of the person involved to the Government of the United States." The phrase "all the evidence" remained, but "reasonable *grounds*" had become "reasonable *doubt*"—directed at the employee's *loyalty,* where disloyalty had been the issue before. *The standard for security was left unaltered.* But the demagogic attacks on the State Department and its personnel were providing the LSB with more incentive than ever to "doubt"— whether with respect to loyalty *or* security.

What had gone on in the collective mind of the LSB since receipt of my letter of June 4 presenting the answer to the last of their posers is something that I can never know, or even imagine, with any degree of certainty. But by letter of June 27, 1951, LSB Chairman Conrad E. Snow informed me that my replies, "together with other available evidence," had been considered by the Board, which had however decided "that charges be formulated against you."

There were first general, catchall charges that: "you are a member of, affiliated with, or in sympathetic association with, the Communist Party"; or that "you are . . . a person who consistently believes in, or supports, the ideologies and policies of the Communist Party"; and that "within the meaning of Section 393.2.d of said [State Department] Regulations and Procedures you are a person who has habitual and close association with persons known or believed to be in the category set forth in Section 393.2.a of said Regulations and Procedures to an extent which would justify the conclusion that you might, through such association, voluntarily or involuntarily divulge classified information without authority."

Sections 393.2.a and 393.2.d, setting forth certain categories of security risks, were as follows:

393.2.a. A person who engages in, supports, or advocates treason, subversion, or sedition, or who is a member of, affiliated with, or in sympathetic association with the Communist, Nazi, or Fascist Parties, or of any foreign or domestic party or movement which seeks to alter the form of government of the United States by unconstitutional means or whose policy is to advocate or approve the commission of acts of force or violence to deny other persons their rights under the Constitution of the United States; or a person who consistently believes in or supports the ideologies of such a party or movement.

393.2.d. A person who has habitual or close association with persons known or believed to be in categories a or b to an extent which would justify the conclusion that he might, through such association, voluntarily or involuntarily divulge classified information without authority.

It could readily be inferred from Snow's letter that the Board considered that those last two provisions might be particularly applicable in my case. In short, the "contact" with Chambers was still the Board's prime concern.

The bill of particulars set forth by LSB Chairman Snow comprised ten specific charges, the first eight of which were identical word for word with "allegations" a through h of the December 26 interrogatory. A shift in the order of one listing was the only difference. The part comprising the last two charges read:

> The specific charges are that you . . .
>
> 9. Have or have had close and habitual association with the following named persons: [11 names] [1]
>
> 10. In 1932 delivered a sealed envelope to the office of the editor of the *New Masses* magazine, a Communist periodical, in New York City for transmittal to one Grace Hutchins, an avowed Communist employed by the Labor Research Association, an affiliate of the Communist Party.

The original allegations "by various informants" had been converted into the Board's own charges against me. There had been added to the blacklist the names of six ad-

---

[1] I omit here the names of the eleven persons. It appears probable that in the listing of individuals the LSB employed the same rough standard as that governing its identification of "objectionable" organizations, namely that it sufficed for an organization to have been "cited as subversive, Communist, Fascist, etc., by a government agency, committee, or other authoritative source." I find the Board's standard objectionable in principle and in law, and thus refrain from support of its implied proposition that the named persons fell into category 393.2.a of the State Department's "Regulations and Procedures."

There will however be found in the text below, in circumstances where inherent logic appears to give warrant (because of publicity already attending the subject person's name), several exceptions to this self-imposed restraint.

ditional persons, all of whom I had identified before the Wood Committee as known to me. The previous wording of the final item had been altered to my disadvantage by addition of the phrase "a Communist periodical" as descriptive of the *New Masses,* by identification of Grace Hutchins as "an avowed Communist" instead of "a reported Communist," and by the characterization of the Labor Research Association as "an affiliate of the Communist Party" where before, as the Labor Research *Bureau,* it had been designated as "an alleged Communist organization." I was still charged with having delivered "a sealed envelope," but all reference to a "document" had been dropped.

My four sworn statements in response to the interrogatory, and the long survey of my reporting record, had thus failed to get the elimination of even one of the specific points brought forward against me by the LSB. My position had actually deteriorated, by reason of the Board's general charge of membership, affiliation, or "sympathetic association" with the Communist Party, and by reason of the Board's further weighting the *New Masses* charge against me.

I received an additional blow: the pertinent Congressional Act of August 26, 1950, Public Law 733, duly cited by Snow in his letter with copy enclosed, provided that the Secretary of State (*inter alia*) "*may,* in his absolute discretion and *when deemed necessary in the interest of national security*" (emphasis supplied) suspend an employee brought under charges. There was no doubt with respect to the discretionary character of the authority; but although my visit to the *New Masses* had occurred nineteen years before and the last cited date in the specific charges against me was 1940, Snow's letter further notified me that "by reason of the charges set out above you are being suspended from active duty in the interest of national security pending adjudication of your case."

The Snow letter was supplemented by a second letter of June 27, signed by Elbridge Durbrow as Chief of the Division of Foreign Service Personnel "For the Secretary of State," informing me that I was suspended from active duty effective that date.

The Department's own rules provided that "any officer or employee who is summarily suspended in the interest of national security shall be . . . informed of the reasons for his supension to the extent that the interests of national security permit." Durbrow's letter, which referred to General Snow's letter of the same date notifying me of the Board's charges, also said simply that I was suspended "by reason of these charges." I was, in effect, presumed guilty until proved innocent. But I had still not been informed of the nature of the presumed disloyalty, or of the character of any alleged security breach.

After 23 years in the American Foreign Service, I stood charged with being disloyal to the United States Government and, moreover, with constituting a security risk to the Department of State. The Executive Orders of 1947 and 1951 respecting loyalty have already been cited. That of 1947 contained a directive that "maximum protection must be afforded the United States against infiltration of disloyal persons into the ranks of its employees, and *equal protection from unfounded accusations of disloyalty must be afforded the loyal employees of the Government*" (emphasis supplied). This latter provision was reemphasized by the President in a letter of July 14, 1951, to the Execu-

tive Secretary of the National Security Council in which
he said:

If these provisions of law are to achieve their purpose of protecting the security of the Government without unduly infringing
on the rights of the individual, they must be administered with
the utmost wisdom and courage. We must never forget that the
fundamental purpose of our Government is to protect the rights
of individual citizens and one of the highest obligations of the
Government is to see that these rights are protected in its own
operations.

The State Department's Regulations and Procedures,
amended as of May 4, 1951, provided in detail the loyalty
and security standards to be employed, defined the categories of security risks, and set forth factors to be given
consideration in determining such security risks. Several
of those provisions are worthy of special note. It was provided *inter alia* that, in cases where the LSB might make
charges against the employee, and the employee did not
answer the charges in writing, "no inference or presumption should be assumed by the board because of the failure
or refusal to reply to the notice of charges." If the employee answered the charges in writing but did not
request a hearing before the Board, "Before making the
determination . . . the board in its discretion may, if a
hearing is deemed necessary, request the officer or employee to appear for a hearing, but the board cannot
require him to appear, and no inference or presumption
should be assumed by the board because of a failure or refusal of an individual to appear for a hearing."
In cases where a hearing might be held, "Strict legal
rules of evidence will not be applied at such hearing, but
reasonable bounds shall be maintained as to competency,

relevancy, and materiality." And finally, "In arriving at its
decision, the panel shall take into consideration the fact
that the employee may have been handicapped in his defense by the non-disclosure to him of confidential information or by the lack of opportunity to cross-examine persons
constituting such sources of information."

By its own Regulations and Procedures, in sum, the Department of State had defined and formally established the
procedures for the exercise of the "absolute discretion" accorded to the Secretary by Public Law 733. The authority
granted by that Public Law was no longer to be viewed as
a naked instrument for purely arbitrary use, once it had
been clothed with elements providing for particular procedures.

The administration of the State Department's loyalty-
security program was by that time under pressure from
certain political elements antipathetic both to a sober legal
functioning of the administrative apparatus and to the evident intent of the men who drafted the relevant law and
regulations. Board Chairman Conrad E. Snow had served
in World Wars I and II and bore the retired rank of brigadier general; but he was also a member of the bars of New
Hampshire and of the District of Columbia, and from 1919
to 1940 had been partner and owner of a law firm. His
credentials could be presumed to render him virtually im-
pregnable to any demagogic charges of sympathy with radicalism. The Board was generally reputed in 1950 to have
tried to administer the loyalty-security program with a
maximum of sanity and a minimum of ill effects for the
State Department. Apparently because of that reluctance
to hunt and burn witches, it had recently come under attack. Not surprisingly, Senator McCarthy was in the forefront of the Board's critics. Oddly enough, however, the

Loyalty Review Board, cloaked with the function of post-auditing loyalty cases passing through the loyalty boards of the several government agencies, was also critical of the State Department's Board—for not having found as large a percentage of "disloyal" employees in State's ranks as had been discovered in certain other agencies. That good record, instead of being deemed reason for reassurance, was seemingly viewed as a suspicious circumstance.

The Loyalty Review Board further had administered a verbal rap on the knuckles to the LSB for the latter's clearance of Foreign Service Officer John S. Service after completion of the interrogatory process alone, without a hearing—although a hearing was not by any interpretation mandatory under the regulations. The Board obviously was not going to repeat that "mistake" in my case. McCarthy was continuing his charges against State Department personnel, and even if the Department administrators did not believe his statements, they couldn't afford to disregard a United States Senator.

There was another highly important factor in the situation: the officials responsible for administration of the Department's loyalty-security program were only sketchily informed with respect to the personnel and functions they were charged with judging. Wilbur Carr, who had administered the Department in the old days, had been a living part of the organization for 45 years, and had been thoroughly acquainted with both personnel and operations. His 1951 counterpart, Deputy Under Secretary of State Carlisle H. Humelsine, was a young ex-Colonel who had been in the State Department only five years. To him had been delegated the Secretary's authority for administration of the loyalty-security program involving the careers of professional Foreign Service officers, some of whom had been working in the Government service abroad for 15 to 30 years.

LSB Chairman Snow, whose technical position in the Department was that of Assistant Legal Adviser for Political Affairs, had likewise served in State only since 1946. To all indications, neither he nor Humelsine was expert in Foreign Service practices, the history of political developments in various parts of the world they now considered from the distant perspective of 1951, or particularly, the tortuous development of Communism in the relatively inaccessible and little known Far East. In essence, they found themselves dealing with strange personnel, and strange subjects, in a domestic political situation properly labeled "explosive." A particular Board consisted of three persons selected from a standing panel of nine men, of whom a number were usually experienced Foreign Service Officers and would presumably constitute leaven in the loaf. However, other panel members were outright amateurs at a task requiring the services of the finest professionals if the needs of both security and justice were to be served.

In addition, especially in those cases that became public knowledge, the Board was poorly sheltered against the stormy winds of politics. Therefore, the exercise of the overall authority, and also the immediate adjudication of the individual cases, reflected the emotional suspicions and the fears of the McCarthy era. Orderly legal impartiality was in such cases *not* the norm; the process was primarily political. It was almost inevitable that the result would often fall somewhat short of incorporating the "utmost wisdom and courage" that the President thought essential.

VI

Guilty until Proved Innocent

Attempts of the courts to fathom modern political meditations of an accused would be as futile and mischievous as the efforts in the infamous heresy trials of old to fathom religious beliefs. It is true that in England of olden times men were tried for treason for mental indiscretions such as imagining the death of the king. But our Constitution was intended to end such prosecutions. Only in the darkest periods of human history has any Western Government concerned itself with mere belief, however eccentric or mischievous, when it has not matured into overt action; and if that practice survives anywhere, it is in the Communist countries, whose philosophies we loathe.

Communications Association v. Douds, 339 U.S. 382, quoted by U.S. District Judge Luther W. Youngdahl May 2, 1953, in decision throwing out four of seven charges against Owen Lattimore.

Theoretically, the LSB's charges, and the Department's suspension of me from active duty, were confidential. Actually, given the simultaneous suspension of both myself and Foreign Service colleague John P. Davies, the odds were that the matter would in due course come to public attention, for both of us were high-ranking officers, and both belonged to the China Service. On July 12, under pressure from newsmen who had got wind of the matter and discovered the name of Davies, the Department of State announced the two suspensions, with the explanation that "suspension is a mandatory legal requirement (Public Law 733) in any case in which a hearing is held." As noted above, Public Law 733 did not in fact make suspension mandatory, and there were loyalty-security hearings of Foreign Service and departmental officers held subsequent to July 12, 1951, *without* suspension of such officers. Nevertheless, in my case, no error on the part of the concerned administrative officers was ever rectified. The inherent bureaucratic tendency is to hold to the course of action even if that course is later clearly demonstrated to be in error; and the higher the level at which the original decision was made the tighter is the adherence to the doctrine of infallibility. The degradation of the career specialist under the impact of McCarthyism operated to strengthen that tendency in the postwar American bureaucracy.

The information issued by the State Department regarding Davies and myself naturally got considerable press attention. "State Dept. Aide is Contradicted," "2 Acheson Aides Suspended," and "Clubb Now Admits He Knew Chambers," blared the headlines. The pro-Chiang Kai-shek Chinese-language press in New York covered the matter in more extravagant terms. Those newspapers presumably felt that, since few non-Chinese would be reading them, they could discard inhibitions. Their attitude can probably be taken as a reasonably close approximation to that of the China Lobby—if somewhat more naked. The *Mei Chou Jih Pao* ("American Daily"), treating the cases of Davies and myself on July 14, 1951, just after the Department's revelation, headed the pertinent news item "Again Two Pro-Red, China-harming Special Agents Discovered in American State Department." The news story asserted that "it is admitted that those persons have committed the excesses of being pro-Red and harming China," and observed that the State Department's action confirmed that there was basis in the charges which (by this version) Senator McCarthy had leveled against both men in recent years. The same paper on July 16 purported to cite Un-American Activities Committee Chairman Wood as authority for the statement that, in addition to having had exchanges with Communist Whittaker Chambers, I had also, when with the Consulate General at Hankow, had exchanges with "the American Red woman profligate Smedley."

As might have been expected, Congress reacted immediately to the news. A member of the House Un-American Activities Committee suggested that Whittaker Chambers ought to be called again before the Committee to testify in regard to me. Senator McCarthy promptly leaped into the act. According to the current press report, the Senator said that Davies' name was among those he had handed to the Senate Foreign Relations subcommittee ("Tydings Committee"), which the year before had investigated his charges that the State Department was harboring Communists and fellow travelers. (The majority report of the Committee found that the Senator had been guilty of a "fraud and a hoax.") The news item continued:

Senator McCarthy said he also had a file on Mr. Clubb. But he added he "didn't feel I had enough on him at the time" to request an investigation.

As for the two suspensions, Senator McCarthy said: "This is one of the first healthy indications that the State Department is becoming afraid of the McCarran committee and is going to start cleaning house."

The House Un-American Activities Committee on July 13 issued a press release reporting briefly that, in December 1948, Whittaker Chambers had testified before it that "he had met an individual whom he recalled as Oliver Edmund Chubb." The account continued:

Chambers said according to his recollection, that Chubb at the time of the meeting was second or third secretary to the United States Consulate in Hankow, China. Chambers stated that this meeting took place in the office of *New Masses* in New York City and that he recalled that Chubb was carrying a message to Grace Hutchins, the details of which he did not remember. Chambers further stated that when Chubb entered the *New Masses* office he asked for Walt Carmon, who had been the former editor of *New Masses*."

I now at last had Chambers' basic story. And I of course duly noted that, according to the Congressional Committee's official report, Chambers had testified that I carried not "a sealed envelope" but a *message*, "the details of which he did not remember."

The press release went on to give the essence of my own testimony of March 1951 before the same Committee. Representative Harold H. Velde, a Republican member, charged that the Committee Chairman's action was "most unfair," saying that the Republican members of the Committee had not been given an opportunity to participate in my hearing; and he said that he would insist that "minor investigations" be temporarily shelved in favor of complete investigations and hearings "in the matter of direct Soviet influence in the present and past Democratic administrations." Representative Bernard W. Kearney, another Republican member of the Committee, told reporters: "I am in favor of reopening the investigation of the State Department concerning possible Communist infiltration there."

In announcing the two suspensions, the State Department spokesman had said that "Suspension . . . does not indicate that a person is guilty of misconduct or is a security risk. . . . the purpose of a hearing is to ascertain the complete facts and thus hearings are for the protection of both the Government and the individual." Given the vagueness and flimsiness of the charges against me, it could hardly have been argued with conviction that my remaining at my desk would have constituted a "clear and present danger" to the security of the United States. But the specific charges had not been made public, and the LSB's governing urge to "play safe" was also not publicly known. And the governing regulations provided, after all, that suspension would occur "when deemed necessary in the interest of national security." The grave implications of my suspension were therefore hardly to be diminished by the Department's characterization of its actions as "mandatory;" its self-serving "explanation" could not be expected to disabuse the public mind of the logical assumption that suspension of a high-ranking officer was no mere bureaucratic formality. If the Department had really intended to protect both itself and Davies and me, it had manifestly chosen the wrong tactics. As a matter of fact, however, appearances suggested that some person or persons in the Department lacked the basic desire to provide for me the safeguards prescribed in the pertinent regulations.

The next step was to be the hearing before the LSB. Legally, of course, I might have refrained from attending such a hearing; I could have chosen to stand pat on the various sworn statements and the long survey of my record already submitted, for the Board had brought no new charges against me and I truly had nothing more of significance to add in regard to the old allegations. But I assumed that the Board couldn't shake off its apprehensions with respect to any matter touching upon the state of one's thinking about Chinese or Russian Communism, or any matter in which Whittaker Chambers was known to be involved. I was convinced that the legal provision that "no inference or presumption" should be drawn from a refusal to appear would have little or no weight in the Board's thinking, that it would in practice infer and presume my guilt if I refused to appear. I quite appreciated that, by virtue of the April 28 Executive Order, the accused was essentially charged not with countering evidence of guilt, but with overcoming any "reasonable doubt" that might lurk in the minds of his examiners; that is, he was presumed guilty until he might establish his innocence. I therefore indicated that I would present myself at the hearing, and set to work at preparing for the ordeal.

I had consulted both with the Board's Chairman and with friends about the desirability of employing a lawyer to help me prepare a brief and to represent me at the hearing. General Snow, however, left me with the impression that, since the hearing was not a legal action, a lawyer's aid made little difference; and he assured me that if I needed such guidance at the hearing the Board's own legal officers would help me. My friends were divided. Some, especially in view of the amorphous nature of the

charges, thought that I alone could do as much as any lawyer. Others advised that I get a lawyer in any event. Being
unable to comprehend the reasoning that led the Board to
take formal action against me on June 27, I had lost some
more of my trust in the Department's administrative processes. I nevertheless was convinced that the evidence of
my record was incontestably in my favor; in addition, lawyer's fees would have been a burden. Moreover, Canon 5
of the "Canons of Professional Ethics" of the American
Bar Association reads: "The primary duty of a lawyer
engaged in a public prosecution is not to convict, but to
see that justice is done." Snow himself was a lawyer—and
had moreover indicated that the Board's legal officers
would act impartially, not as prosecuting attorneys.

I therefore decided simply to consult a lawyer for background advice, to prepare the brief myself, and to present
my case accompanied by a colleague who had the same
access to confidential material as I. Dr. John F. Melby,
who had entered the Foreign Service in 1937 and had
served in both China and the Soviet Union, generously
agreed to act in the capacity of my informal representative.

The work began, with my family ardently helping. The
new blows that had rained down on us on June 27 and
after were hard, but mother, wife, son, and daughter all
faced our difficulties courageously. Part of their fortitude
no doubt derived from the conviction, expressed almost
daily in our household, that "It just isn't possible that you
won't be cleared." The more I and my family worked on my
defense, the better it looked. Mariann had abandoned her
easel in January, lacking the heart for her customary paint-
ing activities after receipt of my interrogatory. Now, she
did the typing of the nonconfidential draft of the defense

brief. Oliver and Zoë did reading for me at the Library of Congress. It was naturally hardest for my mother, whose age prevented her from participating directly in the work at hand, but her distress was somewhat mitigated by her being with us and observing with what good heart the family was preparing for the battle.

The LSB and the Department's administration were presumably likewise at work on the case. When I contemplated the smoldering world, and the work there was for skilled hands to do, I could not be other than aghast at the misdirection of energy and brains, and thought of the last line of Edna St. Vincent Millay's poem "Toys"—"And all the time, death beating the door in." Nevertheless, one had to follow the prescribed routine, and trust that the matter would be brought to an expeditious, proper conclusion. But—and the "but" remained for Mariann and me to face in our private councils—we had to admit, on the evidence of our eyes and ears, that the times truly seemed out of joint in the United States; and in those circumstances one could not be certain that innocence and a fine record would be enough. After all, many of the 300,000 witches burned in Europe from the thirteenth to the eighteenth centuries were probably innocent, and some must have had excellent records of sobriety and social accomplishment.

Our position in local society changed. First of all, we at once appreciated that we had been stigmatized. The Department's spokesman on July 12 had apparently tried to give the impression that only security charges were involved, but actually the process was concerned with both my security and my loyalty. Our social life therefore suffered injury both from our natural impulse of withdrawal and from the reserve of others. In our case, the change was perhaps less than one might have expected, for excepting those members of the Wood Committee who had sat in on its executive session with me in March, none outside the State Department knew what the charges against me might be. We received no vituperation over the telephone, no scurrilous letters, as did some of our colleagues who had been exposed to public view. But a number of people put guards over their friendliness, and there were the few acquaintances who now failed to recognize me. After all, "guilt by association" was a principle that had come to be accepted by some Congressional committees—and by a part of the public.

But this was what would be termed, in war, a "local condition." From our friends and colleagues in many parts of the world we received expressions of sympathy and support. The language of the messages varied, but one word appeared more frequently than any other to describe the correspondents' reaction to the charges made against me— "shocking." And from that beginning, the letters went on to weave an even pattern:

"The news is incredible. . . . it seems that my feelings are more than my pen can handle and I can think but to write over and over again—damn, damn, damn."

"It is a terrible thing that a man of your distinguished career must go into formal hearings in order to put an end to malicious rumors which have been circulated anonymously."

"It is a pretty harrowing experience to devote one's life to government service, to struggle to preserve one's independence and quality of thought, and then to face allegations of disloyalty or security risk."

". . . . it would appear that the virus of McCarthyism is spreading to appling proportions. . . . At a time when morale in the Foreign Service generally is . . . at a fairly low ebb among the

FSO's, . . . the continuance of this sort of thing will probably lead to the conclusion that it is rather less strain after all to stay home and work for Quaker Oats or something."

"The curious behavior of public opinion in this country since, at least, the McCarthy speeches of last year has had the effect of making me feel increasingly unclean."

". . . . I am deeply disturbed at the inroads that ignorance and intolerance have made into the fabric of American life. Undoubtedly you were brought up as I was—to believe in intellectual initiative and integrity, and to respect individuals who made an effort to inquire and to learn. It is truly alarming to find a considerable sector of public opinion ready to condemn the learning process."

"I keep thinking of the state of mind portrayed by Anatole France in 'The Gods Are Athirst'. Perhaps we have progressed a bit from the days of the French Revolution, though: from the guillotine to mccarthyism."

"Your case seems to me to savour of the witch-hunting (without the witch and without the manifestations) of early Puritan days in your country."

"The line of reasoning of those placing charges against you would seem to be that if one read the writings of Confucius or the Koran it would definitely prove that one was not a Christian, or if one would have conversation with a murderer as to the cause of his action it would make that person likewise a murderer."

"Unfortunately, it is probably true that it will never be possible to silence such charges as have been leveled against yourself and many of our friends. Too much is at stake for the Chiang regime, a fringe of Republican politicians, and a group of professional and amateur smearers."

"What you are being made to go through is a sad commentary on the psychological pass to which partisan politics by a few asses has brought our country."

"Your present position in the Department is, of course, a very vulnerable one at the present time. I had thought that if anyone could be safe from attack it would be you. One feels that if a person of your integrity and discretion can be thus attacked no one is safe."

A foreign friend wound up on a note gloomier even than the rest, as follows (in translation):

"The evil is that, behind the social machine, there is often a sordid human machination, a desire to injure not only to pull therefrom a personal profit (which would be all the same not excusable) but also to act by virtue of the principle 'it does not suffice that one should be happy, it is still necessary that the others be unhappy.' Add to this that, to quote another of my classics, 'we live under a regime of police mythology.' At the bottom, there is calumny, malicious or stupid rumor; on this there comes to be grafted a bureaucratic and inhuman interpretation."

This was the general tenor of the many friendly messages. The communications generally ended with something of this nature: "delighted to be of any possible assistance in combating preposterous insinuations."

We were buoyed up by the sympathy and support of those courageous "men of good will." We worked on, trying to develop a logical force adequate to brush away the elusive cobwebs which were the LSB's accusations. Soon after receipt of the charges, I had asked the Board to clarify and amplify those charges, so that I might better come to grips with them. In a communication of July 3, 1951, it responded as follows:

Regarding your request for further clarification and amplification of charges 1 thru 8 and charge 9(e), it may be stated that charges 1 thru 8 relate to specific comments from the testimony of persons allegedly in official or social contact with you during the periods designated. The generality or specificity of such comment, as the case may be, the testimony of such persons in its entirety, as well as all other evidence made available in the case, including that adduced by interrogatory and hearing will, of

course, be carefully considered by the Board in reaching a decision in the case.

It was of no help to know that the "generality or specificity" of comments taken from the testimony of the LSB's
anonymous informants would be "carefully considered"
by the Board in reaching its decision: When translated,
this bureaucratic gobbledygook simply meant that I was
denied the opportunity to know in what context, and by
whom and for what purpose, the comments were made.

On July 20, I was asked whether I would be willing to
advance the date of my hearing from July 31 to July 25, so
that my case could be disposed of at the same time as that
of John Paton Davies. I considered the state of my prepa-
rations for the hearing, which had been based on the anticipation that I still had ten days before me, and informed
the Board that I couldn't undertake to be ready in that
shorter time. The hearing was therefore held as originally
scheduled. I then met, for the first time, the members of
the Board who would sit in judgment on me: General
Snow, the Chairman; Ambassador Fletcher Warren, a
Foreign Service officer whose career dated back to 1921;
and a young ex-Lieutenant Colonel of World War II,
Francis Murphy. Lieutenant Colonel Murphy, like Brigadier General Snow and Colonel Humelsine, had been in
the State Department for approximately five years. None of
the three Board members had ever served in the Far East.
John W. Sipes sat with the Board as Legal Officer, Lawson
A. Moyer as Assistant Legal Officer; both young men, like
Snow and Murphy, had joined the State Department only
after the war. Those were the men charged with determining whether I, who had spent twenty years in the Far East
as Foreign Service officer, had had "pink tendencies" in

Peking, China, in 1934–35, and similar issues. Deputy
Under Secretary of State for Administration Humelsine
was in overall authority.

The five sat on one side of a long table, confronting me
in accepted tribunal fashion. The reporter brought up one
flank. I and my colleague-associate Melby faced them from
a lonely position well across the room. I had confronted
various tests before, but with factors that could be calculated at least approximately. This time I found myself in
an encounter with the imponderable, a mystery created of
elements outside my knowledge; and at issue were high
stakes—my career, my reputation, and the happiness of my
family.

The LSB sat in the joint capacity of accuser, prosecutor,
judge, and jury in a matter where the accused was not enabled to know what it was all about. As supporting my
comprehensive survey of June 22, at my request the Office
of Chinese Affairs forwarded to the Board 323 voluntary
reports, dispatches, and telegrams on which the survey
was based. Those documents thus became part of the dossier. (I had on June 22 listed 215 additional communications of my drafting on the twin subjects of Chinese
Communism and Sino-Soviet relations, for the LSB's reference.) I would present witnesses to support the documents
and my own testimony. The unknown persons whose
statements the LSB had used as charges against me were
not present. Throughout the hearing, the Board of its own
initiative never identified any of its informants to me. Nor
were the charges ever put into their original contexts. In
addition to having been refused the right of confrontation
and cross-examination of my accusers, I was even denied
the right of access to the full text of the accusation; further-

more, it would become apparent in due course that the LSB upon occasion had substituted wording of its own invention that significantly altered the purport of the charge—to my disadvantage.

But there I was, present at the hearing, to review the data already handed over and ready to submit to examination by the Board. The hearing began. The Chairman read the charges. Due note was taken of my request for amplification of the charges, and of the nature of the Board's reply. It was recorded further that "it was also indicated to Mr. Clubb during the discussions that Charge 3 is comment apparently obtained by the FBI from his personnel file in the Department." It was left unsaid, but it could be deduced, that the FBI had then communicated the Department's own data back to the Department's LSB, which thereupon found it appropriate to convert it into a formal charge against me. The information attributing to me "pink tendencies" had evidently been forwarded to the Department through established channels some 15 years before, but had then been weighed and found wanting in the light of what was known about me. Since at least two more of the charges evidently also came from old efficiency reports, however, and were of the same general vintage, the anachronism of charge no. 3 did not stand out as especially remarkable. It was more remarkable that the LSB had been able to unearth so little that was unfavorable to me in reports covering 20 years and presumably three continents—reports coming from all types of persons, malevolent as well as benevolent, liars as well as honest men.

The preliminary formalities over, General Snow observed that "At this point we usually turn the hearing over to the party or his representative or counsel to conduct the hearing." The Board in effect rested its case on the bare charges. At no point in the proceedings did it present evidence in support of the charges.

I undertook my defense, prefacing my presentation by the request that there be inserted into the record a part of the testimony of Foreign Service Officer George F. Kennan in the hearing of John P. Davies. One of Ambassador Kennan's observations seemed especially relevant:

> I feel it absolutely essential to the conduct of foreign relations in our country and in this Department that the Government be at liberty to tap the honest and best judgment of all the men who work for it. If there ever creeps into our system an atmosphere in which men do not feel at liberty to state the facts as they see them, knowing that the greatest crime they could commit would be to state them as they did not see them; then, in my opinion, the successful operation of the democratic foreign policy will be out of the question.

The charges against me fell into three natural groups— political unorthodoxy, dangerous associations, and a visit to a leftist magazine 19 years before. For tactical purposes, I divided the specific charges into five categories:

(1) that I associated with Communists in Hankow in the period 1931–34;

(2) that I was "friendly" toward the USSR, 1935–37;

(3) that I was possessed of various political attitudes varying in shade from "pink" to "100% pro-Red," and had been "friendly" toward Communism, at various times from 1931 to 1940;

(4) that I had had "close and habitual association" with a number of named persons; and,

(5) that in 1932 I had "delivered a sealed envelope to

the office of the editor of the *New Masses* . . . for transmittal to one Grace Hutchins. . . ."

Regarding the charge of association with Communists in Hankow in 1931–34, I pointed out that there were no known Communists, Chinese or foreign, who lived openly in Hankow in the period under discussion. It was then that the Nationalists were carrying out the most stringent measures against all Communists or suspected Communists in the areas under their control, and the only "Communists" we saw in Hankow were those Chinese executed along the road the foreigners took to go to the Race Club—on charges of "Communism" made as readily as in the United States during the McCarthy era. I gave the names of three leftist foreign journalists who had visited Hankow during my tenure, and said that the Department's informant might have believed them to be Communists. But the Board Chairman said that "the statement of the informant in question was general, not specific," and further identification was impossible. So weak was this charge that the LSB pursued the matter no further.

The next general charge was that I had been " 'friendly' toward the USSR" in 1935–37. Since I had been in Peking at the time, it was only with the greatest difficulty that I could imagine how I might have manifested that "friendly" attitude toward a sovereign state geographically removed from me. True, I and my family had in 1937 returned to post from home leave by traveling via the USSR—a circumstance that could well have been judged suspicious by some of the more rigidly anti-Soviet, and one that may have caused the Board's unnamed informant to reach his global conclusion. But no evidence was introduced that attributed overt acts or express statements to me. Nor was there cited any Departmental directive to the field instructing Foreign Service Officers to be unfriendly to, and remain aloof from, things, ideas, and persons Soviet. On my part, following the pattern of my January 22 letter, I cited to the LSB as directives of the United States Government, presumed effective for Foreign Service Officers as well as others, official statements by the President and the Assistant Secretary of State on the occasion of American recognition of the Soviet Union in 1933, and a number of other pronouncements before and after World War II. I ended that survey of officially expressed policy by quoting the Ribicoff Resolution passed by both houses of Congress on June 20, 1951: one *week* before the Board charged me with having been "friendly" toward the USSR in 1935–37, Congress reaffirmed "the historic and abiding friendship of the American people for all other peoples, including the peoples of the Soviet Union. . . ."

With a delicacy that may not have been fully appreciated, I chose not to review wartime pronouncements on the Soviet Union by leading American political figures; I limited myself to the observation that I was sure the Board would agree that official American policy had remained friendly to the USSR during the war years—a full decade after the time I was myself charged with having been "friendly." And I concluded that I should not have been deviating from the official "line" at any time from 1933 to 1945 (excepting perhaps August 1939–June 1941) had I in fact been "friendly" toward the USSR; "and that I should have been in full conformity with powerful sentiment had I been friendly toward the Russian people at any time from Senator Borah's speech, March 3, 1931, to the Senate, to the date of the passing of the Ribicoff Resolution." It

was difficult to perceive how American officials were to be
sure of what the policies in question might be, if talking
out of both sides of our mouths was to be the national practice and if words no longer bore an honest meaning. But
past words regarding the USSR seemingly conveyed little
significance to the Board in 1951—even when the attitude
attributed to me also lay in that same past. The charges
themselves indicated that, for the Board, the contemporary
Cold War spirit and concepts governed.

I developed my argument to include the next set of
charges, as hard to hit as wills-o'-the-wisp, that I had been
possessed of demonic attitudes ranging from "pink" to
"Red." I admitted my interest in the Russian language and
Russian history, and offered no apologies. I freely admitted friendliness for the Russian people, and went on to
add that I was similarly friendly toward the Chinese, Japanese, and Turki peoples—toward all peoples. I remarked:

It is possible to see in this connection how the LSB's informant,
by a process of thought transference, well known alike to psy-
chologists and politicians, might have considered that my interest
in the Russian language, and my friendship for the Russian people, and my study of the course of revolution in China, were
equivalent to "friendship toward Communism," that is, looking
at the matter in the context of the charges against me, biased in
favor of Communism.

I explained in general terms my attitude toward the Soviet Union and Communism. I said that I made no claims
to omniscience, "either 20 years ago or now," and added:
"I would say in my defense that, by my own estimate, I
have made fewer mistakes about either the USSR or Communism than a large number of people who have never
studied the subject." I quoted a bit from Thomas Jefferson's inaugural address of March 4, 1801:

When right, I shall often be thought wrong by those whose positions do not command the whole ground. I ask your indulgence for my own errors, which will never be intentional; and your support against the errors of others, who may condemn what they would not, if seen in all its parts.

I said that, while I had attained to some knowledge of the USSR and Communism by 1935–37, I had learned a lot more in the fifteen years that had elapsed since then. Finally, I asserted bluntly that:

despite the gaps in my knowledge in my earlier years, and despite the natural confusion that ensues in a situation respecting which a large number of authorities express widely differing views, my thinking on the subject of both the Soviet Union and Communism, as set forth in the pertinent Department files of my work in the form of the despatches and other communications now in the hands of the LSB, has not erred substantially in analysis, estimate, or prognostication.

For its use in checking on my challenging assertion, I submitted to the Board two documents, *Blueprint for World Conquest* (containing among other things the "Program of the Communist International") and the COMINTERN resolution of September 1, 1928, entitled "The Revolutionary Movement in the Colonies and Semi-Colonies." I doubt that the LSB members had previously made a careful study of those Communist documents, or other parallel Communist doctrine. I further surmise that they made no such study during my hearing, or afterward, for all of my challenge. In a process where doubt is the main factor, and the tribunal purports to be concerned with the feelings, sympathies, and mental attitudes of the accused at a period far removed in both time and historical development, concrete data would clearly be deemed of little significance.

I now undertook the task of proving the contention that my analyses, estimates, and forecasts regarding both the USSR and Chinese Communism—presumed to be of major concern to the LSB—would be shown by the written record to have been substantially correct. I asserted that the question could easily be resolved, "for we now have established history as a body of reference for most of the period during which I reported events and gave my opinion of their significance." The files of the Department contained abundant, incontrovertible evidence. The record reflected my thought indelibly, and that thought portrayed much of the troubled times of a China in revolution. The LSB had not been a part of those times, but I had. And so had witnesses I produced.

So I brought the record for the LSB right down to my memorandum of December 18, 1950, dealing with possible new dangers facing the United States in the period immediately ahead instead of in some distant future. I had continued to produce other memoranda in 1951, until my suspension on June 27, but I stopped my survey with 1950: I judged that the Board, given its nature, would suspect that any writing after receipt of the interrogatory on January 2 would have had due regard for the established political line—insofar as it could be discovered. I ended the survey with the comment:

In the final analysis, one must stand on his record in cases like the present, and I stand on mine. My reporting to the Department over a period of twenty years to my mind is full and adequate refutation of charges which, in essence, allege bias and disloyalty. Had I been biased, I should not have been accurate. Had I been disloyal, I should patently not [have] gone to such infinite pains to try to communicate to the Department of State what I thought the purposes of the Chinese Communists and the Soviets might be.

I supplemented this examination of the record with the testimony of thirteen witnesses who either appeared personally or submitted sworn statements. Those witnesses had observed me in both official and nonofficial functions for periods ranging from five to twenty-three years; most of them had known me for periods of time closer to the latter figure. Those who testified in person submitted themselves to the cross-examination of the Board, all in marked contrast to the Board's informants, not one of whom was ever brought forward to confront me. Ambassador Edwin F. Stanton, sometime Assistant Director of the Division of Far Eastern Affairs, had known me since 1932 and had served with me variously in Peking, Hankow, and Shanghai. He submitted an affidavit that paid especial attention to my work on the subject of Communism, stating in part:

Mr. Clubb was one of the first members of the Foreign Service, certainly in China, to realize that the terrible and sinister force of communism was likely to be a threat to the freedom of mankind, a threat to world peace and a threat to the United States. His vision and foresight led him to undertake a study of the Russian language and to make a thorough exploration of communism in general and of Chinese communism in particular. His reports to the Department of State while he was stationed at Hankow contained much very valuable material concerning the motives, objectives, organization and plans of the Chinese communists. . . . [Regarding the charges contained in the LSB's letter of June 27, which "have the appearance of rumor, hearsay and gossip"] I do wish to emphasize in the strongest manner possible, that Mr. Clubb's interest in and study of communism, his contacts with communists, his reports regarding communist activities were made for the benefit of the Department of State, his Government and his country.

Most of my witnesses, naturally, were from American officialdom. But an affidavit submitted by a missionary educator who had known me during my tours of duty at Japanese-occupied Nanking and Shanghai in 1939–41 and who testified that he had been familiar with my work and reputation from 1932 through 1949, offered an example of sentiment from the nonofficial American community in China:

My own experience of Mr. Clubb's work, his conversation, and his personal associations supports entirely his consistent reputation as a loyal and effective representative of American interests. In eighteen years of frequent mention of Mr. Clubb by all sorts of persons, I heard of no act or word in support of Communist interests or injurious to American interests. In that time, 1932–1949, I know of two, and only two, items over which any raising of eyebrows occurred, and those I now report frankly.

First, in or about the period 1931–1933, when the National Government of China was undertaking extensive campaigns to suppress the Communists southeast of Hankow, Mr. Clubb's political reports from his post at Hankow called attention to generally unrealized potentialities of the Communist movement in that area, which was frequently more effective in organization and in methods than was the greatly superior force of the National Government. Such information was not pleasant to most of those who received it, including myself; for it presaged long years of civil war with dubious outcome. But the careful search for facts and the honest reporting of them through regular official channels was increasingly recognized as an important service to our own Government and to American interests generally.

Secondly, Mr. Clubb's prompt, firm stand in 1949 with regard to Communist treatment of American official property in Peiping was first questioned by some Americans in China as perhaps too hasty, too stiff, when an experimental effort by American interests to get along for a time with the new Communist regime seemed tentatively the lesser of evils. But further consideration consolidated approval for Mr. Clubb's position based upon general confidence in his record and upon his position and acquaintance with Communist practice—notably his tour of duty at Vladivostok—and also upon realization that superior officers in Washington were standing strongly with him in his action at Peiping.

The statements made in this affidavit, including the central paragraph . . . dealing with my experience of Mr. Clubb and of his standing among fellow-officers and the American residents in China, carry the plain meaning of their words. They are also to be understood in the light of events in China during the past twenty years. In this time, Communist power has developed from small beginnings, long ignored by most of us, to present dominance. Mr. Clubb, neither an advocate nor a tool of Communism, examined the entire Chinese scene with the weakness of the National Government and the threat from the Communists. He sought persistently to know what the Communists were doing, how they made their appeal to their fellowcountrymen, what their proximate destiny might be. This was a service not adequately appreciated and not adequately utilized. Such work made it possible to see the trends, the diagram of changing forces, over against which general, military, and economic policy could be based.

In the eyes of American residents in China, Mr. Clubb did meritorious duty, both in the intelligent finding and report of facts, and in the defence of American interests vis-à-vis the three types of de facto authorities with which he had successively to deal—Chinese National, Japanese military, Chinese Communist.

VII

Dangerous Thoughts

The accused was told that, in the Holy Office, no one was arrested without sufficient evidence of his having done or witnessed something contrary to the faith or to the free exercise of the Inquisition, so that he must believe that he has been brought hither on such information. Therefore, by the reverence due to God and his glorious and blessed Mother, he was admonished and charged to search his memory and confess the whole truth as to what he feels himself inculpated, or knows of other persons, without concealment or false witness, for in so doing he will discharge his conscience as a Catholic Christian, he will save his soul and his case will be dispatched with all speed and befitting mercy, but otherwise justice will be done. . . .

This brought an exceedingly effectual pressure to bear upon the anxious prisoner, especially when the system of delay, whether calculating or merely procrastinating, left him for months, and perhaps years, to lie in his cell, shut out from the world, brooding over his fate, and torturing himself with conjectures as to the evidence so confidently assumed to be conclusive against him. He was simply admonished to discharge his conscience, being kept in the dark as to the crimes of which he was accused, and left to search his heart and guess what he had done to bring him before the terrible tribunal. This had the further utility that in many cases it led to confession of derelictions unknown to the prosecution, his im-

passible judges coldly accepting his revelations and re-
manding him to his cell with fresh adjurations to search
his memory and clear his conscience.

H. C. LEA, *A History of the Inquisition in Spain* (N.Y.
1907), Vol. III, p. 39.

I had to wrestle with the LSB examination concerning my political beliefs and attitudes. I agreed with
the suggestion of one of the Board members that I had
been a "liberal" in the 1930s. In response to another question, I willingly conceded that I also had been pro-New
Deal. It is notorious that in some quarters President Roosevelt's policies were violently opposed. Thus I felt it incumbent upon me to attack the concept, implicit in well
over half of the Board's charges, that the casting of political epithets at a man automatically transformed him into a
villain. I went on to argue that name-calling could not
usually be accepted as a technically accurate description.
History of course abounds with material to support my
thesis, and I cited examples of calumny directed at Washington, Jefferson, and Lincoln. I could of course have adduced contemporary instances of name-calling in American domestic politics, but I refrained.

It is easily demonstrated that, in politics, it has long
been true that "Orthodoxy is my doxy; heterodoxy is another man's doxy." And there are always those who, using
the primitive yardstick *post hoc ergo propter hoc,* damn
honest men as directly responsible for the events that they
might forecast in reports to their governments.

It was evident that the phraseology used in some of the
allegations against me expressed a political opprobrium a
particular informant might feel for a point of view I held;

nevertheless, such informants apparently avoided the realm of what the Board termed "specificity." It would appear rather that the LSB expected me to accommodate it, in the fashion of authoritarian States, by confessing specific sins to fit the general epithet and then crying *"mea culpa! mea culpa!"* and heaping ashes on my head in pretended penitence. I did not do so. I did not deny that my political thought might have differed from the Board's informant's in a particular case (or, as far as that goes, from the Board's), but I did not confess to having "sinned" by differing.

Again, however, the testimony of my witnesses should have been reassuring to the LSB—if it desired reassurance. One witness was a U.S. Army officer who had known me for twenty years and had served with me at Peking in the end, when he had headed the Department of the Army Language School located at the post. He was currently assigned to the Intelligence Division of the Army General Staff on duty at Washington. The Board probed to get his appreciation of my political reporting:

Q Well, over these years that you have known Mr. Clubb and years that have been spent in Intelligence work for the Army, you have undoubtedly seen his reporting and his work over the years. What is his general reputation in G-2 as to accuracy and objectivity of his reporting?

A He is considered very sound, very reliable, and an impartial reporter.

Q At any time has the Army considered there is any bias in any of his reporting?

A On the contrary, his reports were always given a very high reliability. That is especially true during the period when he was in Peking when the Communists held the city. I saw practically every wire which he sent after I got back here, and he was still in Peking.

Later, the Chairman took up with the witness the matter of my political attitudes, and there was the following exchange:

THE CHAIRMAN: Colonel, certain informants have made statements about Mr. Clubb as to his attitude toward Communism and the USSR during the '30's. . . .

It is said by an informant that prior to 1940 he was mildly red and espoused doctrines of a Communist nature.

THE WITNESS: He never gave me that impression, sir. . . .

THE CHAIRMAN: And you never heard other people say that either?

THE WITNESS: No, sir.

THE CHAIRMAN: Another statement is in the early '30's he showed a marked preference for some Communistic principles.

THE WITNESS: I think I knew him in the early '30's, and I never got that impression, sir. . . .

THE CHAIRMAN: . . . From 1934 to 1935 informant said he had distinct pink tendencies.

THE WITNESS: I was in China from 1934 to 1936, and engaged in such type of work, sir, that I am sure if that had existed I certainly would have known it.

All but one of my witnesses testified, from their varied experience of me in China, that they had never heard of the reputation alleged by the Board. The one exception was Ambassador Clarence E. Gauss, who had been my superior at Peking, Shanghai, and Chungking. Under questioning by my representative, John Melby, he was led into the area of my political leanings. After a few initial exchanges, Gauss came to grips with the issue:

Well, now, gentlemen, we might just as well get down to facts. I was Chargé at Peking when Clubb reported to me for duty there as Third Secretary in 1934. Now, prior to Mr. Clubb's arrival in Peking there had been stories that he was inclined to be "pink." Who those stories came from I couldn't remember at this

day. But I do recall talking to someone of the China Corps. . . .
I asked him about Clubb in Hankow. And the suggestion was
made to me that it would be a good idea if when Mr. Clubb reported to me in Peking I were to give him a word of good advice
to suggest that he be careful of his associations, because the reputation that had reached me concerning him in Hankow that he
might be a little "pink" arose from his too close association there
with, oh, people—I don't mean Chinese. I mean foreigners, non-
Chinese, who were inclined toward the left. Now, not Communists. It wasn't a suggestion that he was associated with Communists but inclined to people toward the left. . . .

Now, then, that is why I say that I would have been sensitive
and was sensitive during all of my association with Mr. Clubb
after that of any tendency in his reporting or in his relations or association with the pinks, reds or anything else.

A short interval later, Gauss summed up: "I have trusted
him absolutely. I would never have sent him to Tihwa if I
hadn't. I wouldn't have had him very long in Chungking if
I hadn't, or in Shanghai or anywhere else." Then Mr.
Murphy took up the questioning of the Ambassador, with
an unexpected result. Referring to an interview between
an FBI agent and Gauss in July 1950 (the month I assumed
my post as Director of the Office of Chinese Affairs),
Murphy noted: "During your talk with the agent, according to his version of the conversation, you mentioned that
he had showed a marked preference for some communist
principles in the early 30's." This was the LSB's charge
no. 4. Responded Gauss: "No. I probably told him that this
was the reputation he had when he came to Chungking
[sic] in 1934. There you are. And it's the question of the
accuracy of a report."

Murphy quoted the FBI man again. Gauss commented:
"Well, I would think that your agent has not made an ac-

curate report of my conversation with him regarding
Clubb." Murphy returned to Charge no. 3:

> MR. MURPHY: . . . in an inspection report dated January 11,
> 1939 at the time when you were Consul General at Shanghai, you
> reported that when Clubb first came to the Embassy, which was
> then the Legation, at Peiping from Hankow, that Clubb had dis-
> tinct "pink" tendencies but that by January of 1939 he had be-
> come better adjusted, better balanced.
> THE WITNESS: Did I say he had "pink" tendencies, or did I
> say he was reported to have?
> MR. MURPHY: That's why I'm reading this. "Had 'pink'
> tendencies."
> THE WITNESS: Had "pink" tendencies?
> MR. MURPHY: Yes. This is taken from a report dated Jan-
> uary 11, 1939.
> THE WITNESS: Well, my recollection now is that I could only
> say that he was reported to have "pink" tendencies, because I
> don't see how I could say that—
> MR. MURPHY: *This is not a verbatim extract from your re-
> port.*[emphasis supplied]. . . .
> MR. MURPHY: To clear up some of the points I am interested
> in, to your knowledge, your personal firsthand knowledge, have
> you ever perceived any "pink" tendencies or communistic incli-
> nations on the part of Clubb during your observation of him?
> THE WITNESS: No. And that is what I told the FBI man.

Thus the source of two more of the LSB's charges
against me, numbers 3 and 4, had been *by chance* identified. But the source himself had testified that both
charges were incorrectly attributed to him, that the reports
had come to him only as hearsay, and that during the three
times he was my superior he had never seen evidence to
confirm them. The Board had attributed to the ambassador
who knew me so well two (at least) of its charges, but had
not checked the validity of its versions with him even

though he resided in Washington. In one case, the FBI interviewer had evidently misquoted Gauss; in the second instance, the Board itself had seemingly misquoted him—although it had the pertinent Department record at hand. The Board also, although attributing to Ambassador Gauss allegations adverse to me, in disregard of the pertinent regulations had failed to ask him to testify before it as to those allegations. By great good luck, *I* had asked him to appear in my own behalf.

Next came the matter of my allegedly "close and habitual" associations with various persons blacklisted by the Board. My associations of the 1930s were generally known to my superiors, for, as Ambassador Gauss had described the situation in Hankow particularly, we foreigners in China lived in a goldfish bowl. If it is difficult to prove one's innocence of an undefined heterodoxy, it is next to impossible to combat a procedure by which one may be found guilty, through association, of whatever a blacklisted person might be confidentially *suspected* of. I was not told why individual persons might in 1951 have been deemed dangerous associates for a Foreign Service officer in the 1930s. Some had, it is true, been recently "cited" in Congressional or other investigations, but so too, over the years, have Presidents, Secretaries of State—and even Senators. And the Board, driven by the same philosophy that led it to lift various allegations from their larger context, made no effort to judge the sum total of my associations.

The essential weirdness of the procedure was disclosed in the hearing on the blacklisted eleven. The first person on my list was Agnes Smedley, then deceased. When I first met her in Shanghai in 1931, she was an accredited correspondent of the entirely respectable journal *Frank-furter Zeitung*. She had already written an autobiography, and would in due course write three books on the Chinese revolution. Her acquaintanceship was extensive, her political and professional interests were well known. Under date May 4, 1934, she received from Secretary of State Cordell Hull the following autographed letter of introduction addressed to American Diplomatic and Consular Officers:

> Sirs:
> At the instance of the Honorable Robert F. Wagner, Senator of the United States from the State of New York, I take pleasure in introducing to you Miss Agnes Smedley of New York City, who is about to proceed abroad.
> I cordially bespeak for Miss Smedley such courtesies and assistance as you may be able to render, consistently with your official duties.
>
> Very truly yours,
> /s/ *Cordell Hull*.

After the date of that letter, I had met Agnes Smedley several times, at Hankow, Peking, and New York. Miss Smedley openly professed her sympathy for the Chinese Communists in the 1930s and worked in the field with them in the period when they were collaborating with the Nationalists in the war against Japan. But *after* World War II, she was charged by the Defense Department with having been a Soviet spy. Challenged by the offended writer, the Department retracted—but of course the charge lived on, and now that she was dead it could pass for common currency without danger of contradiction. She was thus more fearsome dead than she ever had been when alive. I had not seen Miss Smedley since the 1930s, but my scant early contacts with her were a subject of burning interest to the Board, for in my response to their interrogatory I had identified her as the "Agnes" who had given me the 1932 letter of introduction to Walt Carmon. I was able to quote Freda Utley, who *had lived with* Agnes Smedley at Hankow during the war period, as describing Miss Smedley as "one of the few truly great people I have ever met." Although that was from Miss Utley's book *China at War*, written in 1938 after her conversion to the ranks of the ex-Communists, it did not perceptibly check the Board's pursuit of the subject. Agnes Smedley was to interest them to the end. Her doxy was not their doxy.

The second name was that of Owen Lattimore. That China specialist and wartime OWI official had in early 1950 like Agnes Smedley been accused, but by Senator McCarthy, of being a Soviet espionage agent. The Senator had early been caused to backtrack from the gravamen of his charge, but Lattimore had nevertheless been smeared with suspicion and was still being kept under attack, and it could easily be guessed that the State Department had blacklisted him on the basis of McCarthy's charge, or something similar; but this I was left to deduce. The Board desired my estimate of Lattimore's thinking. An exchange in regard to the book *Pivot of Asia* gives the tenor of the inquiry. The Board said that, according to the ubiquitous "informant," Mrs. Lattimore had supplied the publishers with a list of persons "who were friendly to Lattimore, and who apparently held similar views with respect to United States foreign policy in the Far East," from whom she thought the company might secure favorable comments on the book for sales promotion purposes; my name had been included in the list. The transcript records the following:

MR. MOYER [Legal Officer]: This is a broad question, and I don't intend it at all to be unfair, but could it be said that you apparently held similar views with reference to the United States foreign policy in the Far East as Mr. Lattimore?

THE CHAIRMAN: That is pretty general. I don't think that question is quite fair. It involves an appraisal of the whole opinion of a writer of prodigious extent on foreign policy.

MR. MURPHY: Were you referring only to the "Pivot of Asia"?

MR. MOYER: I am referring to that particular book, because the allegation only concerns that.

THE CHAIRMAN: Let's put it this way. Did you read the book?

MR. CLUBB: Yes, sir.

THE CHAIRMAN: Did you agree with it?

MR. CLUBB: You wish to know whether I agreed with conclusions rather than fact, I suppose.

THE CHAIRMAN: Yes.

MR. CLUBB: Quite frankly, my general recollection of the book is that it had very little in respect to American policy in regard to Central Asia in it. It was Sinkiang, you see, that it was discussing. The book comprised a brief introductory part by Mr. Lattimore, and then a number of chapters, and certain ethnological studies. . . . Frankly, I don't remember the American policy parts of it.

THE CHAIRMAN: Then the question can't be answered.

MR. MOYER: I don't think the informant is necessarily speaking of the particular book [cf. Mr. Moyer above]. The informant presented Mr. Clubb's name as one who held similar views on matters in the Far East. I may ask if that is generally accurate or inaccurate.

THE CHAIRMAN: I think it is too difficult.

MR. MURPHY: I would like to know if he is familiar with Mr. Lattimore's views. If he isn't——

THE CHAIRMAN: Do you know what Professor Lattimore's opinion on American foreign policy is?

MR. CLUBB: I am afraid I couldn't say yes or no to that, for the very simple reason . . . I have read about seven books of Mr. Lattimore's over a period—considerable period of years.

Now, in my opinion the thinking of Mr. Lattimore has changed somewhat, has been something in the 1930's, changed somewhat in the 1940's, and maybe is something else again at the present time. And for somebody else to say that it is believed that I am in line with what Mr. Lattimore thinks would put me in a very difficult position, and I do point out it was somebody else that said it, not I.

MR. MOYER: That is why I wanted your comment on the allegation.

MR. CLUBB: This may sound, if you will, a little challenging, but it is the only way I can put the response. If you will tell me what Mr. Owen Lattimore considers American policy to be or his attitude in respect to American policy, I will try to answer you.

MR. MOYER: I am afraid you put me in a spot with that question.

The inquiry into my alleged sympathy with the views of Lattimore on American Far Eastern policy ended there. It is noteworthy, however, that (1) the book *Pivot of Asia* was not the work of Lattimore alone, but the LSB evidently began its inquiry on the assumption that it was, (2) the Board members undertaking the questioning had evidently not themselves read the book and assumed on the basis of the hint got from an "informant's" report that it at least dealt in passing with American policy regarding the Far East—which was not the case, (3) although themselves ignorant of the contents of the book, and also apparently unable to define Lattimore's position respecting American Far Eastern policy, it seems certain that had I simply said that I "agreed with the book" or that I viewed American Far Eastern policy "just as did Owen Lattimore," the Board would have given me a black mark.

The third person listed was a Frenchman whom I had first known in Shanghai 1939–41; I had met him again after

the bitter war had shunted me along strange byways and
had penned him in Shanghai, where he carried on underground work for the Free French. He brought to his
then profession of journalism unusual linguistic abilities
and an omnivorous interest. I gave a brief description of
our relations and indicated in conclusion that "I naturally
do not know why the Loyalty Security Board has questioned me respecting my relations with——." The response came:

THE CHAIRMAN: Mr. Clubb the reason why——is mentioned
in the charges is that the Board has information before it that
one——was on the suspect list of the French intelligence as a
Communist, and that——had told the informant that you had furnished information to him on previous occasions, that is, to——.
That is all the information the Board has on the subject. Did you
ever give information to——?
MR. CLUBB: Not classified information. I naturally had had
various conversations with Mr.——. I had good relations with all
of the press in Shanghai and other places. I never gave classified
information to anybody who was not entitled to have it.
THE CHAIRMAN: He might have well and properly have said
he received information.
MR. CLUBB: That is quite true. I believe that I have enough
knowledge and experience about China so that I could give information to a large number of people. But giving information is different from giving classified information.
THE CHAIRMAN: The informant alleges that he visited the
home of——on occasions and found you present at the
home. . . .
MR. CLUBB: Yes, I have visited his home.
THE CHAIRMAN: I think that takes care of the allegation.
MR. MOYER: To your knowledge, did Mr. —— have the reputation of being a Communist?
MR. CLUBB: No, sir—I know of no pro-Communist sympathies or activities on the part of Mr. ——."

The fourth charge designed to establish my "guilt by association" carried me back to 1929–31. There were then some eight Language Attachés at the American Legation in Peking, all of course assigned there by the Department of State. I was one of the eight. Another of those colleagues was now included on my blacklist. This officer was congenial, and an able student. We naturally maintained the relations usual between men engaged in similar work in the same Government office. (There might, in fact, have been some adverse criticism of us put into efficiency reports had we gone about at dagger's point.) In 1931 I was sent to Hankow and Colleague X went to another post in China. Later, he resigned for personal reasons and took up teaching instead (quite sensibly, it seems to me now). He had subsequently again served the U.S. Government in two or three positions of high trust, then returned to teaching. I had never been aware of anything that remotely suggested pro-Communist sympathies or activities on the part of this competent scholar and officer. In any event, I had not since 1931 had anything even faintly resembling "close and habitual" relations with him. The Board gave no hint of the reason for his blacklisting. But a possibility for making a good guess came in connection with the discussion of subject no. 5.

The only name on my list which I could not remember ever having heard before was "Vladimir Mikheev." I made my statement regarding that stranger:

To the best of my recollection and belief, I have never met or known anyone by the name of Vladimir Mikheev. It is noted that the LSB, in its letter of July 3, 1951, replying to my request for amplification and clarification of this charge among others, informed me that, according to information made available to the Board, Vladimir Mikheev was an Australian correspondent for the Soviet News Agency, TASS in 1945. I have never been in Australia, and in the particular year 1945 I was in Vladivostok; leaving Vladivostok in January, 1946, I proceeded to Manchuria and remained there until October, 1947; from Changchun, Manchuria I was transferred to Peping [*Sic*—Peiping], where I remained until April, 1950—excepting home leave in 1948 when I touched neither Australia nor the USSR. I recall meeting no TASS representative of the name Vladimir Mikheev in China in either the pre-War or post-War period.

In a subsequent session, I took an opportunity to seek some elucidation:

. . . I should like to know for my reference when and where it is alleged by the Board's file that I knew and was in close and habitual association with Mr. Mikheev.

CHAIRMAN: In general I can answer your question. The information in the hands of the Board has to do with the spring of 1945. It appears at that time that this Mr. Mikheev displayed a calling card on which there was a message to Edmund Clubb, U.S. Consul, Vladivostok, "Greetings through my friend Vladimir Mikheev."

MR. MOYER: The card was obtained from a third source.

CHAIRMAN: It appears that somebody had written a card addressed to you, introducing Vladimir Mikheev, who was a friend of this person who wrote the card.

MR. MURPHY: He was the Australian correspondent of the "Tass" news agency.

MR. MOYER: The card addressed to you apparently said "Greetings through my friend."

CHAIRMAN: It is not indicated you were the friend of Mikheev.

A. [myself] May I ask if the friend was an American?

CHAIRMAN: Yes, it was——, Director of ——. [The subject of item no. 4!]

A. That would seem to indicate that he had some contact with——, assuming that is correct, but hardly with me.

CHAIRMAN: That is all the Board wanted to find out.

But there was another point that interested me:

A. I don't recall any such person passing through Vladivostok, and is it certain that he passed through Vladivostok, this man Mikheev?

MR. MURPHY: No, the question was designed to determine from you whether you had been in touch with Vladimir Mikheev.

A: I am sure that if somebody came to me with a card of introduction from an American whom I knew and who, by this identification, was at that time connected with the——and that man in addition were a newspaper representative, I should probably have received him.

CHAIRMAN: Did you know Mr. ——? [The subject of item no. 4, whose name had already several times been before the Board and regarding whom I had made a full reply.]

A: Yes indeed, he was a colleague of mine in Peking. We were at the language school together and that for a period roughly two years, and I have already responded in my testimony respecting my contacts with Mr. —— to the general effect that I met him very infrequently after that particular period.

CHAIRMAN: But you have no recollection of Mr. Mikheev bringing you a message from Mr. ——?

A: I have no recollection of even meeting him in Vladivostok, and I think probably I should have remembered it.

CHAIRMAN: I think that takes care of that item.

I had one thing more to say with respect to the point in question:

A. May I point out, just to wind this up, it is my understanding, as a result of a check performed, that Mr. Mikheev got an entry permit——not an entry permit, a visa to proceed to the Soviet Union via the United States in 1945, which would seem to indicate that he did not proceed via Vladivostok.

That ended the question of my allegedly "close and habitual" association, through the medium of a calling card displayed in Australia before the end of World War II, with a citizen of our Soviet ally—and with the American official who gave him the card. If the LSB was that interested, it could readily have ascertained from State Department records—as I had done—that Vladimir Mikheev had been granted an American visa to travel via the United States on his journey from Australia to the Soviet Union in 1945.

There now came the names of six persons who were but casual acquaintances, and with whom for reasons of geography alone I could have had no more than long-distance contacts. Two I had met once or twice in my life, three I had met at most a half-dozen times. The sixth individual was a man who had been stationed at the American Embassy in Chungking, in Government service, in 1942. During my four months in Chungking at that time I had had the usual official and social contacts with him, and I had seen him once or twice in Nanking in the postwar period. In 1948, that officer had been called before his own Department's loyalty board. He was cleared in his hearing, but subsequently resigned and entered the academic field—in England. Clearance through the established process of his own Department, however, had not prevented his being blacklisted by the State Department's LSB, or the LSB's charging me, in that manner implying grave wrongdoing, with having "close and habitual" relations with him.

I wound up my presentation regarding my relationships to those six persons and Mikheev with the comment:

In sum, I have had only the scantiest of relations of any sort with the last seven persons named in the LSB's reference list. It is pertinent to remark in this general connection that, from the time of my entry into the Service in 1928, until my return to the

United States in 1950, I have served in the United States under
assignment only approximately one year in total, that is, eight
months in 1928–29, and four months in 1944; that the rest of my
service has been abroad, with my posts including places as far
from the beaten track as Hankow, Chungking, Lanchow, Tihwa,
Vladivostok, and post-War Mukden and Changchun; that the very
mail service to several of those posts was frequently bad, especially in wartime; that I was physically in the United States, apart
from that one year of service, only on leave status, in the course
of which I generally touched a number of points and stayed long
at none but longest at my home in St. Paul; and that, therefore,
all logic points up the fact that actual physical opportunities for
me to establish "close and habitual" associations with these persons separated from me by thousands of miles have been slight, if
not, indeed, non-existent.

   If the Board had been niggardly as to reasons, a logical
deduction can perhaps be drawn from the circumstance
that of the eleven persons seven were writers and journalists, two were my former colleagues, and two were sometime officials of the Institute of Pacific Relations. *None was
Chinese.* To the best of my knowledge, none of the eleven
persons had ever been categorically identified as a
member of the Communist Party. *All* of them, however,
had been concerned with pursuits generally defined as
"intellectual," and this in fields that were at one and the
same time "controversial" and foreign to the experience of
the LSB. The Board had been confronted by the possibility of my contact with "dangerous thoughts."
   Throughout the hearing, the LSB evinced no interest
in my extensive relations with Soviet government officials
in China, remote Central Asia, and the USSR, but Murphy
was interested in my acquaintanceship with a Soviet TASS
representative in Shanghai and wanted to know all about a

casual meeting in 1932 with one Boris Skvirsky, head of the Soviet Information Bureau in Washington, and what we had talked about. I finally protested:

I may note that the Board in indicating people with whom I have had close and habitual association has not included any of the Soviet diplomats that I have known in various places, Peiping, Shanghai, Changchun, Chungking, Lanchow, Tihwa and Vladivostok, and I have even met some in Moscow. To suggest that I can meet a Soviet diplomat out on the plains of Sinkiang, Central Asia, with no other American around to observe what I see or what I say or what I do, but I can't meet one here in Washington is, I think, . . . drawing an unbalanced picture.

I observed that the Soviet Information Bureau was presumably "legal and acceptable to the United States Government" in 1932.

Later I took the occasion to expand, for the Board's benefit, the record with respect to Skvirsky. He had been mayor of Vladivostok during the Allied occupation of 1918–20. He was seized by the Japanese as one of the occupying powers and turned over to the White Russian leader Semenov. He would doubtless have been executed but for the intervention of the American commanding officer, General William S. Graves. In 1921, he attended the Washington Conference in the capacity of observer for the (interim) Far Eastern Republic (in Eastern Siberia). Subsequently, he became head of the Soviet Information Bureau in Washington, which by all logic operated with the full permission of the U.S. Government. I said: "I relate this merely to indicate that his contacts with American officialdom were clearly very early and that he came here under evidently American auspices, and . . . was still here in 1932." Asked Chairman Snow: "Did he afterwards turn out to be Communistically inclined?" I had to admit that Soviet Information Bureau chief Skvirsky in 1932 was probably a Communist—but I tried to lessen the shock by again inviting attention to the report that his life had been saved in the first instance by General Graves.

The only concrete charge made against me by the LSB was that concerned with the alleged delivery of "a sealed envelope . . . for transmittal to one Grace Hutchins." I now, on July 31, reviewed the whole process of handling the item, from the time it was presented as a question in the interrogatory down to its incorporation in the formal charges laid against me. I ended that review by giving the Board a photostat of the pages in question, and submitted the leather-bound diary itself for physical inspection of the pages bearing the record.

This testimony marked not the end of the matter, but instead the introduction to a whole new series of events. The hearing of the next day, August 1, opened with the members of the Board returning immediately to the *New Masses* item, which was obviously the one uppermost in their minds. Chairman Snow, in his description of the information that they had received, used data and terminology—including the misspelling of my surname and the mistaken identification of me as "Third Secretary" of the Hankow consular office—which made it entirely evident that charge number 10 was based upon statements that Chambers had made to the Wood Committee in 1948. Snow observed that the recollection of the "informant" (Chambers) had been confirmed by my diary entry, "the difference between the two being that instead of a letter for delivery to Grace Hutchins the diary indicates that you produced a letter of introduction to Walt Carmon from

Agnes, whom [*sic*] I presume is Agnes Smedley." "Correct," I said. Then Snow asked for "some explanation from your own memory of what this was all about, what actually occurred." I observed that the meeting was, as the diary entry made evident, "a casual call," and said that I remembered no more of the circumstances than were in the diary. The Chairman pointed to the words "most interesting meeting thus far," and asked: "Now, what was that series of meetings? What could it have been?" I pointed out that in New York I had met one and probably more persons before going to the *New Masses*. The Board then asked me to identify, from my diary entries, the people I had met in New York. I did so. And then Legal Officer Sipes expressed disbelief:

Mr. Clubb, is the Board to understand that in your first answer to the interrogatory and in your supplemental answer filed somewhat later that you had no recollection of making the trip to New York, having returned from China, in 1932, and now on receipt of your diary the indication is that you had numerous meetings and called on a number of people? Is it fair that the Board should assume that you forgot all about these meetings on your visit to New York? And have you established how long in terms of days you were in New York?

In response, I quoted from my letter of January 22. In that "first answer," remarking the difficulties encountered in reconstructing the events of 1932 from memory, and reporting what steps I was taking to clear up the matter, I had simply postponed reply on the *New Masses* item and had requested that the Board grant me further extension of time, "to enable me to exhaust the various existing possibilities for the collection of data which might be relevant to the case in point." That letter concluded with a promise: "I would not fail, of course, to forward a definitive answer . . . or to supply such other pertinent information which might represent the best data available—although falling short of a definitive answer—, as soon as the facts might become available." When my own investigations were completed, I had voluntarily forwarded to the LSB the fullest possible reports of the pertinent circumstances attending the trip, including the diary record. But the LSB, which by all the evidence had accepted his procedure in the first instance, now purported to suspect that it veiled some hidden motive.

There was one thing I had not discovered even by August 1, 1951. Although I had succeeded, after some effort, in obtaining from Department records data showing that I had been in Washington on consultation and in New York on certain dates in 1932, I had been unable to discover any message extending the Department's original authorization so that I might travel to Washington at Government expense. Although I informed the LSB as early as January 22 of my search for the official record so vital for the reconstruction of my 1932 itinerary, and although the LSB in the much later hearing purported to place so much importance on my original inability to reconstruct the matter for it, I learned only after the whole hearing before the LSB was concluded that the file copy of the missing telegram—one dated June 30, 1932, and sent to me at St. Paul—*had all along been in the hands of the LSB.*

There next occurred a series of semantic skirmishes. Seemingly ignoring the circumstance that, apart from Chambers' initial report, all available information of my three-day trip to New York had come from me, Snow and Murphy began a dogged quest for some so-called "independent recollections" of the 1932 trips to New York and Washington. They never said what it was that they desired me to remember independently of my diary record and independently of certain recollections of specific events that I gave them from my memory. They apparently distinguished the mental phenomenon they sought from the usual recalling of specific impression of actualities. That problem was, in the nature of things, insoluble—as any psychologist might have told them. But it was evidently destined to become more important in the Board's collective mind than the charges themselves.

The Board pressed its offensive. Why had I called the *New Masses*, in my diary entry, a "revolutionary organ"? I knew in 1932 that the *New Masses* was "a Communist publication," that "it wasn't pro-American"? Would I remember Walt Carmon as "Carmonsky"? Then Murphy asked that I examine my diary and relate to the Board my full itinerary, and the names of all of the people I saw in the United States in 1932. This request seemed irrevelant to any matter before the hearing and an unwarranted snooping into my private affairs, and I began to question the relevancy of the proposal, only to be checked by a bombshell tossed in my direction by Murphy. He said that "the Board has information in the file indicating that you were a member possibly of the Communist underground during that period" (presumably 1932). Here Legal Officer John W. Sipes qualified this horrific statement with a fuller explanation: describing the recollection of their "informant" as confirmed by my diary entry to have been "in almost all respects . . . amazingly accurate," he reported: "the informant has stated that this whole matter sticks in his mind and he recollects it because of the delivery requested of the letter to Miss Hutchins, because this was his first contact with the Communist underground."

There was a fundamentally false note in the LSB's statement. In all logic, Chambers could not have been referring to Grace Hutchins as being that "first contact," since this was definitely not his first contact with her: she had attended his wedding. On the other hand, if he had been referring to me, there had to be some indication why I, admittedly a stranger to him, could have been recognized in the character described. What was the evidence, even the "sign," that had led him to that conclusion?

There was no hint that the Board was aware that Chambers had testified on June 1, 1949, that while editor of the "Workers' Correspondence" on the Communist *Daily Worker* staff *in 1925–29* he had been charged with guiding the establishment of "underground units." In his book *Witness*,[1] Chambers repeated part of this testimony, stating: "The worker correspondence also resulted in two other experiences: my first party editorship and my first contact with a party underground cell" (p. 229). The same book notes how underground Communists are generally known to each other by "simple first-name pseudonyms," and usually have several such aliases, for security's sake.

It is a revealing commentary on the mental qualifications of amateur spyhunters of the era that the LSB would think worthy of credence, and perhaps accepted even as "amazingly accurate," the tale of a Communist's snowy virginity at a time when he had seven or eight years of party standing. Contamination was to come to the veteran *Daily Worker* and *New Masses* functionary, the Board

[1] Whittaker Chambers, *Witness* (N.Y.: Random House, 1952)

seemed prepared to believe, through the visit to the *New Masses* office of a person who, identifying himself by name and official government position, sought someone else and left "a message . . . the details of which he [Chambers] could not remember." But in justice to Chambers, it should perhaps be recorded that the memories of individual Board members were more than once disclosed in the hearing as inaccurate even for elements of my recent testimony, and that there was a distinct tendency on the part of Board member Murphy to blow up the case and to give things an appearance more terrifying than the innocuous reality.

The Board's springing this startling story on me had the patent purpose of throwing me off balance and getting my compliance. True, the regulations restricted the LSB to "reasonable bounds" as to relevancy, and materiality, which would hardly seem to include Murphy's proposed fishing expedition in my diary. I was nevertheless caught in the unenviable position of all witnesses who would stand on their rights and refuse to answer on the grounds that the investigating apparatus has no authority to ask them: I might be legally justified, but my refusal would be taken as a confession of guilt—for the Board would arrogate to itself the privilege, if not the "duty," of doubling its suspicions. Under the pressure of that logic, I undertook to comply with the offensive proposal that, following my diary account, I give the Board a full report of the places visited and persons met during my home leave of 1932. It would in due course be discovered that my compliance was a tactical error. Relevancy had now gone by the board; more of the regulations would follow it into discard.

The Chairman, on my acquiescence, applied more psy-

chological pressure, giving what he said was the impression of "an independent observer" (himself?):

It seems to me that the diary entry [regarding the visit to the
New Masses] has a "Red thread" running throughout, and that
thread is "revolution." I want to call your attention specifically to
the reference to revolution in the entry. . . .

. . . you refer to the "New Masses," and you say, "Their so-
called revolutionary organ is a horrible rag." You were looking at
it as a revolutionary organ. You were introduced as "Comrade
Clubb." Now, that could only have been a result of something
that was said in the letter of introduction [2] which you had presented which would suggest to the independent observer that
you were indicated in the introduction as a comrade in some enterprise. You were introduced as "Comrade Clubb."

And the immediate topic of conversation was revolution. "He
spoke of revolution." "He spoke of revolution but had no hopes
for it in the United States at the present, bemoaning the lack of
organizers for when [*sic*] the field is prepared and the crops are
ripe for harvest."

The next reference to revolution, possible reference to revolution: "I asked him of conditions in the United States." What conditions?

And, finally, you say: "I feel [*sic*] too much like a stranger to
show the proper revolutionary enthusiasm."

Now, the frequent references, constant references throughout
the entry to revolution, revolutionary enthusiasm, seem to the
uninitiate [the Chairman?] like a "Red thread" throughout the
entry, as though you were making some investigation into the
possibilities for revolution in the United States.

The only mitigating words in the entry are the final remark—
that you were out of your bailiwick and masquerading under
false pretenses, although you say "somewhat" under false pretenses, which suggests the possibility that, even if you were looking for the evidences of revolution, the prospects of revolution in

---

[2] It was of course the receptionist who had introduced me as "Comrade
Clubb"—and she would hardly have read my letter of introduction addressed to someone else.

the United States, you were doing so under false pretenses for somebody else.

The Chairman ended his suggestive analysis of the dire implications of the diary entry by advising me:

. . . I hope you will be exceedingly frank with the Board in this part of your testimony . . . and if you find, on refreshing your recollection with this examination of your diary, that you were actually engaged in some sort of still hunt for possibilities of revolution in this country, either for yourself or somebody else, I hope you will be perfectly frank in saying so to the Board.

The Chairman omitted mention of Grace Hutchins.

I skimmed my diary entries for the period I was in the United States in 1932, which naturally were innocent of any record of wrongdoing. This would clearly have been in the intrinsic nature of things even had I actually been guilty of high treason, for no Communist underground worker would ever have been so abysmally stupid as to record in a diary his various nefarious projects and activities. Chambers has indicated in *Witness* that he told the LSB as much, so my appearance of innocence could not allay the Board's suspicions and fears—they would assume that my very denials would be in line with Communist tactics! At the end of my listing of innocent persons and guiltless places I endeavored to rebut the Chairman's arguments as prosecutor:

. . . it is indicated that there was a "Red thread" that rather runs through that entry. It seems to me that if one were to call at the office of a magazine like the "New Masses," which was known to be at that time radical, you would find naturally something in the nature of a Red thread if there were any record at all. You would not find a Red thread, however, in the record of some entry that I made regarding a visit to, say, a banker or a missionary. . . .

There was a series of meetings, but, as you see, the meetings began actually about the time that I put my foot on these shores. One of my main desires in the course of a return to the United States is to see old friends and meet new people and get new ideas and refresh my knowledge in respect to the United States and thinking that is in course here. . . .

Now, I did refer to it [the *New Masses*] as so-called "revolutionary organ," but I didn't say that I called it a revolutionary organ. . . . But the use of the word "so-called" ordinarily means that it is so called by other people or so called popularly. . . .

It has to be regarded, I think, in all fairness, that, after all, I wasn't writing that particular diary entry with a view to technical perfection. . . . I assuredly had never thought that it would come before a hearing. If I had, I would naturally have tried to be more specific in respect to my reactions to the whole thing, and I would have made naturally a much fuller record.

Now, the circumstance that I was introduced as "Comrade Clubb" was of sufficient unusualness apparently in my mind for me to make a record of it. Actually, of course, if I had been a Comrade or something like that, I would never have noted it down. . . .

I said that there were certain questions that arose, but that the Board's informant, Whittaker Chambers, was not there to answer them—although he should be in a position to answer. I expanded the area of questioning I had suggested to the Board Chairman on March 3:

. . . it should be asked of him how he learned my name, particularly in that form. Did I introduce myself orally or did he get it from a calling card? If I were acting as an underground agent, I surely would not have left a calling card and identified myself to Mr. Chambers or anyone else by that particular means. It hardly seems likely. . . .

Again, had he ever heard of me before? . . . by my recollection of the testimony centering on Mr. Whittaker Chambers, he himself was supposed to be an underground agent at that time. In that event, presumably he would know how other underground agents identified themselves, particularly couriers.

Now, one thing that the Wood Committee report indicates is that Mr. Chambers said I was carrying a message. The word "sealed envelope" is not used in their report. Carrying a message to Grace Hutchins—the details of which he did not remember. Now, in the event that this was an important meeting, Mr. Chambers should remember something about it. And if it were a sealed envelope, how did he have access to the message?

There are other questions. Did he check after meeting me to determine my identity and background? He was supposed to be in the Communist apparatus at that time. And, if so, where did he check and what did he get from his check? And then there is this question that arises out of the circumstance that one version gives it as a message and the other gives it as a sealed envelope. How did he know the sealed envelope was for Grace Hutchins? The Loyalty Security Board has asked that question of me. Therefore, the question should likewise be asked of him. . . .

My hackles had begun to rise:

Now, I carry a commission of the President of the United States which evinces a certain amount of confidence in my reliability. I am here testifying voluntarily under oath before the Loyalty Security Board. You have a charge which arises from an allegation from a man who was a member of the Communist Party admittedly, of the Communist underground also admittedly. It seems to me that Mr. Chambers, if he has more to say in respect to the matter in point, should appear or should be interrogated.

Mr. Murphy of the Board took up the defense of Whittaker Chambers:

MR. MURPHY: I might mention here that the courts of the country have evidently accepted Chambers' testimony as being valid.

Chambers has furnished a signed statement under date of May 1950 in addition to his interview with the FBI. His recollection of the incident in general—and I am not quoting directly from his letter—is that you visited the "New Masses" on an occasion in 1932. He doesn't pinpoint the month. He says that you told him you were on leave here in the United States and you were going home to visit some relatives in Minnesota, and you delivered to him a message, as he recalls it. He doesn't state this categorically. He says he believes that it was a letter that was to be transmitted to somebody else, a third person.

MR. CLUBB: I beg your pardon. Did you say a message?

MR. MURPHY: Yes. He said you delivered a message, as he recalls it, in the form of a letter for delivery to a third person. He believes that, according to his recollection, the person was Grace Hutchins. At that time she was known, at least to Chambers, as a Communist and still is. Evidently he got the impression that you were surprised at finding him there, and he also got the impression that you had been to the "New Masses" at some time before. He doesn't say why, but he states this. And that you discussed the Communist situation in China. And he also points out that you mentioned to him more or less in passing that prior to your present assignment—this is in 1932 to Hankow—you had been on duty in Peking. . . .

I thought you would be interested in knowing the detail of his recollection. It's fantastic that he remembers things so precisely. But evidently he does.

Now the reference to "Communist underground" was left out!

I was now in possession of some additional information touching on Chambers. He had, then, not only testified before the House Un-American Activities Committee in 1948 with respect to my 1932 visit to the *New Masses,* but had in addition been interviewed by the FBI and in May 1950 had submitted a signed (not sworn) statement (inferentially to the Board) repeating the essence of the story he had already related to the House committee. By Murphy's own account, Chambers in his statement had said only that I delivered to him "a message," which he believed was in the form of a letter "to be transmitted to someone else, a third person." And Chambers' recollection was that the addressee was Grace Hutchins.

But the LSB in its interrogatory had stated that I was alleged to have delivered "a sealed envelope" to the *New Masses;* and the Board had inquired regarding "the nature of the document transmitted." In its formal arraignment the LSB had charged that I had delivered "a sealed envelope to the editor of the 'New Masses' magazine . . . for transmittal to one Grace Hutchins." The Board had manifestly arbitrarily expanded upon Chambers' testimony. Where was one to fit in the LSB's attribution to Chambers of the observation that he recalled the 1932 occasion because of the request that a letter be delivered to Grace Hutchins, since (in the Board's words) "this was his first contact with the Communist underground"? Why had Chambers not informed the Wood Committee of his "first contact with the Communist underground"? But that *was* the *Board's* version, and it had already offended by distortion of other reputed "allegations" by unnamed "informants." Might it not once more be employing its own select phraseology? What had Chambers *really* said?

With Murphy's new description of the matter, I asked some more questions of the absent Whittaker Chambers, but with no more response than before. The Board instead advanced a little farther:

MR. MURPHY: Would you want to read to the Board the entries that you have in your diary for the period during which you were in New York other than the one you have already supplied? You were in New York from July 7th, probably the evening of July 7th, through the 11th [sic]. . . .
MR. CLUBB: Well, may I say this: That I furnished the Board as an exception to what you might say is a principle. This I

regard as a personal diary. It's a personal diary and there are certain personal comments in that that I just wouldn't want to give to the Board. That is the long and short of it. I sometimes have phrased my comments rather cogently. And I see no particular reason to parade all of my thoughts or all of my soul before the Board insofar as it is not pertinent to the hearing. But if you want to have the language of my reports on my contacts there, I think I could give you that.

I read them some entries relating the physical circumstances of meetings with people, omitting parts recording the reactions of those people themselves to the world of the 1930s. This done, the Board came to the point which it presumably had been leading up to all along:

THE CHAIRMAN: Would you be willing that the Board, without making it any part of the record, should peruse the omitted portions of your diary during the New York trip just for their own satisfaction?

My first compromise had had the usual result: the camel, his nose once in, wanted to get all the way into the tent.

At my request, we went off the record. I pointed out that I had met the questions and charges of the LSB, and answered them to the best of my ability. I said that if the Board had other questions to ask, I would do my best to answer them. That evidently was not enough: the Board members desired to look at my diary, not to seek the answers to any questions they might have formulated, but "just for their own satisfaction." The governing loyalty regulations seemed clear to me, and I gave my reply for the record:

I believe that I have responded fully to the questions put by the Board. I have given to the Board all of the information that is in the entries for that particular period covering the visit to the

"New Masses." It is my belief that there is nothing else in the diary touching upon the "New Masses" and I believe, therefore, that I should prefer to respond to the question which has just been put, in the negative.

The Board had confirmed, just before we resumed the "on-the-record" status, that although Murphy had taken the position that the whole diary be made available, its proposition should remain as defined by the Chairman in the first instance. This was given especial interest by subsequent developments. The rest of August 1 was taken up, in main, with finishing the testimony of my witnesses. At the end of the day's session, the Chairman announced "The case is closed." But it wasn't.

VIII

"Quick, Thy Tablets, Memory!"

You have indeed received the Federal unction of lying and slandering. But who has not? Who will ever again come into eminent office, unanointed with this chrism? It seems to be fixed that falsehood and calumny are to be their ordinary engines of opposition; engines which will not be entirely without effect. The circle of characters equal to the first stations is not too large, and will be lessened by the voluntary retreat of those whose sensibilities are stronger than their confidence in the justice of public opinion. . . . Yet this effect of sensibility must not be yielded to. If we suffer ourselves to be frightened from our post by mere lying, surely the enemy will use that weapon; for what one so cheap to those in whose system of politics morality makes no part?

THOMAS JEFFERSON, letter to Judge James Sullivan, May 21, 1805.

I had been outraged by the LSB's demand for access to my private diary. The Fourth Amendment is explicit in its prohibition against "unreasonable searches and seizures" of personal papers, and the courts have held that mere suspicion is not sufficient warrant for the government to violate that prohibition. In a case in point, the Court observed that:

Anyone who respects the spirit as well as the letter of the Fourth Amendment would be loath to believe that Congress intended to authorize one of its subordinate agencies to sweep all our traditions into the fire and to direct fishing expeditions into private papers on the possibility that they may disclose evidence of crime.[1]

To my surprise, however, most of my colleagues with whom I discussed the issue tended to react about as follows: "You are right in principle, *but* your refusal to turn over your diary will weigh against you, so perhaps you ought to find a way to meet the position of the Board." It was only a minority that said "You did exactly right—to Hell with them." Then, in an interview with Deputy Under Secretary Humelsine, he told me to consider that, if I continued to refuse my diary to the Loyalty Security Board, this might be prejudicial to my case. He went on to admonish me to reflect on the effects for myself and my family of an adverse finding. Humelsine was charged with direction of the Department's loyalty-security program, and with review of the LSB's findings in each particular case, so the attitude of both the Board and himself was now made quite clear to me.

I next saw Secretary Acheson, and told him that I desired him to understand my position, which (I believed) was in accord with the letter and spirit of the Department's loyalty-security program as evidenced by its own

[1] *Federal Trade Commission* v. *American Tobacco*, 264 U.S. 298, 305–6 (1923). A Court ruling of the Nixon era was in line with that position: "The historical judgment, which the Fourth Amendment accepts, is that unreviewed executive discretion may yield too readily to pressures to obtain incriminating evidence and overlook potential invasion of privacy and protected speech." *U.S.* v. *U.S.D.C.*, E.D. Mich. 40, U.S.L.W. 4761, 7767 (June 19, 1972).

Regulations and Procedures. The Secretary agreed that I was technically and morally correct. He then attached the persistent "but," and suggested as had the majority that in the existing practical situation I might wish to find a compromise solution. The Secretary presented only soundly reasoned arguments, not veiled threats like his deputy Humelsine. I was nevertheless left without any solid support in the Department for the position which, all agreed, was right in principle.

I decided to follow the line of thought developed in my interview with Secretary Acheson, and immediately drafted a letter to the LSB. Before I could deliver it, a new development occurred: on August 9, the House Un-American Activities Committee subpoenaed me to appear before it, "and to produce all diaries in [my] possession, the entries of which were made during [my] employment with the United States Government." The deliberations of the LSB by regulation were supposed to be confidential, even from members of Congress. The natural question arose: how did the Wood Committee happen to develop a fresh interest in my diaries so promptly after my refusal to produce them for the LSB? The first summons to a hearing before that Committee, on March 14, had come close on the heels of my report to the LSB of my initial failure to solve the puzzle posed in their interrogatory regarding the Grace Hutchins matter. One could only hazard logical inferences, but some chronological sequences were beginning to look like more than coincidences.

On the following day, August 10, I sent to the Board my letter offering a compromise proposal:

"My diary is personal, private, and confidential, comprising as it does my personal record of contacts and relations with friends

and acquaintances, their and my unadorned comments on phenomena and personalities of 19 years ago, my marital relations,
and my philosophical and speculative meanderings varying from
the light-hearted—even frivolous—to considerations thought
serious in 1932. The Board's proposal that I deliver to them that
diary for checking of the New York entries comprised no new
question in cross-examination of me, but by full implication was
designed to give the Board opportunity to corroborate my testimony as given under oath. This seemed to me at the time inadequate reason to surrender to the Board that diary as requested;
and, it still seems to me inadequate reason, especially given my
basic assumption and belief that it is not the explicit or implicit
intent of the present loyalty security procedures that any officer
facing charges of disloyalty or bad security shall be caused to surrender to the Board his private papers, including private diaries,
for inspection, or undergo prejudice to his case.

Careful reflection on this matter leads me nevertheless to an
appreciation that my above-noted refusal may lead the Board to
conclude that there *might* be something of relevancy to Charge
No. 10 hidden in the section under reference, and that my case
consequently, for all of the provisions of the governing regulations, might suffer prejudice. Consequently, in order to relieve
myself of any possibility of prejudice in this respect, and having
particular reference to the Board's question of August 1, 1951, I
am prepared to make a proposal which I believe will substantially accommodate the interest of the Board, as reflected in that
record. In making this proposal it must be understood that this is
the limit to which I can go in view of my own guiding principles.

I proposed that a third person should read that portion of
the diary covering my 1932 New York trip and testify to
the Board *only* whether it contained data regarding my
visit to the *New Masses* office in addition to that already
supplied the Board and/or "data indicating that I visited
New York (or elsewhere) on a Communist mission."

On the same day, I invited the attention of the Department to the fact that my diaries contained matter that the
Department might not desire to have made public through

the medium of a Congressional committee. Again the responsible official was Humelsine—under his other hat as officer in charge of the Department's administration. I suggested that the Department might wish to check the diaries on policy grounds, but I made one proviso: that, if I surrendered the diaries to the Department for such check, my action would not carry with it any consent, explicit or implicit, for the transmittal of those same diaries to the LSB. The two matters were separate and distinct, and I intended them to remain so.

On Saturday August 11, I received a reply from the LSB stating that "The Board has considered your letter and has determined to reopen the hearing in your case for the purpose of responding thereto and for the further consideration of your case." And it fixed a new session for Monday, August 13. A letter received the same date from Humelsine directed me: "In order to permit the Department to determine what official interest, if any, it has in these diaries you are instructed to turn the diaries over to me for inspection, *after which they will be returned to you.*" (Emphasis supplied.) I immediately turned over such of my postwar looseleaf diaries as I had at the Department at the time, and offered to return home and produce the rest that same day. I was informed that this was unnecessary. On Monday morning, before proceeding to my hearing, I delivered the remainder of the looseleaf diaries. The next day, August 14, I turned over the two bound volumes for 1932 and half of 1933.

In the hearing of August 13, Chairman Snow referred briefly to the offer contained in my letter, and then said:

The Board would not be satisfied with that type of commission [*sic*] of the diary. The Board feels that *in order to satisfy itself as* to whether or not the diary confirms the testimony you have already given [emphasis supplied] it should be given possession of the '32 diary for examination, as I stated at the hearing the other day, not for the purpose of putting any portion of the diary into the record unless we should find something therein that we would feel was a proper part of the record,[2] in which case we would confer further with you before putting it in. . . . So the purpose of this morning's session is to make further inquiry of you whether or not you are willing to let us peruse the '32 diary.

A. [myself] I understand that the original proposition of the board was that they should peruse the immediate portions of my diary during the New York trip, which was July 7 to 10, 1932.

Q. It would seem that that is a rather narrow period because there may be something in the diary antecedent of that which would disclose the purpose of the trip. The purpose of the Board is to examine what is in the diary that was connected with that trip. But just to limit it to the entries during the period of that trip might be a little narrow. . . .

A. In short, the Board at the present time desires to expand its original request to include the whole of the 1932 diary?

Q. I think that is a fair statement.

A. I regret to state my position is as set forth before, Mr. Chairman. I am quite prepared to answer all of the Board's questions, all of the Board's charges, and I think I have, and I was prepared to put forward this proposition as being one which would substantially meet the desires of the Board. But I frankly see no reason to hand over a personal, confidential record for the perusal of the Board. It does not seem to me to be a material part of the case and it does not seem to me that I have been presented with any new question or any new charge or any variation of the present charges that I have failed to answer fully.

Q. What is your present position, then, to deny the diary to the Board completely?

A. Yes, sir, except under the condition I have set forth here [in the letter of August 10].

[2] The qualifying clause beginning with "unless" had not in fact been included in the Chairman's original proposal.

The Board did not judge this repulse to be sufficient reason to adjourn the session. Murphy and Snow joined forces, in a patent attempt to impress upon me the seriousness of the matter. Again they marshalled "The Witness" in support of their maneuver. Said Murphy:

Chambers has testified under oath and subjected himself here to examination. Part of the examination was devoted to an effort to find out exactly why he told the FBI that he had spotted you as a member of the underground. That is where you fitted into his recollection. He testified again under oath, based on his recollection, . . . a very clear impression that you were a member of an international mechanism or system connected with the Communist movement. He used the term "underground" as a label and I believe he was fair in his testimony in making it clear that it was a way of describing it.

His memory has been established as very accurate both by your testimony in this case and by other information in the file. . . .

Murphy shortly afterward sought to add to my understanding of "the way the Board is approaching this problem of accepting [sic] your diary." "It is as much to establish the record on your behalf," he said, "as it is *on behalf of the Government or any other agency.*" (Emphasis supplied.)

I had now learned, by the LSB's oblique channel, that Chambers had appeared before it and testified against me, without my being accorded the right of cross-examination (presumably, by reason of Chambers' refusal to confront me). I commented that Chambers had admitted to multiple perjury, that he himself simply referred to "recollections," and remarked that "I myself want to be pretty careful of my own recollections before I become very categorical." The Chairman protested: "All we have asked for from the beginning is the best of your recollection. We understand as well as anyone that recollections over a period of 18 years are not accurate, are not supposed to be accurate. We have only asked for the benefit of the best recollection you have. . . ."

In his argumentation, Murphy characterized Agnes Smedley as "a Communist," and identified the *New Masses* as "a known Communist literary center," to which, he said, I had gone "seeking Walt Carmon, a known Communist, [and] while there talked to Michael Gold, a known Communist. . . ." Shortly afterward, he conjured up another bogey to frighten me: "The Board also has other information indicating that at least one source of information to a known spy ring in the Far East was a Foreign Service Officer. I want to make clear that *at the moment* there is no implication that you are tied in any way with that particular element, but the information is before the Board [emphasis supplied]."

I responded that Agnes Smedley might have been known to the Board as a Communist but had not been known to me as such—and apparently was not so known to Secretary of State Hull as late as 1934 when he issued a letter of introduction to her. And she had given me *her* letter of introduction to Carmon in 1932. I said that

. . . in respect to Mr. Walt Carmon and Mr. Michael Gold, I have no present recollection that they were described to me as Communists. They may have been known to Mr. Whittaker Chambers as Communists. He, I believe, was at that time supposed to be a member of the Communist underground. He would presumably have known Communists. Whether or not they were generally known as Communists at that time, or whether or not they are generally known as Communists at this time is something that I, myself, couldn't rule on.

I attacked Murphy's other sinister implication:

> . . . in respect to the known spy ring, that spy ring was not
> known, of course, to anybody . . . until 1941 when Sorge was
> captured by the Japanese. At the time he was captured . . . we
> and the Soviet Union were essentially allies in the struggle
> against Germany. He was spying on behalf of the Soviet Union,
> one of our allies. . . . It was only in 1941 and '42, in short, that
> anything was known about that spy ring. Whether Miss Agnes
> Smedley knew about it, I don't know. Whether Mr. Lilliestrom,
> whom you cited as an American Foreign Service Officer, knew
> anything about that spy ring, I don't know, but I can tell you this,
> I didn't know anything about that spy ring until the name Sorge
> came out a long time after I knew for the first time Miss Agnes
> Smedley. And as I say, that information apparently was not
> available either to the Secretary of State or to Senator Robert
> Wagner. . . .

The Soviet agent Richard Sorge was of course spying on
our then enemy, the Japanese. The Board persisted in
bringing up Chambers' testimony that I had seemed "surprised" to meet him instead of Carmon at the *New Masses*.
I finally observed that before I met Chambers I had encountered both the secretary at the desk and Michael
Gold, and had presumably already learned that Walt Carmon was not there; so, "if I was still surprised by the time
I met Mr. Whittaker Chambers, either my capacity for surprise must be very considerable or Mr. Chambers' discern-
ment must be very acute. . . ."

We went on. On July 31, I had remarked the Board's stiff-
ening of the charge by its designation of the *New Masses*
as "a Communist periodical," and had pointed out that the
Fish Committee had not so listed it in 1930, that the 1935
report of AFL's William Green to the State Department on
Communist propaganda in the United States had said only

that the *New Masses* had been a recipient of Garland Fund benefits, and that there existed no Attorney General's list at the time so it could hardly have been included there. I had proposed:

In view of the circumstance that the designation of the periodical in question [as "Communist"] tends to constitute a weight in the balance against me, it would seem proper to suggest that, unless there is legal basis for such description of the "New Masses" in 1932, the LSB might desire to make a correction. That it was at that time Communist in orientation is, of course, a matter of common knowledge.

The Board now took the occasion to reject my argument:

CHAIRMAN: You have admitted yourself [before the Wood Committee] that you understood at that time that it was a Communist paper.
A. That is my impression.
CHAIRMAN: That is enough, isn't it?
A. No, I don't think it is, not if you are establishing its status by law, because I am not the legal authority to rule on the status of the "New Masses."
MR. MURPHY: It might be well to establish in the record that the man, Chambers, admitted Communist at that time, himself described it as a Communist publication, testified under oath to that effect.
MR. SIPES: *Stated it was generally regarded as such.* [emphasis supplied]
MR. MOYER: There is no legal way to determine the character of an organization except by the testimony of informants who knew something about it.

Moyer, in speaking of "informants who knew something about it," presumably referred to Whittaker Chambers, and not to the Fish Committee or William Green.

Chambers' book *Witness*, which at that time had not yet
appeared, might have solved that particular problem with
his presumably authoritative statement that, until he took
over the *New Masses* editorship, "Communist control was
masked. I edited as a Communist." Chambers' name did
not appear first among those of the magazine's several editors until the May 1932 issue. In the July issue the name of
Carmon, previously listed as Managing Editor, was dropped; there was no successor. Chambers says that it was in
June 1932, "while I was preparing my third issue of the
New Masses" (then a monthly magazine), that he received
a call from "Comrade Bedacht" which resulted in his
entering the Communist underground. Bedacht told
Chambers that he would have to leave the *New Masses*,
and had until the following day to think it over. Chambers
met again with Bedacht, inferentially on schedule, and his
refusal was met with Bedacht's words "You have no
choice." He met his contact man the same day. Chambers
told the latter, at the end of their meeting, that he was
going to the *New Masses* office. His Communist colleague
said "It had better be the last time." Chambers left the
New Masses office "about six o'clock" that same day, and in
the company of his colleague met another man, "Herbert,"
who repeated the charge never to return to the *New
Masses* and added that "This is a military command."
Chambers remarks in his account that Point One in underground organizational techniques is discipline: "Absolute obedience was the rule of the underground. Whatever
I was told to do was a military order, and I must obey it as
such." (Quotations in this paragraph from pp. 268–83 pas-
sim.)

So there was, by clear implication, no way out. The unmistakable purport of Chambers' account is that he left the *New Masses* for good in June 1932. And, still according to Chambers, his departure did not go unnoticed: "My disappearance from the *New Masses* had caused a scandal. There had been charge and counter-charge on the floor of the John Reed Club. One 'non-party' element had demanded to know if the party had 'liquidated Chambers.' A loyal Communist had shouted that Chambers had probably walked out of the *New Masses* as he had walked out of the *Daily Worker*." (*Ibid.*, p. 288.)

Either Chambers had been an underground agent in the service of the Fourth Section of the Soviet Military Intelligence as he claimed (*ibid.*, pp. 32, 288), or he had not. Max Bedacht in May 1957 denied Chambers' story that he had recruited Chambers into the underground, stated that he had never had any contact with the Soviet military, and remarked significantly that in testifying before grand juries and the House Committee on Un-American Activities, and in FBI interviews, he had never been questioned about Chambers.[3] If Chambers had in fact played the claimed conspiratorial role, as Congressional committees and the LSB in 1948–52 apparently believed, his calendar for his subversive activities was logically to be accepted in the absence of contradictory evidence. It was presumably due to the confusion attendant upon his disappearance that the *New Masses* kept his name on its masthead through September 1933, when the magazine went out of existence

[3] Meyer A. Zeligs, *Friendship and Fratricide: An Analysis of Whittaker Chambers and Alger Hiss* (N.Y.: Viking Press, 1967), pp. 120–22. See also in this general connection the revealing portrayal of the "imaginary" character Gifford Maxim in Lionel Trilling's novel *The Middle of the Journey* (N.Y. 1947).

as a monthly [4]—long after Chambers by his arithmetic had vanished into the "deep underground." There would have to be some other explanation, however, for Chambers' being physically in the *New Masses* office in *July* 1932, when I met him, well after he had by his own account left the place forever. But in the 1950s there was a special dispensation provided for the self-contradictions of ostensibly penitent "ex-Communists." So the Board avowedly viewed Chambers' memory as "very accurate," and according to Murphy the courts of the country had "evidently" accepted Chambers' testimony as "valid." My request for correction of the LSB's weighted wording of Charge No. 10 was fruitless.

This wrangle was finally sidetracked by the Board's asking whether I had "in 1932 . . . looked with favor on the Chinese revolution." One more cat was let out of the bag:

MR. SIPES: . . . Mr. Chambers has testified that you favored the Chinese revolution, in your conversation with him you made statements which led him to the positive, clear conclusion, that one of the points he had a clear recollection of was that you favored the Chinese revolution.

I pointed out that "I happened to be working for the United States Government and my loyalties were to the United States Government," and cited my 1932 report as setting forth my estimate of the Chinese revolution. This led to another exchange:

MR. SIPES: Would you agree that it is at least conceivable, Mr. Clubb, that an officer might well express his judgment and his estimates of, say, the Chinese revolution in a paper or in a

[4] The *New Masses* was succeeded on January 2, 1934 by the weekly *Masses,* with nearly complete change of editorial board. Chambers *then* indeed was not listed among those present.

new masses

VOLUME 9   SEPTEMBER, 1933.   NUMBER 1

Editorial Board: JOSEPH FREEMAN, WHITTAKER CHAMBERS, HUGO GELLERT, WILLIAM GROPPER, MICHAEL GOLD, LOUIS LOZOWICK, MOISSAYE J. OLGIN, JOSHUA KUNITZ, HERMAN MICHELSON.

CONTRIBUTORS :—Phil Bard, Emjo Basshe, Jacob Burck, Whittaker Chambers, Robert Cruden, Jack Conroy, Adolph Dehn, Robert Dunn, John Dos Passos, Kenneth Fearing, Ed Falkowski, Hugo Gellert, Eugene Gordon, Horace Gregory, William Gropper, William Hernandez, Langston Hughes, Joseph Kalar, I. Klein, Joshua Kunitz Melvin P. Levy, Louis Lozowick, H. H. Lewis, Norman Macleod, A B. Magil, Scott Nearing, Myra Page, Paul Peters, Walter Quirt, Louis Ribak, Anna Rochester, E. Merill Root, James Rorty, Martin Russak, Esther Shemitz, William Siegel, Upton Sinclair, Agnes Smedley, Otto Soglow, Herman Spector, Bennett Stevens, Joseph Vogel, Mary H. Vorse, Keene Wallis, Jim Waters, Art Young. Published monthly by NEW MASSES, Inc., Office of publication, 31 East 27th Street, New York City. Copyright 1933, by NEW MASSES, Inc., Reg. U. S. Patent Office. Drawings and text may not be reprinted without permission. Entered as second class matter, June 24, 1926, at the Post Office at New York, N. Y., under the act of March 3, 1879.

Subscribers are notified that no change of address can be effected in less than a month.

Subscription $1.50 a year in U. S. and Colonies and Mexico. Foreign, $2.00. Single Copies, 15 Cents; 20c abroad

What It Means to Be a Communist In Yugoslavia

Translated by Louis Adamic

TRANSLATOR'S NOTE:—*While in Yugoslavia, during the past year I met some of the 15,000 men and women, Communists and other revolutionaries, who had been tortured in recent years by police sadists in the employ of King Alexander's military-fascist dictatorship, ba----' b?* ---- --~ *capitalist powers and in~ ----- nance* ---- ~~ ---- ---- *th*

wasn't certain just where X lived but possibly could locate him, suggested we go out.

We walked around awhile. Turning, I noticed a few paces behind, two local detectives, whom I knew by sight. The Bel- ---- -tecti-- urged me to exert n ---- ---- ---- X. I stalled ---- ----came undi ---- ---- n' he look'. ---- ---- ---- -~- '

Masthead of **New Masses**, September 1933

report to the Department in one way, and certainly it seems possible that he could entertain personal views and convictions which he might express to someone else privately or in another way?

A. I don't think you would continue to carry on a deception like that over a period of 20 years, Mr. Sipes. Quite frankly, if you consider the accuracy of my prognostications and my estimates and my reporting, I think that you will agree that in substance it is pretty good. That is my estimate of it.

When the Chairman announced adjournment, I asked permission first to put some questions. For one thing, I was still interested in that "sealed envelope":

A [myself] . . . I should like to ask . . . whether in view of the testimony of Mr. Whittaker Chambers, which has apparently been both in 1948 and 1950, that I carried a message, there is other testimony either from him or someone else indicating that I carried a sealed envelope, as indicated in the Board's charge. . . .

MR. MURPHY: Chambers' original information to the FBI in 1950, as reported to the Board, the language he used was "He delivered a letter, 'he' being Mr. Chubb or Clubb." . . . he stated "He delivered a message to me in the form of a letter, I believe, for transmittal to a third person." Chambers has qualified his information as to the type or form of the message, and in his testimony the other day he made again clear that he was not testifying and could not testify as to the form of the message, whether it was a letter or a package of some sort, or an oral message delivered by you.

A. In short, he did not testify at any point, so far as you have determined, that there was a sealed envelope.

MR. MURPHY: I don't recall that he used those words.

MR. MOYER: We asked that question, I believe.

MR. MURPHY: He testified clearly that he does not recall the type or form of the message. I am talking now about his most recent testimony, but I think that is consistent with the signed statement he furnished the FBI because he qualified it there by saying "I believe." . . .

A. And it is not alleged by other source that I carried a sealed envelope?

MR. MURPHY: That is correct.

The Loyalty Security Board had used its own suggestive phrase "sealed envelope" in framing charge No. 10 against me. It was moreover glaringly evident that the Board's earlier inquiry regarding the nature of "the document transmitted" was likewise a figment of that unjudicious body's fertile imagination. But this was not the only time that some "went a-whoring with their own inventions" in connection with my case.

There was another matter which to my mind was still unsettled. As recorded above, I had early felt that a certain colleague who had served with me at Hankow and Shanghai was quite possibly one of the witnesses against me, and in my response of January 22 to the Board's interrogatory I had set forth the circumstances of a clash between the two of us at Shanghai. That officer now occupied a high administrative position in the Department. The Board, in character, had given no hint that the individual in question was in any way connected with my case. Nevertheless, I had on July 17 formally requested the LSB to invite him to appear at my hearing "as a material witness." On July 25, Chairman Snow had replied, citing Loyalty Review Board memorandum No. 41 of February 28, 1951, requiring (in Snow's words) "that every informant be invited to testify who (1) is personally identified, (2) who has given pertinent information adverse to the employee, and (3) has not expressly indicated an unwillingness to testify; further that such testimony be given before the Board in the presence of the employee and his counsel if the informant is willing and otherwise be given before the Board not in the presence of the employee or his counsel." Then

Snow said: "While Memorandum No. 41 has been com-
plied with in your case, the Board has no subpoena power
to compel the presence of any witness in a case before the
Board."

The logical inference was that the officer in point had
been invited to appear, but had refused to do so. In the
July 31 session, I again set forth, for the formal record, the
circumstances of the Shanghai clash, supporting my account with the sworn affidavit of someone who had witnessed the affair. General Snow took the occasion to expand upon the matter:

THE CHAIRMAN: . . . It is suggested in your outline here, in
your testimony that you requested this Board to invite Mr.
B—— to appear before this hearing as a material witness.
MR. CLUBB: Yes.
THE CHAIRMAN: The Board, in accordance with its fixed
policy, does not invite favorable witnesses. It leaves that to the
employee himself to make his own defense.
I am free to say that although Mr. B—— has been interviewed
in this case, his testimony on the whole is not unfavorable; therefore, he is not included in that category.

Shortly afterward, this exchange occurred:

THE CHAIRMAN: I think it is fair to you to state that Mr.
B——'s testimony to the FBI was that he did not regard your interest in communism in any sense as a manifestation of disloyalty
on your part; that he would not consider you disloyal to the
United States. That is the basis of my saying that the testimony
on the whole was favorable.
MR. CLUBB: I am very glad to know that.
THE CHAIRMAN: What has been referred to is an efficiency
report which he made for you. Were you familiar with that report?
MR. CLUBB: No, sir.

THE CHAIRMAN: In that it is said to be stated that you, he is quoting, were formerly classified by Chinese colleagues as "mild Red" and espousing doctrines of a Communistic nature.

Murphy thereupon disclosed more of the matter with this interpolation: "Do you have some comments on B——'s remarks in his official report on you. The report is made in August, 1950, in which he makes that statement. That is a matter of an official report in the Department." And the discussion was directed once more to the matter of my general reputation in the early 1930s.

Three things were now clear: (1) my Shanghai colleague had supplied the allegation that had been converted into the Board's charge no. 6; (2) his report had been given to both the FBI and the Department, in at least the latter instance after my last return from China; (3) the LSB, which had used B——'s report as an adverse charge against me, had clearly implied in its July 25 letter that he had been invited to testify in my presence but had refused to appear; but now, on July 31, the Board purported in effect (if in equivocal terms) that it had *refrained* from even inviting that officer, on the facile grounds that "his testimony *on the whole* is not unfavorable" (emphasis supplied). And it was noteworthy that Snow had failed to cite B——'s testimony as to whether I might be considered a security risk—quite apart from the issue of my loyalty.

Having discovered the identity of the author of charge no. 6, as the session was drawing to its close I asked the Board whether the same man was also the source for the charge that I was "100% pro-Red" at Shanghai in 1940. The Board responded that the charge in question "does not come from a colleague or Foreign Service Officer, either present or former." I let stand my observation of the first session: ". . . the charge is false on its face and false by the record; and because of its fundamental falsity I suspect that it was motivated by some personal malice, or else was simply a calloused, unquestioning repetition, in a common variation, of the original slanderous statement given public utterance by Mr. B——."

I posed another question:

"A. And the charge that I associated with Communists in Hankow in 1931–34?

MR. SIPES: It comes from, as near as we can identify that, two or three sources. That charge comes from several sources within the Service.

A. All of whom, however, fail to name the Communists?

MR. SIPES: Yes."

So the record in that respect was left with my general rebuttal, and the testimony of an old acquaintance (resident for 31 years in China, India, and Australia as a representative of the British-American Tobacco Company of London), who deposed that, at Hankow:

. . . we were members of the same social clubs and were familiar with the associates of each other and were well acquainted with the mental attitudes and views of each other upon public questions and especially upon the question of Communism; that affiant knows of no communistic leanings, associations or ideas of the said O. Edmund Clubb and says that the said O. Edmund Clubb did not associate with communists nor express any sympathy for them or their ideals or political activities and theories.

And, when all was said and done, there was the hard fact that there were no known Communists present in Hankow in 1932.

In the hearing, then, I had identified positively the sources of four of the charges against me, and was able to make an "educated guess" in regard to the authorship of two or three others. It had been made clear that some of the charges had been taken out of context, at least two had been corrupted, and the LSB itself had heavily loaded the Chambers story to my disadvantage. Moreover, the first eight charges, attributing various political attitudes to me, seemed probably all to have been inspired by some early Hankow gossip among those who looked askance at my report on Chinese Communism. Some of the reports that reached the LSB must have contained a solid context that put the rumors in perspective; in others, political ignorance was obviously involved; finally, personal malice seemed to have been involved in at least two instances. The Board showed no signs of being able to separate one from the other.

On August 14, therefore, after the third hearing session, I wrote again to the Chairman of the Board. After reviewing the pertinent correspondence and the record of the transcript, I came to the crux of the matter:

The attention of the Board is invited to the circumstance that Mr. B—— has now been personally identified as the person who originated charge No. 6, namely that I "were [was] classified as 'mildly Red' and espoused doctrines of a 'Communist' nature prior to 1940." I consider that information distinctly adverse to me, as is implicit in the Board's use of that allegation as a charge. It is therefore now formally requested that the Board extend an invitation to Mr. B—— to appear as an informant "who has given pertinent information adverse to the employee," in accordance with the provisions of the cited regulation, to testify before the Board in the presence of myself or counsel or representative. It is further requested that any refusal of Mr. B—— to appear shall be made a matter of official record.

It is requested that if this procedure is not followed, charge No. 6 be cancelled by the Board.

The Board never replied to my letter. The elusive Mr. B—— never appeared to confront me.

A few days later, on August 16, Whittaker Chambers appeared before the McCarran (Senate Internal Security) Subcommittee, and was led to testify again in regard to our now-well-advertised meeting of 1932. In view of what he was already reported variously to have told the House Un-American Activities Committee in 1948, the FBI in 1950, and the LSB in 1951, it was of especial interest to have, for the first time (following identification of me by Messrs. Morris and Mandel) his own direct public testimony:

Mr. Morris. Mr. Chambers, did you ever meet Mr. Clubb?

Mr. Chambers. Yes, I did.

Mr. Morris. Will you tell us the circumstances of your meeting Mr. Clubb?

Mr. Chambers. Probably in June, in May or June of 1932, while I was editing the New Masses.

Mr. Morris. That is 1932.

Mr. Chambers. 1932. While I was editing the New Masses, which is a Communist-controled magazine, there came into my office a young man who asked to see Walt Karmon [sic]. . . .

This stranger seemed rather disturbed not to find Walt Karmon, in the office where he expected him.[5] Walt Karmon, in fact, wasn't any longer in the building, in the New Masses. The man, the stranger, told me his name was O. Edmund Clubb.

Senator Ferguson. Would you recognize a picture of him?

Mr. Chambers. *I can no longer identify a picture of Clubb. If you realize that I spoke to him not more than 15 minutes in the*

---

[5] A shift from the record of a "surprised" reaction cited by the LSB, and noted in *Witness*. It appears not to have occurred to Chambers that any visible manifestation of emotion on my part might have been directed toward him rather than toward the absent Carmon. My diary entry covering the *New Masses* visit indicated fairly clearly, after all, that I found Chambers unpleasing in appearance, "a shifty-eyed unkempt creature."

year 1932, I think it is simply impossible to make a positive iden-
tification [emphasis supplied]. . . .

Mr. Chambers. Nevertheless this man told me his name was O.
Edmund Clubb, that he was a consular official of some kind at
Hankow, I believe, that he was on leave of absence, and that he
had some kind of message which he wanted to deliver. The difficulty about my recollection of Edmund Clubb or Oliver Clubb
is that I can no longer remember what that message was or even
to whom it was to be delivered, but there has stayed in the back
of my mind an impression which I will not testify to positively
that the message was written and that it was for Grace Hutchins.
Grace Hutchins is an open Communist, a member of the open
Communist Party, has run on the Communist ticket in various
elections, and is well known to be a Communist. But I cannot
testify more positively to anything along those lines. Clubb then
sat talking a little about China. Naturally I don't recall what our
conversation was over that length of time, but I do remember that
we talked about Hayang [*sic*] Arsenal. . . . I have a further recollection, which I hesitate to make positive, that the message was
from Agnes Smedley, but again I can't really testify to that positively.

Senator Ferguson. That is your best judgment, is it?

Mr. Chambers. *I find it impossible, with the play of so many*
influences on my mind, because people are always asking me
questions, bringing me information, and there are actually areas
of my experience where I can no longer distinguish between
what I once knew and what I have heard and learned in the
course of testifying [emphasis supplied]. I have given many
thousands of words of testimony by now, as you know.

Mr. Morris. But there is no doubt about the fact that Clubb
came into the New Masses office.

Mr. Chambers. There is not the slightest doubt about it. He
further told me that his parents lived in Minnesota and that he
was going there to spend at least part of his leave with them.

Mr. Morris. Can you amplify any more about whether or not
Clubb at the time was a member of the Communist organization?

Mr. Chambers. *I have no knowledge whatsoever* [emphasis
supplied].

Mr. CHAMBERS. 1932. While I was editing the New Masses, which is a Communist-controlled magazine, there came into my office a young man who asked to see Walt Carmon.

Mr. MORRIS. Who is Walt Carmon?

Mr. CHAMBERS. Walt Carmon had been in effect the managing editor of New Masses before I became editor.

Mr. MORRIS. Did he have any connection with the Communist underground?

Mr. CHAMBERS. Walt Carmon may or may not have had connection with the Communist underground. I don't know. He was a Communist.

This stranger seemed rather disturbed not to find Walt Carmon in the office where he expected him. Walt Carmon, in fact, wasn't any longer in the building, in the New Masses. The man, the stranger, told me his name was O. Edmund Clubb.

Senator FERGUSON. Would you recognize a picture of him?

Mr. CHAMBERS. I can no longer identify a picture of Clubb. If you realize that I spoke to him not more than 15 minutes in the year 1932, I think it is simply impossible to make a positive identification.

Senator FERGUSON. You cannot identify the picture.

Mr. CHAMBERS. I feel that other impressions bear on it, and I should not make an identification of him positively.

Senator FERGUSON. All right.

Mr. CHAMBERS. Nevertheless this man told me his name was O. Edmund Clubb, that he was a consular official of some kind at Hankow, I believe, that he was on leave of absence, and he had some kind of message which he wanted to deliver. The difficulty about my recollection of Edmund Clubb or Oliver Clubb is that I can no longer remember what that message was or even to whom it was to be delivered, but there has stayed in the back of my mind an impression which I will not testify to positively that the message was written and that it was for Grace Hutchins. Grace Hutchins is an open Communist, a member of the open Communist Party, has run on the Communist ticket in various elections, and is well known to be a Communist. But I cannot testify more positively to anything along those lines. Clubb then sat talking a little about China. Naturally I don't recall what our conversation was over that length of time, but I do remember that we talked about Hayang Arsenal. As you probably know, Hankow is one of three cities which lie close together—originally called the Wuhan cities where the Communists made their last stand when Chiang Kai-shek first swept them out. I have a further recollection, which I hesitate to make positive, that the message was from Agnes Smedley, but again I can't really testify to that positively.

Senator FERGUSON. This is your best judgment; is it?

Mr. CHAMBERS. I find it impossible, with the play of so many influences on my mind, because people are always asking me questions, bringing me information, and there are actually areas of my experience where I can no longer distinguish between what I once knew and what I have heard and learned in the course of testifying. I have given many thousands of words of testimony by now, as you know.

Mr. MORRIS. But there is no doubt about the fact that Clubb came into the New Masses office.

Whittaker Chambers testifies before the Senate Internal Security sub-committee, August 16, 1951

Later, in *Witness*, Chambers included a few lines repeating the simple anecdote of a young man who, in 1932, "walked into my office in the *New Masses* one day . . . [and] seemed surprised not to find Walt Carmon. . . . We sat talking for a while about the Hanyang Arsenal, . . . and then he went on his way." (p. 270) This The Witness tagged in his text as "an odd experience," without explaining just what was so odd about it. But a footnote explained that, since the lines had been written in 1950, there had been developments:

. . . one day, in our local newspaper, I saw a picture of Oliver Edmund Clubb, a U.S. consular official in China who had recently returned to the United States after the Communists captured Peking. I said to my wife: "I know this man. He paid me a visit in the *New Masses* office in 1932. But they have his name wrong. It should be Chubb." I mentioned the fact because it amused me that my memory could retain an impression of someone of no particular importance (I then supposed) and details of a conversation held fleetingly almost two decades before. Out of the same sense of amusement, *and for no other reason* [emphasis supplied], I mentioned the incident in a casual conversation with two F.B.I. friends.

Chambers was "startled" by a "burst of interest" displayed by his FBI friends in his memories of the man Clubb.

Presently, an investigator for the House Committee on Un-American Activities called and questioned me about Clubb. Presently, Clubb testified before that Committee. He had no recollection of visiting Whittaker Chambers in the *New Masses* office in 1932. . . . The State Department's Loyalty Board requested me to testify before it about a month later in the Case of O. Edmund Clubb. . . . Before my belated answer . . . had reached the Board, one of the higher officials of the State Department

telephoned me. Warmly, he reminded me that we had a great
mutual friend. Generously, he offered to send a car to fetch me if
I would testify at once at the Clubb hearing. I agreed to testify. . . . The sudden urgency surprised me as much as the sudden warmth which again enfolded me when I reached the State
Department.

The hearing began. Usually in a hearing it is possible to detect
a logic and purpose in the questions asked. The questions put to
me that day mystified me completely. Among other questions, I
was asked if Mike Gold had been present at my conversation
with Clubb, if Mike Gold had been present at all at the *New
Masses* that day in 1932. I was asked if Mike Gold on meeting a
stranger would be likely to call him "Comrade," [6] what the geography of the *New Masses* building was like, if there were revolutionary posters on the wall. Two points, in particular, puzzled
me. I could not understand why I was asked if a Communist
would keep a diary (my answer: no). I could not understand the
degree of importance which was obviously attached by the Loyalty Board to the case of a man whose rank in China had not been
especially exalted.

For I did not know two facts that I was to learn shortly after.
The first fact was that Clubb, on his return from China, had
abruptly been upped to head the State Department's China desk.
The second fact was that he had kept a diary. In the course of his
hasty departure from China that diary had passed into the hands
of the British authorities. Always great readers of diaries, the
British read this one and found an entry to the effect that, in
1932, O. Edmund Clubb had had a conversation with Whittaker
Chambers in the *New Masses* office. Other entries provided the
basis for the mystifying questions at the hearing. This diary the
British had turned over to the American authorities. . . .
(pp. 270–71n)

Chambers' footnote purports that he knew me from the
picture he saw in a newspaper in 1950. The text itself

---

[6] Was it the LSB, or Chambers, who forgot that it was the *New Masses*
receptionist, not Gold, who greeted me as "Comrade"?

would indicate that he had remembered me before seeing the picture. In any event, by August 1951 my image had so slipped Chambers' mind that he would testify to the Senators that "I can no longer identify a picture of Clubb." He apparently also forgot, when writing his book, that he had testified about me to the Un-American Activities Committee in December 1948, some year and a half before he had seen my picture in the press and experienced amusement at his ability to retain "an impression of someone . . . and details of a conversation held fleetingly almost two decades before." It is of course impossible to determine exactly whether Chambers' chief lapse of memory was in 1952 for what he had said in 1951, in 1951 for what he had experienced in 1950, or in 1950 for his testimony of 1948.

For Chambers, presumably, those discrepancies were all to be explained by the mental phenomenon reported to the Senate Committee. But given its high admiration for, and abiding faith in, Chambers' "amazing memory," the Board must have been given a sore blow when it learned that he could no longer distinguish between what he once knew and what he had "heard and learned in the course of testifying" (perhaps even before the LSB?). It must have been in some such manner that Chambers fell into error in his report that the British authorities at Peking had read my diaries and turned them over to the American authorities. That information was false. I had simply left my diaries with the British for safekeeping when I left Peking, and it was I who had initiated steps to get them back when I felt the need for them—and I who had actually received them. There was no reason whatsoever to suspect that the British had read them. If Chambers did in fact truthfully relay a hearsay story, instead of weaving his account around a bare shred of information, his source had lied to him.

But Chambers was wiser about memory processes than the Board, which in 1951 had not yet had the opportunity to mull over Chambers' enlightening comment in *Witness* on what happens in the human mind. Chambers discussed changes occurring in his own mind over a ten-year period:

> The main outlines of the past persisted as the plan of a structure can be traced in its ruins. But dates, time intervals, faces, names, happenings tended to run together or disappear. . . . some things have undoubtedly faded forever. Nor is it possible to say whether they may be important or not. For there seems to be no order of importance in what the mind retains and what it forgets. I may remember distinctly after years something completely trivial—a gesture, a wry remark, a shadow on a wall—and be incapable of recalling an important address, like the photographic workshop in Washington. (p. 512)

Regarding the famous documents put into safekeeping by Chambers in 1938 as his "life preserver" vis-à-vis the Communists, he recorded that in the decade that passed before he received them back, "The heap of copied State Department documents, the spools of microfilm, had sunk from my memory as completely as the Russian regiments of World War I sank into the Masurian swamps" (p. 512). One would deduce from the position taken by some of the LSB members that the Board would have listened to that story from Chambers without challenge, but it is quite clear from the record that it would never have accepted a memory lapse of those dimensions from me.

Thus it appears that in 1948 Whittaker Chambers included in testimony to the Un-American Activities Committee a minor anecdote, which he would later include in a manuscript telling the story of his life. In 1950, when I returned from Peking, Chambers was "amused" at his power of recollection, upon seeing my picture in his newspaper, of a minor incident of long before. He indicated that in the first instance he would have accorded the anecdote no more than casual mention. It was only with the manifestation of interest by the FBI, the Un-American Activities Committee, "one of the higher officials in the State Department," and the LSB, in 1950 and after, that The Witness felt impelled to add a footnote. There, even as in his testimony of August 1951, Chambers essentially confirmed his account of 1948 as reported by the Wood Committee. The LSB, by all indications, started with that same simple story and then went on to conjure up and explore a phantasmagoria of "sealed envelope," "document," and a mysterious "Communist underground." But at last, in August, we all came out by "the same door where in we went."

Chambers' testimony of August 16 must have impressed the Board in some way or other. It never mentioned him or the *New Masses* again, and would in due course be off on another scent. But I was now to reappear before Congress. On August 20, I confronted the Wood Committee a second time. On this occasion the committee met in full public session. To satisfy the requirements of the subpoena, the State Department had delivered to the Committee the diaries I had handed over the week before; technically, it was as if I myself had put them into the Committee's hands. The diaries were admitted into the record for identification only, and the Committee limited its inquiry to the entries respecting my trip to Washington and New York in 1932. The main subject of the interrogation was still my contact with the *New Masses*, and with Whittaker Chambers.

We retraced again the outlines of the 1932 New York trip. This had now become familiar ground to me, but there was so little to it that the refrain had become somewhat tiresome—for me at least, and possibly for some who had heard the story before. In the circumstances, where so much was at stake, the suspect could hardly experience actual boredom, however, and in his anxiety there might easily flash through his mind Ogden Nash's little prayer: "Oh to be Machiavellian, oh to be unscrupulous, oh, to be glib! Oh to be ever prepared with a plausible fib!" The wily stratagem appears on occasion to have served "favorable" witnesses well—but then, they enjoy an immunity ordinary mortals do not. Pedestrian as it was, I told my story again.

The hearing was long, and my testimony was frequently punctuated by the popping of flashbulbs. One committee-member was critical of my having failed to report to my superiors Michael Gold's having *no* "hopes" for revolution in the United States in 1932, apparently not appreciating that sentiments rather more subversive than that had probably appeared in every issue of the *New Masses* that year. Only one Congressman evinced interest in the fact that I had in 1932 alerted the Government to a revolution in being—the Chinese revolution—but even he did not inquire what heed had been given to the alarms I had actually sounded. The Committee went through the usual process of probing into my contacts with various persons, and the day's long session ended.

I was called back briefly on August 23 and confronted with two more names, and then the Committee excused me. The Congressmen had pursued the matter to its normal conclusion seemingly without becoming unduly apprehensive regarding the magnitude of the threat that my having entered the doors of the *New Masses* office in 1932 might have posed to the national security. I quit the Committee chamber feeling that even though the Committee members remained uninformed regarding the competency that had given me such a good record in the Foreign Service, they were more judicious and sober—and less mistrustful by far of my bona fides—than was the Loyalty Security Board. But then, of course, they didn't have to worry about Deputy Undersecretary Humelsine, the Loyalty Review Board, or partisan Senators.

The day after Chambers' testimony of August 16, the McCarran Committee's counsel, Robert Morris, had telephoned to say that Chambers had given testimony of concern to me and to invite me to appear and give my own version. I had replied that I should be happy to do so. No date had been definitely fixed for my appearance before the Senate committee. On August 21, between the two Wood Committee sessions, Morris informed me that the McCarran group would meet with me at 5 o'clock. Since it was already after 3 o'clock, I was caught without papers ready or lawyer at hand; but I consented to appear—and made a dash for the lawyer then helping me with my Congressional hearings, the very Irish Gerard D. Reilly. Reilly was engaged for the hour set, and was disturbed at the prospect of my appearing alone even after he had telephoned Morris and been told that the matter was mainly routine and could be expected to last about half an hour. I nevertheless held to the belief (which I should have been conditioned against long before) that since I was appearing as a voluntary witness to tell a story that was simple and already known to the Senators the hearing could hardly be a serious or complex matter. I confidently argued that I preferred to meet the Senators at the hour fixed, and have done with it. Reilly finally agreed, if still with obvious reluctance. I hurried home, grabbed a portfolio of material, and got back to the Senate office building in time to keep my appointment. I was accompanied by Mariann, but she was not permitted to enter the Senate hearing room with me, and had to wait, with her anxiety, outside in an antechamber.

Senator McCarran was absent, and another Senator presided. Other Senators wandered in and out during the session. One might have thought that the hearing would begin by a request for my comments on Chambers' testimony, but this did not occur. The Committee was technically concerned with its investigation of the Institute of Pacific Relations, but little attention was devoted to that matter. The investigators themselves had no charges to make against me, evidently, or complaints that I had in the past done—or failed to do—anything in particular. That did not prevent my receiving a grilling that patently gave little consideration to my status as a public official who had served the United States Government in difficult posts for over twenty years, or for the sometime American doctrine that a man is to be deemed innocent until proved guilty. Well into the hearing, the chairman asked for the LSB's charges against me. It was confirmed, in response to my question, that this request stood even though the loyalty-security processes of the Executive branch were confidential. I handed them a copy—and the Senator asked "Is this all?" I assured him that that was all there was to it. With the charges in hand, the Committee went to work on the further development of the matter of my associations. The ordeal dragged on. And Mariann waited anxiously outside.

The hearing lasted three hours instead of the "half-hour" Morris had foreseen and ended, I am sure, without great benefit either to the store of the world's knowledge or to the taxpayers. At the very end of the session, I succeeded in handing over to the committee copies of a number of articles and speeches I had presented on a subject it might have thought relevant—Chinese Communism. This evidence was accepted, but without visible enthusiasm. I naturally have no way of knowing whether any one of the Senators who had found it necessary to look into my views ever took the time to read those samples of my thought on the subject of Communism. The hearing ended, however, without my being able to present my reply to the testimony of Whittaker Chambers.

As a Government official, I had faced—at various times and under differing circumstances—"tribunals" of Japanese military captors, Chinese Communist courts and arbitration boards, the State Department Loyalty Security Board, and the House Un-American Activities Committee. The Japanese were hard and threatened me in an effort to obtain their ends, but they were enemy military and we were at war—and with due respect to fundamental proprieties they refrained from the ultimate use of the superior physical force at their command. The Chinese Communist organs, while adhering to their own regulations and according me settlements that met the letter of their pertinent labor codes, were arbitrary and personally insulting. The Wood Committee, as far as my three contacts with it went, was both reasonable in approach and efficiently concerned with the witness before it. The State Department's LSB had committed manifest breaches of the official regulation that "reasonable bounds shall be maintained as to competency, relevancy, and materiality," and for all of Chairman Snow's initial assurances of legal impartiality, the Board's bona fides in my case had already become suspect. Now, with this hearing before the Senate Internal Security subcommittee, my experience was rounded out. I discovered, as have so many people of various nationalities in the twentieth century, how much easier it is in the end to meet an enemy in strenuous and dangerous contest, confident in the support of one's associates and one's government, than it is to face the slings and arrows of one's own compatriots. The difference lies in what happens to the heart.

IX

High Court of Suspicion

Conscious that your charges against Mr. Jefferson cannot
bear the light of inquiry and the test of argument, you
resort to *suspicion* as your dernier stronghold. If evidence will not convict, let us only suspect him to be an
infidel, and then we ought not to promote his election,
*"conscience is not safe while there is a doubt or suspi-
cion."* Destroyed he must be at all events, and if we cannot conquer him in fair battle, let us take him off by
poison or assassination. If argument will not prevail, if
evidence should fall short, why, then we must resort to
the vagaries of the imagination, and conscience will de-
cide against him, for it prefers the company of suspicion
and fancy to the society of reason and evidence. I will
venture, sir, to say that this high court of suspicion in
which you propose to try Mr. Jefferson, is a tribunal unknown to christianity, to common sense, or common justice. Its model can only be found in the bloody tribunals
of the inquisition, or in the infernal judicatory of Rhada-
manthus, as described by the poet. Gnossius hoec, Rha-
damanthus habit durissima regna, Castigatque, audique
dolos, subigitique fateri. [Gnosian Rhamanthus holds his
iron sway; he chastises, and hears the tale of guilt, exact-
ing confession of crimes . . .] Virgil.

"GROTIUS" (De Witt Clinton), *Vindication of Thomas
Jefferson* (1800)

It seemed that my various hearings were probably over. The Wood Committee had dismissed me, and the McCarran Committee evidently had no real interest in me. Snow had not formally closed the LSB hearing again on August 13; but, I had answered all the charges and rejected the demand for unrestricted access to my diaries, so there was presumably nothing left to talk about in that quarter. If the LSB were to act as promptly as it had in the case of Davies, who had already been cleared, I should have my decision in about one week after the last session. And had not the Board itself in mid-July indicated a desire to expedite the matter, so that both cases could be gotten off the calendar?

There was still uncertainty respecting the ultimate disposition of my diaries, now back in the custody of the Department. I had taken a firm stand on principle against either giving the LSB direct access to the diary entries respecting my 1932 visit to New York, or granting it the right to undertake a general fishing expedition in my 1932 diary in line with its latest proposal. I had naturally envisaged the practical possibility that the Department, in the course of performing its check for reasons of policy, would go farther and give its security staff access to them. But I knew that the diaries contained nothing detrimental to my position, and assumed that any such invasion of my privacy by the Department would in the end result in no more than the security personnel's giving an "all clear" signal to the LSB. And Humelsine's pertinent letter of August 11 had directed that the diaries be turned over to him for inspection, "after which they will be returned to you." There was no apparent reason suggesting that the matter could not now be expeditiously concluded.

Oliver had come to Washington after graduation, hoping to be able, in view of his knowledge of China and the Chinese language, to enter the Naval Officers Candidate School at Newport, Rhode Istand, for special training. The publicity attending my case could hardly have helped his application. His hopes were in any event dashed. He stayed with us for his birthday, August 11, and then returned to Minnesota to join the Marines as a private. He and his grandmother left to the tune of our reassuring "now don't worry, everything is going to be all right." Mariann, Zoë, and I were left to count the days until the Board's decision came. Days passed, then weeks. Then in mid-September, with still no word from the Board, I telephoned Humelsine, who had been one of those who had professed a desire to "expedite" my case in the first instance. I pointed out that the weeks were passing, and asked when the Board might be expected to act. His reply was brief, but reassuring—"soon."

A report sifted down from one of the Washington dinner tables. A senator had spoken as if he knew the contents of my diaries. Those diaries, he said, had indicated clearly that I wasn't a Communist—there was no worry about that—but they'd "have to do something" about my sleeping with two or three women every night. Either the senator had embroidered imaginatively upon information received, or his State Department source had lied to him: there was nothing in the diaries to substantiate any suggestion of sexual promiscuity. In fact, the same July 9, 1932, entry that recorded my meeting with Chambers carried another item:

Burner proposed a bit of a stag party for tonight, but I couldn't quite see that. I wasn't sure whether t'would lead to women or bad brew or both, but I wanted neither. (Might as well admit I *want* women, but it doesn't fit in with the present marital agreement, so I risk the development of inhibitions. Probably not much danger so long as I keep at work and so long as Mariann and I get along so very well.)

I had turned my diaries over to the presumably security-conscious State Department for a confidential check—only to have a grossly distorted version of their contents leaked to Washington dinner tables. Through the veil of the Department's make-believe, there could sometimes be perceived, if only dimly, forces that seemed bent on my destruction.

Prominent in the history of the Spanish Inquisition and the Soviet purges alike is the feature of keeping the victim in ignorance of the charges and in long suspense. The procedure has the evident purpose of "softening up" the suspect, and better preparing him psychologically to make a confession. As the weeks went by without any sign of life or movement from the LSB, we could only reach the conclusion that either the Board was afraid to act until the FBI had checked all persons whose names had been found in my diaries, or there existed somewhere in the loyalty-security hierarchy a desire to punish me, after a fashion, for my refusal to grant the LSB access to my diaries. All men dislike admitting mistakes, and the Board had clearly erred in trying to equate rumors against my record, and in blowing up out of all proportion the 1932 visit to the *New Masses* office. Given particularly Chambers' own latest testimony, the Board was left with its *New Masses* item quite demolished. But analyzing the situation with Mariann, I observed that the longer the waiting period lasted, the more the loyalty-security administration would feel impelled to produce some justification for its actions, which would otherwise appear crassly stupid.

Ten weeks dragged by without word from the Board. For relief from the strain, Mariann and I left Washington to visit some friends in New York and New England. Our first stop was New York City. On November 2, the day after our arrival, I received from the Board a telegram calling me back for a new session on "matters under consideration." I phoned the legal officer of the LSB and said that I would appear. Our trip was off. On November 6 I faced the Board again.

It is to be recalled that after my presentation of the diary excerpt dealing with my visit to the *New Masses* Board Member Murphy had introduced an opening wedge for the LSB's broadening interest in my diaries (*faute de mieux?*) by asking whether I would read to the Board the entries for the several days that I was in New York in 1932, and that immediately after my *partial* satisfaction of that request the Chairman had asked whether I would be willing "that the Board, without making it any part of the record, should peruse the omitted portions of your diary during the New York trip just for their own satisfaction," and that I had refused. On August 10, however, I had put forward my compromise proposal to let a third party read the diary entries covering the New York trip and testify to the Board. Then, on August 13, there had come the Board's demand for access to the whole of the 1932 diary— and my refusal of that expanded proposition. Later in that session, when the matter came up again, Assistant Legal Officer Moyer had remarked that, "Of course, you realize the Board does have to make a decision and an independent reviewing authority would have to be thoroughly fa-

miliar with the evidence before the Board, and the Board
has expressed an interest in . . . the period covered by
your general home leave period of time, and that the diary
entries go beyond, possibly, your visit to the 'New Masses'
and include any contacts that you made during the
period."

It was thus made evident that the Board now not only
desired to have free access to the whole of the 1932 diary,
*but also to put diary extracts unrelated to their charges
into the official record,* for the reference of any "independent reviewing authority." I commented at the time on the
expanded demand: "May I point out, gentlemen, that . . .
in China . . . the merchant starts with a high price and
goes down to a lower price. He doesn't start with a low
price and go up. Now the proposition put forward by the
Board was limited distinctly in the official part of the proceedings to the New York trip, which was July 7 to 10,
1932."

And I had held to my compromise proposal of August
10.

Now, on November 6, when I met with the Board again,
Chairman Snow began the session by remarking that "At
the request of the Department you have made such of your
diaries as you have in this country available to the Department, is that correct? " I confirmed that it was, but noted
the circumstances which had led to that action. And then
the Chairman:

Now, then, let me state for the record that the Department in its
discretion has seen fit to turn over the diaries for the examination
of the Board, and I will say, Mr. Clubb, that the Board has found
a great many matters of interest to the Board in the diaries, a
great deal of which is a matter that should be presented in your

favor at this hearing. You understand, of course, that the Board is only interested in arriving at the facts, and there are certain facts recorded here that seem to be highly in your favor and should be made a part of the record so that your case may stand completed in the record. So we would like to run through the diaries with you, bringing out for the record such portions of the diaries as the Board has noted, both favorable and perhaps unfavorable, so that the whole thing may be complete in the record. Let me first, for the record, establish just what diaries we have here.

The Chairman at that moment had *all* of my available diaries physically before him, for the wartime and postwar years as well as for 1932–33. The purpose of the new session was thus crystal-clear. But I was still not prepared to acquiesce in the Board's arbitrary invasion of my privacy. I protested:

Mr. Chairman, . . . my position in respect to the diaries and access of the Board to the diaries remains as before. In short, as a matter of principle, I oppose the consideration by the Board of my diaries. That was my position in the first instance, and as stated on July 31, I believe. It was my position on August 13th where I made a categorical and clear refusal. . . . I know and I knew that there were certain elements in that diary that would establish clearly, even for the satisfaction of the Board, that I was not and am not a Communist. Nevertheless, I think that principle was clear and the principle was clearly stated by me.

My challenge to the Board's purpose included citation of several specific instances where, in service of my government, I had chosen to act on principle rather than out of expediency, even though the choice resulted in hardship to myself, as when I had rejected the Japanese demand for the keys to the consular safe at Hanoi in 1941 and where I had faced the Communist courts at Peking rather than submit to exorbitant demands on the part of Chinese em-

ployees of the Consulate General. And I took the occasion
to remark incidentally that, although I had delivered my
diaries to the Department because I had thought "my loyalty to the Department demanded that," there had been
a leak to Washington dinner tables from those diaries
while they were in the Department's possession. I characterized the leaked matter as being "in the nature of malicious gossip," and pointed out that "it doesn't happen to be
in the diaries." This, I said, was what happened when
there was an invasion of my privacy.

I noted that none of the Board's informants had charged
me with being a Communist, nor had any member of
Congress so charged—not even Senator McCarthy himself.
I quoted the October 10, 1951, statement of Chairman
Ramspeck of the Federal Civil Service Commission that
"we need a return to a more just appraisal of our public
servants—not a witch hunt or a condemnation proceeding
in the press, on the radio, on television and in denunciatory speeches, including some in the halls of Congress."
My career, I said, "has been irreparably damaged by the
circumstance that the loyalty process has taken place at all.
My public standing has been very effectively damaged." I
also quoted a speech made on September 6 by General
MacArthur:

This drift toward totalitarian rule is reflected not only in this
shift toward centralized power, but as well in the violent manner
in which exception is taken to the citizen's voice when raised in
criticism of those who exercise the political power. There seems
to be a determination to suppress individual voice and opinion
which can only be regarded as symptomatic of the beginning of
of a general trend toward mass thought control. Abusive language
and arbitrary action, rather than calm, dispassionate and just
argument, ill-becomes the leadership of a great nation conceived

in liberty and dedicated to a course of morality and justice. It challenges the concept of free speech and is an attempt at direct suppression through intimidation of that most vital check against the abuse of political power—public criticism. If long countenanced by free men, it can but lead to those controls upon conviction and conscience which traditionally have formed stepping stones to dictatorial power.

I volunteered the assumption that the LSB had no intent of pursuing what the Japanese called "dangerous thoughts," and I added that "it isn't quite clear to me just what purpose would be served, frankly, by exploring with the Board the intent of thoughts put down at random, and sometimes carelessly, as long as twenty years ago, taken particularly out of context." I said that I was there to answer its questions, but that "my presence today should not be taken as approval or warrant, explicit or implicit, of access to my diaries, whether the access results in favor to me or disfavor. . . ."

General Snow said that he thought the Board understood my principles very well—but he ignored the one at issue. He asserted that the Board had no intention of taking entries out of context, and then immediately shifted any responsibility for misinterpretation to my shoulders: "That is the purpose of this examination, to have the entries in context so you may feel quite free—the diaries are here—to add any context that goes along with any entry so we will have a clear understanding for the occasion of the entry and what your purpose was in making it."

He did not note either the occasion for the Board's first interest in the diaries, or the limitations which he as Chairman had originally proposed should govern the Board's inspection of them. Nor did he mention the commitment given in Humelsine's letter of August 11 that, after inspection *by the Department*, the diaries would be returned to me.

Without further ado, the Board went into action. The first question was about Agnes Smedley, already discussed at such great length. The Chairman started out as if she had never been mentioned before:

THE CHAIRMAN: Now, referring to the period 1932 to 1933 as covered by your diary, would you state for the record just what your relations were with Agnes Smedley during the years 1932 and 1933 in outline. Who was she and what were your relations with her?

MR. CLUBB: May I invite the attention of the Chairman to the fact that I have already stated my relations with Miss Agnes Smedley in response to the first interrogatory and also in some detail in my hearing on July 31st.

THE CHAIRMAN: You have nothing to add to that?

MR. CLUBB: I have nothing to add to that unless the Board has some questions to ask.

THE CHAIRMAN: Very well, we will ask specific questions.

MR. SIPES: Is the Board to understand, Mr. Clubb, that your position is that you have already given us a review of all your contacts with Agnes Smedley in previous testimony?

MR. CLUBB: I think I have given you a pertinent survey. I can't say I have told you everything I know or everything I ever thought about Agnes Smedley, but I don't think there is any point in bringing in a lot of irrelevant material, and if the Board has some particular questions I will be glad to have them asked.

The Board asked some specific questions. Just what had been my purpose in showing to Agnes Smedley my paper on Chinese Communism? Had there at any time been "intimate" correspondence between Agnes Smedley and myself? Had she ever offered me a secret code or secret address for correspondence? (The Board had before it several diary entries touching on those points, but presumably they felt there was no harm in testing my memory—to see if it measured up to that of Whittaker Chambers? Where did Agnes Smedley live in Shanghai, and had I seen her after her 1934 visit to the Soviet Union? Those questions were easy enough to answer—if one could reconstruct the context of 1932.

In 1932 American *consular* offices ordinarily had nothing to do with secret information: secret political matters were the concern of the Embassy in the nation's capital. Consular offices were concerned primarily with the promotion of commerce and the protection of American rights and interests, and only secondarily with political reporting; furthermore, their most important representative functions required them to deal with no more than local officials. The Hankow office thus would not have been in possession of "secret" information in 1932. There was at that time, in fact, no other classification for consular reports than "confidential" and "strictly confidential," indicating respectively that, in the commercial surveys published periodically by the Department of *Commerce*, such reports might be used but without attribution to the author, or not used at all. It was a common and accepted practice for consular offices of the period to make nonconfidential reports available to American businessmen and journalists. Ambassador Warren knew the difference in procedures of the present and those of 20 years earlier, and remarked the fact. But how could military men like Snow and Murphy, who had been in the State Department only five years, know what practices were authorized for consular offices in China in 1932?

My report on Chinese Communism had not been a regular office report, but was a study prepared on my own time and put into official channels as of possible interest. For source material I had relied primarily upon the Chinese- and English-language press, with some additional data drawn from the few Communist publications (including *Pravda*) that I was able to get my hands on, supplemented by information obtained from missionaries and others. It had absolutely nothing to do with American "national security." I had freely shown it to a number of people outside governmental channels. But Snow demonstrated that he, for one, had not read that 124-page report, or, if he had, had forgotten it:

THE CHAIRMAN: Have you put a copy of that essay of yours into the record?
MR. CLUBB: Yes, sir. That is a part of the dossier, part of the file that has been turned over to the Loyalty Security Board.

I had early indicated to the LSB that this particular item of evidence was important, even critical, as probably having been the specific thing of which colleagues might have been thinking when they dubbed me "pink." I had long been reconciled to the possibility that some of the critics of my early work on Chinese Communism had not troubled to read my reports, or else belonged to the ostrich school of thought. But in the circumstances it did seem inordinately to increase the sum of my difficulties if the LSB Chairman, more than nine months after I had cited the report as something that had caused, I believed, a small number of my colleagues "to find differences in thinking between themselves and me," and three months after I had submitted it to the Board as material to the case, should still remain uninformed regarding even its presence in the dossier.

As regards "intimate" correspondence, I conceded ignorance of what the LSB meant by the term, but said that I had exchanged a number of letters with Agnes Smedley in 1932 particularly. Miss Smedley happened to be an excellent source of information regarding the Chinese revolutionary movement, in which she was deeply interested. It was as a result of my contacts with her, and of course with other persons as well, that I obtained information highly useful for preparing my reports to the United States Government, and various periodicals of such interest to the State Department that it requested the Hankow office to make arrangements for it to receive the same material. And then there was the circumstance that, in 1934, the Department had expressed the wish that I continue my reporting on the subject of Chinese Communism—which I had done. In my work, I had been concerned with obtaining accurate information for transmittal to the U.S. Government; and the people who gave me information knew well that this was my official function. But the LSB evinced not the slightest interest in the competency or in the accuracy of my reporting; instead, it showed itself primarily concerned with the ideological orthodoxy of my sources of information.

In *Witness*, Chambers reported on an effort to establish contacts with the Chinese Communists:

The contact with the Chinese Communists seemed on the point of splendid success. Just as we were seeking it, Agnes Smedley happened into New York on her way to Russia from the Kiangsi Communist area. . . .[1]

[1] I have never heard of Agnes Smedley's being in the Kiangsi Communist area in 1934, when I was still reporting on events in that area and would ordinarily have learned eventually of the visit of an American journalist to a region so hard of access. Given the heavy fighting in progress in that sector all through 1934, until the Communists were forced to withdraw

I knew of Miss Smedley as the author of *Daughter of Earth*
. . . and as a persistent spokesman for the Chinese Communists.
I asked Peters to arrange a meeting for me with her so that I
could introduce a friend (Don) to her. I said that it would be unnecessary for Peters to go along. . . . I met her in an Automat on
72nd Street in New York. Peters had not told her whom she was
going to meet and she was extremely surprised and distrustful at
meeting a stranger.[2] She was equally distrustful of Don. We
separated without agreeing to anything, and Don never got his
contact with the Chinese Communists. (p. 366)

Given Chambers' reputed authority in the Communist
underground of the period, it seems singular that his efforts were so fruitless—if Agnes Smedley as well as
Chambers had the Communist connections alleged in
some quarters.

The Board abandoned Agnes Smedley. The Chairman
then began recording extracts from my diaries. Although
the Board was purportedly interested primarily in my
movements, acquaintanceships, thoughts, and attitudes of
the 1930s, the Chairman spent most of the time with the
diaries beginning in 1944. There was no discernible endeavor to remain even near the general area of the charges
against me: the process had patently become a fishing expedition. Apparently all of my observations on China and
the USSR weighed most profoundly with the Board. Anything that might have been judged by a suspicious Japanese gendarme to constitute "dangerous thoughts" was
also grist for its mill. Despite the previous limitation fixed

westward in October of that year, Chambers' locating of Agnes Smedley
in Kiangsi is inherently improbable. She probably came from Shanghai,
which had been her residence for some time.

[2] Note that Chambers reports that Agnes Smedley, too, was "surprised" at
meeting him. Surprised—and distrustful.

by the Board itself relative to the character of its interest and the discreet manner in which it proposed to handle diary material, all entries extracted by it went automatically into the record.

The Chairman made one offer that he presumably felt to be generous: I might profess amendment of views in respect to one matter in point. After reading one of several comments (which in this case happened *not* to be my own) on the corrupt and reactionary character of Chiang Kai-shek's group, the Chairman said:

In these cases, where I'm quoting your opinion of the Nationalist regime, if at any time you have had occasion to change your opinion, I would be glad if you would note it. Otherwise the opinion stands as stated.

My reply was:

My opinion in respect to the Nationalist regime has, of course, been set out in considerable extent in the course of my reports to the Department and it is supported, but only supported by and perhaps qualified a little bit, by these other personal records that I have made. . . . my opinion in respect to corruption and inefficiency of the Nationalist regime was paralleled at that particular time by the opinion of other rather outstanding American officials, including as the most recent perhaps in that particular period General Wedemeyer.

I felt no need, and took no occasion, to amend the record set forth in my diary.

One of the notable tactics employed by the Board members as they coursed through the wartime and postwar diaries was the persistence with which they sought my opinion on the political leanings of various well-known people they met in the diary pages. Their profession to the contrary notwithstanding, I sensed that they *were* acting as

an investigating organ, possibly with the idea that some
other agency might benefit from my comments gleaned in
such a process as this. I was being called upon, while
myself in the dock, to add my testimony to other dossiers
in those blacklists which, by the geometrical process of
"guilt by association," were currently growing so rapidly
in the files of United States Government agencies. But at
last, with myself and diaries presumably thought squeezed
dry, the Chairman said "I have now completed the extracts
from the diary that I had taken note of that I thought
should be made part of the record."

The session thus ended with the recording of extracts
from my diary for the 1944–50 period, when I had occupied
various positions of considerable responsibility. There had
been gross violation of my privacy, but I nevertheless felt
that the portrayal of my powers of observation and analysis
respecting Far Eastern developments was impres-
sive, and on my arrival home I reported to Mariann that
the prospect looked good. But the hearing resumed on
November 7 in a manner that I felt at once to be suspect.
Although Snow the day before had purported to have finished extracting diary entries for the record, he now returned without explanation to 1932. Although he had
brushed aside my initial protest by saying that "the Board
has no intention or desire to exercise any kind of thought
control over anyone," everything even faintly tinged with
politics for that pre-New-Deal era was now subjected to
the closest scrutiny. There was a spate of questions concentrated on my 1932 thinking, and the Chairman fished
out comments by other persons. When I suggested that it
was hardly necessary to read into the record comments by
friends on various personalities "where they don't reflect

on the case or the charges against me," the Chairman replied: "My purpose in reading the entire item into the record is simply for completeness. I just want it to appear that the entire item for that day has been read." This, then, was the new application of the regulations respecting "relevancy." It was also, indubitably, a search for "dangerous thoughts."

I had realized that, in challenging again in the November 6 session the Board's right to delve into my diaries at all, I had done something which it must have hoped I would avoid. Because of that challenge, and by reason also of the LSB's various breaches of the applicable Regulations and Procedures, the Board would be at a technical disadvantage should the matter go to the Loyalty Review Board. It would remain at such a disadvantage—unless, of course, it could be shown that I was really a wolf in sheep's clothing. I therefore was warned by the Board's increased pressure on November 7, and assumed that the members had talked the matter over at the end of the previous day and, perhaps after consultation with Humelsine, had undertaken new maneuvers. So, while I again worked over old memories in an attempt to respond adequately to those new questions about my youthful attitudes and beliefs, I watched the Board members for a clue as to the LSB's purpose.

The full entries of the diaries for my 1932 Washington and New York trips were read into the record, with all personalia included. I had told the Board before that there was nothing in the parts I had omitted that was relevant to either the *New Masses* visit or any alleged "revolutionary" activities on my part. This was discovered to be the fact. I had attended a symphony concert, the movie *Grand Hotel*

and the Pulitzer Prize play *Of Thee I Sing;* and I had
dined with friends. The Board members went on, and recorded lengthy extracts from entries describing our trip
back to Hankow. They found nothing to reward their
quest.

There nevertheless seemingly remained, undying, the
suspicions that Chambers had *originally* planted deep in
the collective mind of the Board by recounting his contact
of minutes with me in the dim past. In apparent disregard
of the sworn testimony of men who had known me for
years—*my* witnesses—the Board members continued to
wrestle to the end with the "mildly pink" and "pro-Red"
terms their informants had used, and strove to have *me*
explain why such terms had been cast my way. This was a
preposterous reversal of all normal procedures: not permitted to confront the persons whose comments, perhaps em-
bodied in reports that would have offered a context of distinctly different complexion (as had been proven in the
case of Ambassador Gauss), *I* was being called upon, in
the informants' absence, to present rationales for their allegations.

The Chairman came to the final entry in the 1932–33
bound volumes: that of June 30, 1933. There, I had commented critically on the growing German Nazi movement,
expressed skepticism regarding the possibility for success
of the New Deal, and ended my (once) private soliloquy:

So, the final battle between Capitalism and the *next* "New
Order" in the history of man's progression from his cave home.
There will be a repression of liberties on every side. But, it
seems to me that the essence of democracy must finally be given
back to the human race, altho the outward form will be altered, if we are to enjoy any of the things that have been dear to

the heart of man, and fought for, ever since we became conscious of social organization. Art, literature, poetry, music, philosophy—all the things that come from freedom, these must be given back to us in some new interpretation of democracy. If not, if humans are to be guaranteed their bread by a smoothly functioning machine but are to be denied all freedom for fear that the order of the Machine—Capitalistic or dictatorial Communism—will be disturbed, it would be better that homo sapiens decently commit suicide. The "divine spark" which has hitherto made him personable and interesting would have been put out.

Well, he will die some day. It is commonly supposed he will freeze to death, or that his earth will dry up beneath his feet and he will die of thirst, or that he will perish in some derangement of the Cosmos which affects the solar system, but it is quite conceivable and possible that he will destroy himself much sooner by the use of the lethal weapons he has invented for internecine brawls. Gas, light-rays, the use of intra-atomic energy, all have in them great possibilities in this direction. It is not *probable* that he will so destroy himself at this stage in the transition to other political forms, but the possibility cannot be ignored.

It is to be granted that it is all tremendously interesting, and that the primal emotions that are being stirred leaves few cold spectators of the scene. The present "peace movement" in the colleges is a phenomenon which would seem to contradict this statement, but it is to be recalled that pacifists usually have to fight to uphold their beliefs if they do not renounce them for the occasion, when the question comes up for final settlement. So it is that those who want peace and democracy will have to fight for them. It will be war, and revolution, and then—¡quien sabe!"

The Chairman asked whether I had any comment on the last passage, and I simply remarked that World War II and revolution had in fact ensued in line with my forecast, and that the German domestic strife of 1932 had led to actions against the human race which were beyond our comprehension at the time. And I commented somewhat wryly that my reference to intra-atomic energy had no connection with the current atomic-energy program, so that I was not liable to charges of breach of security in that regard.

The Board did not pause to admire that quip, but started off on another tangent:

CHAIRMAN: Now this diary that you have turned over is, I take it, in fact exactly the same form in which it came to you?
A. Yes, sir.
THE CHAIRMAN: You made no alteration of it?
A. No sir. . . . I might say for the purposes of the record that in writing out diary entries I have never, ordinarily speaking, gone back over them to read them after having written them out. You will therefore find in those entries things that were put down sometimes carelessly with sometimes typographical errors or repetitions which were not corrected and, as I have said, it didn't represent a striving for absolute accuracy so much as a putting down in a rapid manner some thought that might have occurred to me at the end of the day.

In its rummaging about my diaries, the LSB had run into a number of the typographical errors I had just remarked upon, and the Chairman now reported that the Board had discovered two entries dated August 14 and 15 in the midst of the April 1951 entries. How did I explain that? I responded that it looked like "pure absent-mindedness." The Chairman commented: "The curious thing to the Board is that the August dates happen to be the very dates on which your diary was demanded." Snow clarified this statement to mean the date demanded by the LSB. His chronology was in error: the Board's demand for access to the 1932 diary (apart from the initial approach of August 1 aimed at the entries from the July 1932 visit to New York) had been on August 13; *and I had actually delivered the looseleaf diaries to Humelsine on August 11 and 13.* The "curious" coincidence that General Snow obviously intended to suggest therefore did not exist. I reminded him of the correct date. Nevertheless, it soon became evident that a new, dark suspicion had crowded into the scene: the LSB now suspected that I might have altered certain entries in the diary that I had refused to give the Board in any event.

The LSB bored in. I began—and here I erred, given that Board—to think out loud and explore the matter in an effort to dispel the Board's evident suspicion. I asked to see the offending page (the LSB was always in possession of the diaries), and those immediately preceding and following. I pointed out that the sheet in question contained one entry for April 16 and the next was April 30, and that the ribbon track was appreciably dimmer for the later date; and that the track of the beginning of the sheet fit in with the preceding page, and that of the end of the sheet fit that of the succeeding page; and that I'd have had no reason to alter diaries I hadn't intended to give the Board—or, in practical fact, time to rewrite over a weekend those voluminous diaries (which the LSB had apparently taken over two months just to read). The Board worried the point as a terrier would a rat. I stated ten times, in the course of the next hour, that to the best of my recollection and knowledge the page had not been recopied.

After the session, I checked my memory with Mariann's. The April 16 entry was made on Mariann's birthday, and I had just returned from Minnesota. There, on April 14, I had given a talk on "American Relations with the Far East" before a statewide conference on U.S. foreign policy. The talk attracted the attention of Senator Hubert H. Humphrey, who had it inserted in the Congressional Record, a copy of which I had earlier supplied the Board

to help in its quest for the pattern of my political thinking.
Did the Board now believe that, at a date when I was already confronted with its interrogatory, and during a brief
trip when I made such a speech, I would have indulged in
unorthodox activities and recorded them in my diary—and
then altered the entries, if not on August 14 and 15, when
they were no longer in my possession, then at some other
less "curious" date? Mariann's and my speculation was far
less Mephistophelian: I had also seen Oliver while in
Minnesota; his birthday was in August, and we hazarded
the guess that simple thought transference plus a possible
alliterative confusion might easily have resulted in such a
typographical slip—in circumstances where I frequently
wrote up two or more entries at the same time, as after
making a trip.

But I had to meet the suspicions of the Board. The next
morning, in the presence of Legal Officer Sipes, who had
custody of the diaries, Mariann and I jointly inspected the
diary paper and typewriter-ribbon track, and the entries,
for the whole first half of 1951. The type record was clear
as day to inspection. The Board convened, and I reported
the check of memories and diary pages, and reiterated my
denial that there had been any recopying. At her own
request, Mariann came forward to testify as to the matter
in point, but left with an unanticipated reaction of horror
that came from facing the five men like a prisoner in the
dock. She hadn't previously realized quite what a Board
hearing was like.

Whittaker Chambers, it will be recalled, indicated that
his own hearing before the LSB had been a confusing experience: "Usually in a hearing it is possible to detect a
logic and purpose in the questions asked. The questions
put to me that day mystified me completely."

That the hearing had not lost all of its confusion by the November sessions is perhaps indicated by this statement from Legal Officer Sipes in the new merry-go-round:

I am at some loss to grapple with this because, as I understand your testimony, it is your recollection that you didn't recopy. However, if you did, with the recollection that you did recopy, you couldn't shed any light for us as to what the nature of it was that may have been eliminated, if you did. So we are left up in the air as to what the content of your observations, if any, were with reference to General Li [Tsung-jen].

There was no gainsaying that we were all, at times, up in the air as to what it was all about.

Before the adjournment of the November 7 session, to portray the temper of 1932 and to put my cited thoughts into the historical perspective of that particular year, I had again quoted to the LSB some pertinent observations by contemporary political figures. The deep pessimism of their estimates, charged with a foreboding sense of impending calamity, more than matched the somberness of my own youthful comments. And after sketching anew the political environment of 1932, beyond any power of the LSB's forgetfulness, I gave the Board a brief exposition of what I thought was meant by "loyalty" and "freedom." This need not be thought gilding the lily. As administered by the Department of State, the loyalty program was manifestly fuzzy and distorted as regards both the concept of loyalty and some of the freedoms defined in the Bill of Rights—including the constitutional prohibition against seizure of private papers. Again I used sage words of other men, philosophers and authors, to bring out the significance of the problem. I quoted President Truman, who had struck out hard several times in 1951 against the mounting partisan attacks, and in a letter of September 2 to the President of the American Chemical Society had written:

> The increasing frequency with which emotional attacks are made against men and women whose ideas now are—or once were— different from those of the majority is most dangerous. Reckless, irresponsible criticism, if it goes on unchecked, could soon confine us to a mental straight-jacket. Clear and calm thinking is just as necessary on political and economic matters as it is in the chemical laboratory. Many of the ideas, social and scientific alike, which now seem axiomatic were once regarded as radical. Progress will come to an end if Americans are ever afraid to experiment boldly with new ideas.

The Secretary of State had added his voice to that of the President, and on October 18 denounced "criticism which springs from narrow political motives, criticism which is reckless and heedless of the national interest, criticism which is directed to untrue attacks on the personal character and personal loyalty and devotion of many among us."

I felt that I did well to introduce those elements into the record, for it was glaringly obvious that the LSB's judgments were being formed in the McCarthyite environment of 1951, instead of with reference to 1932. The President and Secretary Acheson were probably thinking primarily of attacks on the Administration by opposition Senators. But I had to think of the State Department's own LSB, which had made attacks on my personal character and loyalty, charged me with improper associations, and busily engaged itself for nearly a year in searching my soul (and my diaries) for dangerous thoughts. *From beginning to end of its "adjudication" of my case, however, the Board raised not one question regarding any of my 538 dispatches, cables, and memoranda on the Chinese revolu-*

tion and Sino-Soviet relations that I had extracted from the Department's official files and submitted to it as evidence, or listed for its reference. It raised no questions regarding even my long report of 1932 on Chinese Communism, which had almost certainly originally sparked some of the early speculation regarding my political leanings that had turned up as "charges." The Board in certain instances disregarded the governing regulations by— quite evidently—failing to invite their sources of "unfavorable" information to testify; it actually produced not one witness to confront me, and apparently gave little consideration to the testimony of my own witnesses. The charges were in the main clearly extracted from overall context, and the sources used would doubtless in at least some instances have provided exculpatory evidence nullifying the force of the naked allegation. However, in affront to due legal process, and in violation as well of Chairman Conrad Snow's initial assurance to me that the Board's legal officers were there not to prosecute, but would assist me should the occasion arise, the LSB introduced no exculpatory evidence—except what was turned up incidentally in my own diary entries as read into the record by the LSB in defiance of my protest.

Instead, the LSB had heaped free-ranging suspicions on top of one specific charge of a visit to the office of a leftist magazine, charges of "close and habitual association" with eleven persons the *majority* of whom I had met only a few times (and one not at all), and other vague charges of political heterodoxy taken out of their original context; and in the absence of substantive evidence the Board had sought to have me prove myself guilty, of something—of anything.

Whether the general situation was more suggestive of *Alice in Wonderland* or of an Iron Curtain country was perhaps not of prime importance; the "objective observer" might laugh, or weep, as he chose, but the matter in its essence signalled the existence of a real danger to the United States Government. In a situation in which there was no requirement that the prosecution's witnesses confront the accused and defend their accusations under cross-examination, a foreign lobby, a Whittaker Chambers, or one's personal enemy were all alike offered opportunity to manipulate a gullible Loyalty Security Board and, by planting false reports and fomenting suspicions, to destroy government officials—regardless of a record of years of proved able and faithful service—for ends inimical to the State.

X

"On All the Evidence"

Independent of extrinsic evidence, the Commission finds:

(1) That the conduct of the Moscow trials was such as to convince any unprejudiced person that no effort was made to ascertain the truth. . . .

(16) We are convinced that the alleged letters in which Trotsky conveyed alleged conspiratorial instructions to the various defendants in the Moscow trials never existed; and that the testimony condemning them is sheer fabrication. . . .

(22) We therefore find the Moscow trials to be frame-ups. . . .

(6) The failure of the prosecution to summon important witnesses was also in contravention of Soviet law as defined by Strogovich-Vyshinski:

. . . 1) that to the court sessions must be called to give testimony witnesses indicting the accused or mitigating his guilt, also those witnesses who exonerate the accused, who speak in his favor; 2) that to the court sessions must be called witnesses whose testimony is contradictory to each other or to the testimony of the accused; 3) that to the court sessions must be called witnesses upon whose testimony was based the indictment presented to the accused.

—JOHN DEWEY (Chairman, Preliminary Commission of Inquiry), *Case of Leon Trotsky: Report of Hearings on the Charges Made Against Him* . . . (New York: Harper, 1937), pp. xiii, 30.

The LSB had closed my case Thursday, November 8. Ambassador Warren left the United States to take up a new post at the end of the week. The Board must have reached its decision prior to his departure. I waited two weeks without word from the LSB. My lawyer called Humelsine's office, and was told that the Board's decision would be forthcoming "by next Friday." Nothing happened. A month dragged by. I checked with the Legal Officer sometime during that period, and received the bare explanation that it was necessary to write up the Board's rationale for its decision. One would have thought that the rationale came first, and the decision after, but again reference to *Alice In Wonderland* gives a clue:

" 'Let the jury consider their verdict,' the King said. . . .

" 'No, no!' said the Queen. 'Sentence first—verdict afterwards.' "

Christmas approached. On December 21 I was called to Humelsine's office and handed a letter containing the decision presumably reached six weeks before:

On the basis of all the evidence, the Loyalty Security Board of the Department of State has determined that no reasonable doubt exists as to your loyalty to the Government of the United States. . . . but has determined that you constitute a security risk to the Department of State. . . . The recommendation of the Board was that you be separated from employment in the Foreign Service. . . . I have reviewed the entire record in your case and concur in the findings and recommendation of the Loyalty Security Board. You will be separated from employment in the Foreign Service of the United States subject to the following.

You are advised that . . . you have a right to appeal this decision to the Secretary of State within ten calendar days after receipt of this notice and to be afforded by the Secretary, or his designee, a hearing on the record at a date not earlier than one week after receipt by the Secretary of your written notice of appeal.

You were suspended on June 27, 1951. You will remain in this status pending a final determination of this matter.

The letter bore Humelsine's signature. I read it in his presence, and said that, to my mind, the hearing record showed no evidence of bad security on my part; indeed, it showed the opposite. I asked therefore to be informed of the basis for the decision. Humelsine replied, in what should become a classic in jurisprudence, that "The Board felt that you were less than fully frank," and said that under the regulations neither the text of the Board's decision nor the particular grounds for the "determination" might be given me.

Although I had indeed rejected the LSB's none-too-subtle invitations to bare my soul in a Maoist "self-criticism," the record would show that I had replied directly and frankly, to the best of my ability, to such specific questions as the Board had been able to come up with in pursuit of its vague piddling charges. It appeared to me in fact that it had been the Board and Humelsine who had been "less than fully frank"—putting it mildly—in the handling of my case. But there was no argument to be formulated on the spot against the position Humelsine had set forth, and I left. I pondered over the recollections that Humelsine had early said that any persistence in my refusal to hand over my diaries to the LSB would possibly lead to its finding against me; and that there had been a rumor indicating some unidentified enemies were after me.

In addition to all that my family had endured during the preceding twelve months, they now had to accept this sec-

ond "Christmas present" from the LSB. Given my loyalty
clearance, it naturally was to be inferred that the LSB had
found baseless its charges that I had possessed political attitudes ranging from "mildly pink" to "100% pro-Red,"
even that I had been "friendly" to the Soviet Union and
Communism, some 15 to 20 years before; the Board had
instead "determined" that I constituted a security risk *to
the Department of State*. The problem of divination of the
LSB's rationale was a difficult one. The Department's Regulations and Procedures established that:

The standard for removal from employment in the Department of
State under Public Law 733, 81st Congress, shall be that on all
the evidence reasonable grounds exist for belief that the removal
of the officer or employee involved is necessary or advisable in
the interest of national security. The decision shall be reached
after consideration of the complete file, arguments, briefs, and
testimony presented.

"The following factors, among others," were to be taken
into account in determining a security risk:

a. Participation in one or more of the [totalitarian or subversive]
parties or movements referred to in Section 393.2a. . . .
b. Service in the governments or armed forces of enemy countries, or other voluntary activities in support of foreign governments.
c. Violations of security regulations.
d. Voluntary association with persons known or believed to be in
categories a or b of section 393.2.
e. Habitual drunkenness, moral turpitude, irresponsibility, etc.

Given the specific charges against me, the only possible
construction of the LSB's adverse finding on security
grounds was that my associations were the issue.

But that I did not know, and could not; neither law nor

logic could be relied upon for guidance through the maze of the loyalty-security procedures. The Board panel was now dissolved, its task performed. Humelsine's office had just been adversely criticized by the Loyalty Review Board for the security breach of making public the LSB's favorable determination in the case of Foreign Service Officer John S. Service, and the Department's loyalty-security authorities would remain as inscrutable as the Sphinx to any probings by me. Humelsine's "less than fully frank" was nothing on which to base an effective appeal. Since the initiation of the Department's security program, there had been five appeals against adverse security determinations—and all five had been lost. The initial odds were against any security appellant, for not only did he have to overcome the weight of the first decision and its confirmation by the Deputy Under Secretary for Administration, but his only appeal was to the Secretary of State, by whose authority the LSB and the Deputy Under Secretary functioned. (The Loyalty Review Board dealt with loyalty cases only.) The reversal of an initial adverse determination was thus a major undertaking.

Those being the conditions, I called on Secretary of State Acheson, accompanied by the lawyer who had been advising me, C. Edward Rhetts. We pointed out the impossibility of making an appeal without knowing what matters to treat. The Secretary at first assumed that I had of course been given a copy of the Board's decision, and he had to be told this was not the case. He immediately perceived the insoluble dilemma confronting anyone declared guilty but left in ignorance of both offense and grounds of the decision, and said that he would check the matter. Later that same day, he informed Rhetts that, if I appealed, I would be informed what points were at issue for the appeal process.

On January 4, 1952, I formally appealed from the LSB's adverse determination. Pointing up specifically the legal dilemma in which I found myself, I repeated my request: "that I be advised fully as to the grounds upon which the Board reached its conclusion, and if an opinion or other statement of the rationale of its conclusions was prepared by it that I be furnished a copy thereof in order that I may effectively prosecute my appeal from its decision."

On January 23, I received from the appeal officer designated by the Secretary of State, Nathaniel P. Davis, a letter responding as follows to that request:

I wish to advise you that the Loyalty Security Board does not make known to the employee or his counsel the basis of its decision which is made after consideration of the complete file, arguments, briefs, and testimony presented in the light of the security standard provided in Section 393.1 of the Departmental Regulations and Procedures. Likewise, the Board does not furnish the employee or his counsel a copy of any opinion or rationale of its decision.

However, in the interest of assisting you in the prosecution of your appeal, I wish to inform you that, after a review of the record of your case, the matters which I, as designee of the Secretary of State, consider of primary importance are as follows:

(1) The fact of and the circumstances surrounding your home leave and visit to New York City in 1932, and your recollection in this regard; and

(2) The excision, deletion, extraction, alteration, removal, omission, or rewriting, if any, of any part of your diaries, and your recollection in this regard.

The appeal officer had carefully avoided relating the LSB to the matters that he considered "of primary importance," but the rationale that the Board had utilized as "reasonable grounds" for its adverse determination had now become visible through the veil of secrecy shrouding its lucubrations.

Ambassador Davis was a career officer who was thoroughly familiar with the Foreign Service. In this respect, he differed fundamentally from the two ex-Army men, Brigadier General Snow and Lieutenant Colonel Murphy, who with Ambassador Warren, had sat in judgment on me to date. Moreover, he was responsible directly to Secretary of State Acheson, not to that other wartime Army man, Deputy Under Secretary Humelsine. Davis, like Warren, was senior to myself in years and position. His distinguished service to the United States under difficult conditions had proved his courage and his caliber. I now knew what points I had to attack in my appeal, and I knew my hearing would be before a man who would support his concern for the safety of the nation with an appreciation of the functions of a Foreign Service officer, and his sense of justice with a wide experience of international politics.

The appeal hearing was held on February 1, 1952. Experience had rammed down my throat the harsh lesson that reliance on my record and a willingness to "talk things over" were inadequate defense measures in the Department's loyalty-security processes, and I would not appear alone any more. Rhetts was preparing to go to Europe, and was unavailable. Two other Washington lawyers, Paul A. Porter and G. Duane Vieth of Arnold, Fortas and Porter, were present on February 1 as my counsel. The process began by my reviewing, under Porter's examination, my home leave and visit to New York in 1932. Porter remarked at the beginning of the session that it was quite apparent that the two matters treated in Davis' letter of Jan-

uary 23 "bear on, perhaps, or reflect the findings of the
board below." In logic, Davis could resolve the case to his
own satisfaction only by reference to both the grounds and
the rationale of the LSB's determination. His questions,
therefore, would bear a double significance: they would
be his, as appeal officer, but they would be based upon *and
include* the LSB's argumentation.

I told about my first investigations designed to establish
the precise record of my 1932 journey. There was examination:

AMBASSADOR DAVIS: It seems to me, from reading the record,
that what was troubling the Board at that time, and what has certainly troubled me in the reading of it, is not whether or not you
went to New York. That, as you say, was easy to establish, but I
am troubled by your persistant inability to remember whether
you had gone there and had gone to the "New Masses" office. . . .
. . . to put it quite bluntly, were you telling the whole truth
when you testified that you could not remember anything about
the trip, first, and then that you could remember just a little bit?
. . . It looks . . . as though you were being *less than frank* with
the Board [emphasis supplied]. I do not say it was perjury but
you perhaps were not telling the whole truth under oath, and that
is what is the issue—the question of security. Can this man be
trusted? If he lies under oath to his superiors in his own department, can he be trusted? That is what we are getting at here.

I remarked that the casual incidents of my brief 1932
visits to Washington and New York would naturally not
stand out as sharply in my mind as many events that had
occurred since:

One has to remember after all that 20 years have passed and I
have been through the floods and famines of China, civil wars,
international wars; I have served in the U.S.S.R. And it was not
my purpose to deny that I had been to Washington. It was not my

purpose to hide anything respecting my visit to Washington or
New York. I merely desired, on January 22, to establish the facts
before making my ultimate reply. . . .

MR. PORTER: You made no effort at any time to conceal.

MR. CLUBB: I made no effort to conceal any of the facts of my
visit to either Washington or New York.

MR. PORTER: . . . When you got question number 20, and
then had, as you testified, no independent recollection, then
when you checked and found that your travel orders did not call
for a trip east, could that have put some kind of mental block.
. . . Do you recall that might have entered your mind?

MR. CLUBB: It surely did in that as I noted before in this
sense that it caused to arise something in the nature of a doubt.
Could my original assumption that I had come to Washington
each time possibly be mistaken? But I didn't . . . pay a great
deal of attention to it because I knew that ultimately I would be
able to establish the facts of my visits to Washington and New
York, and it was necessary to establish then . . . the objective of
the inquiry: did I or did I not proceed to the New Masses?

. . . it was difficult for me . . . to first recognize anything in
that allegation for the one simple reason that . . . the allegation
was that I had carried a sealed envelope for a Miss Grace Hutchins. That was the crux of the matter. . . .

Ambassador Davis disclosed more of the reasoning of
the LSB.

I have to determine an appeal from the findings of the Board, that
they do not feel they can trust you. Obviously, one reason, they
do not say so but it is obvious from the record, was that *they did
not feel you were being completely frank with them in telling
them what you remembered and what you did not remember.*
[Emphasis supplied.] That is what I am getting at. Were you
being frank or were you giving only so much as you had to give
to answer their questions . . . tell them nothing for fear they
would misconstrue or because you felt this was an unfair sort of
proceeding or for any other reason, were you being deliberately,
shall we say, verging on perjury?

The LSB had evidently invented a new rule for determination that a Foreign Service Officer was a bad security risk: if he failed, not to answer specific questions and charges, but to convince a suspicious Board that he had told them all he knew regarding the events over a three-day period falling 20 years before, he might be found guilty of "lack of frankness verging on perjury." Porter then asked a question that touched upon a critical element:

MR. PORTER: Would you be willing even at this stage to plead guilty perhaps to a faulty memory?

MR. CLUBB: I should indeed, in the event that that is the charge against me. I have never claimed that my memory was infallible. In fact, if I had thought that it were infallible, I should have never kept a diary.

Davis finally said that he had no further questions in this regard, and we went on to the issue of the physical condition of my diaries. I reviewed the role played by my diaries in the whole affair. I noted that, before departing for the Soviet Union in 1944, I had first cut from my loose-leaf diary of that year certain bits that might have been of interest to the Soviet authorities had the diary fallen into their hands. But the excisions, I said, had been made approximately eight years before, and chemical analysis of the diary paper would show whether they were new or old. There was the question of alteration or rewriting. I pointed out that a motive for recopying the diaries before August 9, 1951, was lacking, given the attitude of Congressman Walter and my position in respect to the Board's (limited) request of August 1, and that there would not have been time between August 9 and the dates of delivery to do the massive job of forgery that would have been necessary.

I observed that one Legal Officer had implied that possibly diary pages had been altered after the diaries had come into the hands of the State Department, and that a question posed by the Chairman apparently evidenced a similar thought; but, I said, physical inspection of the diary pages showed a clear history of the typing from January to June 1951. Recounting for Davis my ten denials of November 7, and the extra one given November 8 for good measure, I repeated that denial that there had been any recopying. I offered again to let science prove my testimony:

> Now, you have something for use as a comparison, I have written a number of letters from January 1951 to June 1951. Most of them were written on my own typewriter . . . those that were written on my typewriter are in the LSB file and can be placed along side the diary pages of approximately the same date and a comparison made. That is a technical problem, which, it seems to me, is possible to solve. . . .

I did not say, but I had been thinking ever since receipt of the letter disclosing the LSB's suspicions against me, that it was nearly incomprehensible that the LSB should have taken action to wreck a career without itself employing all available practical and scientific methods to check its supposition, and without even informing me that an issue in addition to the original charges had arisen. *Nearly* incomprehensible—but not quite.

Davis himself described what had happened on November 7:

> The Board kept questioning you and repeating questions in the same language and slightly different language; they kept boring in, and your answer repeatedly was to the best of your knowledge and belief you had not done so.

Now, that might give the impression that you were avoiding a categorical statement for some reason.

But he took cognizance of my point that the Chairman on August 13 had said, in similar circumstances, that "All we have asked for from the beginning was the best of your recollection." And I invited attention to the psychological fact that the brain has no positive memory pattern for a negative factor, so that there can be no memory for something that never happened. As I testified to Ambassador Davis:

. . . it seems to me quite frankly that if a person speaks to the best of his recollection and his knowledge and what he has been able to derive from his logic, it is hard to demand more from him; because, truly, testimony, no more than facts, does not spring forth in full-fledged pattern like Minerva from the brow of Jove. You have to have a basis for those facts. So, when one is giving, as the Chairman said, "the best of your recollection," frankly, it seems to me adequate; you cannot go beyond. I do not know of any way in which you can go beyond it, unless you depend upon inspiration.

I had used Snow's approved phrase "to the best of my recollection" in my testimony; but he evidently had deemed his own formula inadequate. The matter now progressed speedily. Porter had me repeat my denial in categorical, legal language, and Davis shortly afterward finished with examination of this second issue.

The appeal process had incidentally performed the valuable function of bringing into striking focus the factors on which the LSB had based its determination that I constituted a security risk to the State Department. Although, given the charges against me and the pertinent regulations, it had appeared that the LSB could only have used the technical grounds of my alleged associations (including the accidental, fleeting contact with Chambers) as basis for its adverse security determination, those associations were evidently not, after all, the issue. Given the specific provision of the same regulations that, even where the employee refuses to reply to the notice of charges or to appear for a hearing "no inference or presumption should be assumed by the Board," the Board would have been hard put to prefer a charge that I had been "less than fully frank." In actuality, of course, I had been charged with neither that inferentially pernicious attitude nor with anything involving my diaries.

"All the evidence" for the LSB had patently not been the voluminous records of my work dug from the files of the United States Government, which for the Board seemingly carried no weight whatsoever, or the broad and intimate testimony of men who had known me for years. The Board at the end had abandoned its embroidered charge that I had "In 1932 delivered a sealed envelope to the office of the editor of the 'New Masses' magazine, a Communist periodical, in New York City for transmittal to one Grace Hutchins, an avowed Communist employed by the Labor Research Association, an affiliate of the Communist Party." Instead, they developed a contorted suspicion of my inability to remember, prior to recovery of the pertinent diary, the 15-minute visit in 1932 to that obscure magazine office for the casual purpose of presenting a letter of introduction—to an editor who turned out to be absent. And then, when the testimony of their prize witness, Whittaker Chambers, failed them, they had boggled at my alleged failure to state definitely in my first reply of January 22 whether I had gone to New York in 1932—though that too was no issue. The Board was in addition evidently dissatisfied with the qualification it had itself once defined as satisfactory, that what I said was "to the best of my recollection and belief." Finally, I was evidently suspected of having effected some alteration in the diaries they had seized. In sum, the Board's "reasonable grounds" were two residual, intangible suspicions that caused them to fear that I had been "less than fully frank" with them, that although I had answered all of their questions there might still be some frightful Unknown left unvolunteered and thus unsaid. There was no evidence; there was only an absence of evidence. And so, although the State Department itself had trusted me for 23 years and had shown that trust in many ways, the LSB had recommended my separation from the Foreign Service, evidently because "they do not feel that they can trust you." And this, "in the interest of national security."

The issue in respect to the Board's procedure was strikingly defined in exchanges between Porter and Davis during the former's summation:

MR. PORTER: . . . I think that this is perhaps the most unusual kind of situation or case that has come to my attention, in a rather unlimited experience in dealing with matters regarding the loyalty and security of federal employees and I would like to say at the outset that Mr. Clubb's record in the Department is a matter of established fact, and I am sure you are familiar with it. I am not going to undertake to comment on that, but I would like to direct your attention to what I think the issue that may have been in the minds of the Board below. They were not satisfied. They thought Mr. Clubb made a bad impression, perhaps, and, to put it bluntly, they felt that he was either evasive or perhaps might have even been lying.

Now, I do not want to criticize the Board or indulge in any excursion into their mental processes; but, on the two principal points we have discussed here this afternoon, it seems to me you should take into consideration, if Mr. Clubb was attempting to withhold, conceal or evade, he was not very artistic about it; and, with a man of his mentality and achievements, if he had desired to be less than frank with the Board, I am certain he would have contrived a more ingenious method of doing it. . . .

Any person who is accused of disloyalty—to me, a crime which is akin to treason—naturally goes through a period of great tension and anguish, and I do not think a man even of Mr. Clubb's experiences is immune from the type and character of reactions that I have witnessed in him as well as many others of a less important position or experience, and I am quite certain that whatever impression he may have made on the Board below was based in part upon the natural anxiety and tension that attends this kind of a situation when a man's career is in jeopardy.

Now, also, I will direct your attention to the circumstance that Mr. Clubb, while he had advice of counsel at the hearing below, his counsel was not present, but a colleague in the service was present. . . .

I have read the record and this is no reflection on Mr. Clubb, but I was impressed, again, by the old maxim that a lawyer who represents himself has a fool for a client. It has been my experience in dealing with these matters . . . that the duty of counsel— and they are indispensable in this type of case—is partly that of a lawyer to see that the record is prepared, to see that the exhibits are complete, and to see that the employee responds to the issue. But, again, he has another function; again, I might describe that of a psychiatrist. The reactions of people who are accused of this type of an offense do not place them in a position where they can adequately represent themselves. . . .

Now, I would like to direct briefly to your attention the requirements that are in the security standard. In Section 393.1, the Secretary has determined, in accordance with Public Law 733, that your findings and his findings must be on all the evidence, and that evidence must establish that reasonable grounds exist for the belief that the removal of the officer or employee involved is necessary or advisable in the interest of national security.

Now, I submit that there is nothing in this record, nor anything that has been developed this afternoon, that offers any evidentiary basis for any conclusion or finding that Mr. Clubb should be classified as a security risk; that we cannot make this conclusion, nor do I believe that the Board below is warranted in making this conclusion because of some intangible impression that they may have had. This phrase is not without significance. "All the evidence" could not be empty and meaningless.

. . . this procedure has been established and, therefore, it seems to me that it is incumbent upon the Secretary and yourself to follow the basic principles of due process. That is not to say that you may not consider hearsay, that inferences are not permissible, but just all the evidence means that there must be some probative facts, and not these impressions, that this man is guilty of some of the allegations and the categories that are developed further on in the order.

AMBASSADOR DAVIS: May I interrupt. The rules of evidence, of course, do not apply here. Is it not true that my responsibility as the Secretary's designee in hearing this appeal is to establish, to put it in non-technical terms—in my own mind whether or not Mr. Clubb can be trusted in positions of responsibility. Otherwise I am to pass on a finding that his employment is a security risk, *but what makes his employment a security risk is not necessarily what he may or may not have done in the past. It is what I have reasonable ground for believing he may do in the future. The risk is something for the future.* [Emphasis supplied.]

MR. PORTER: But you have to base that, sir, upon all the evidence. . . .

AMBASSADOR DAVIS: From all the evidence and facts and circumstances; it is put in very broad language.

MR. PORTER: But let me make this clear, that, as I see the term, and the same term is used in Executive Order 9835 on which the loyalty procedures are based and under Section 5 of that order, it is stated that for the protection of the Government, and for the equal protection of the employee, the findings must be made on all the evidence.

I take the position that, the mere fact that the Board believed that Mr. Clubb might not have been telling the whole truth, they must establish that by some evidentiary standard and by some fact upon which this inference can be developed.

AMBASSADOR DAVIS: May I interrupt. The rules of evidence, of course, do not apply here. Is it not true that my responsibility as the Secretary's designee in hearing this appeal is to establish to put it in non-technical terms--in my own mind whether or not Mr. Clubb can be trusted in positions of responsibility. Otherwise I am to pass on a finding that his employment is a security risk, but what makes his employment a security risk is not necessarily what he may or may not have done in the past. It is what I have reasonable ground for believing he may do in the future. The risk is something in the future.

MR. PORTER: But you have to base that sir. upon all the evidence.

AMBASSADOR DAVIS: Yes. Now, if I base that on a finding. it is on my shoulders to determine whether I think he is a liar. I do not believe he told the truth; so, then I can't trust him. Now, that is not following the rules of evidence, but isn't that what I am called upon to do?

MR. PORTER: No, sir; I would not concede that. If you have a subjective impression---

Extract from transcript of the appeal hearing, February 1, 1952

There was further exchange between counsel and the appeal officer respecting this point, and then Porter cited a precedent:

MR. PORTER: . . . at the Nurnberg trials, the President's own tribunal convicted eight Nazi judges because they received secret dossiers from the Gestapo for political prisoners for which there was no opportunity to examine, no opportunity to know the details of the charges.

Well, Justice Jackson, as the head of the President's own tribunal, sent those eight Nazi judges to jail for a period of eight years.

And then this eminent jurist finished his summation:

I said this term ["on all the evidence"] . . . has got to have some meaning . . . and furthermore, I don't believe or do not concede that you, in your own responsibilities, can say, "Well, I have some feeling, I have some uneasiness; I feel uncomfortable about the matter, and, therefore, perhaps there is in my own mind a reasonable doubt." Even that reasonable doubt has got to be based upon all the evidence, and it cannot be some attenuated kind of concept. . . .

It seems to me that the Board, perhaps subconsciously, permitted its own resentment to enter into its conclusions because their belief or their feeling was that Mr. Clubb was not cooperative, was not being exactly precise with them. We have not seen the opinion. We do not know what their findings are. I do not know of the process by which they reached their conclusions.

However, one thing has occurred to me, and that is the fact that, well, here is Mr. Clubb. His diary is under subpoena; he has been before the House Committee, before the Senate Committee, and here is a matter of some controversy. He had the misfortune to labor in a part of the world which has been under, as we all recognize, a great dispute. Those who had some participation there have been targets, and whether those things went on in the Board's mind, I have no way of knowing. . . .

I say, on the basis of this record, there is no more to support a finding here, than where in the case of a chicken thief or pickpocket, given the rudiments of our due process, more specific allegations would be required before an adverse finding could be sustained.

I just want to say one final thing, and that is directed toward the question of morale of our foreign service, and of the government itself. I think perhaps the reason that some of us as private lawyers interest ourselves in these private matters is not only to protect the basic civil rights of persons who may be involved, but also to try to make some contribution against what at times seems to me to have been the real secret weapon of our enemy.

There is nothing in this record but suspicion. . . .

. . . it seems to me, unless there is definite probative proof and something that is more than suspicion both from the standpoint of individual rights and for the good of the service, this finding of the Board below has got to be reversed and Mr. Clubb's vindication upheld.

Davis himself commented upon the regulations and the established procedures, and granted that his finding "must be based on something tangible." He remarked that the finding of the LSB was a part of the evidence, that after presumed deliberations they had voted, "and the *majority* vote was against Mr. Clubb." (Emphasis supplied.) All logic now suggested to me that the military men Snow and Murphy had voted against me, whereas veteran diplomatist Fletcher Warren, who knew what the Foreign Service was all about, had voted in my favor.

Davis soon thereafter announced the end of the appeal hearing. On February 7, six days later, in refreshing contrast to the months the LSB had dawdled, another letter from Humelsine conveyed to me the appeal decision:

On January 18, 1952 the Secretary designated Mr. Nathaniel P. Davis to consider your appeal . . . from the decision of the Loyalty Security Board of the Department of State that you be sepa-

rated from employment in the Foreign Service as constituting a
security risk to the Department of State. . . .

   . . . After consideration of all the evidence, . . . Mr. Davis has
found that no reasonable doubt exists as to your security risk to
the Department of State and that therefore your removal from
employment in the Foreign Service is not necessary or advisable
in the interest of national security.

   The Secretary has reviewed and concurred in Mr. Davis' findings.

Adjudication by another professional diplomat had given
me victory, but I was under no illusions as to my position
in the State Department hierarchy: it was fundamentally
changed. As the *American Foreign Service Journal* had observed editorially the previous August: "The person so
besmirched [by a loyalty process] can never obtain full
retribution, nor can the government regain the full value
of his services." Further, the well-known case of China
Service officer John S. Service had demonstrated beyond
cavil that "clearance" did not at all mean a definite end to
the matter. Service had been dragged through hearing
after hearing before grand jury, Congressional committee,
and LSB, from 1945 to 1951. Cleared six times by the LSB
on the same charges, he was finally discharged summarily
in December 1951 when the Loyalty Review Board decided that any failure on their part to doubt his loyalty
would be extending "the mantle of charity" too far. It was
to take Jack Service years of arduous litigation, with ultimate recourse to the Supreme Court, to win reversal of
the Loyalty Review Board's action and reinstatement in
the U.S. Foreign Service; and his legal costs added up to
seventy thousand dollars. The loyalty of a Whittaker
Chambers and the patriotism and bona fides of a partisan
politician might be considered beyond doubt; but in the

DEPARTMENT OF STATE

WASHINGTON

ADDRESS OFFICIAL COMMUNICATIONS TO
THE SECRETARY OF STATE
WASHINGTON 25, D. C.

FEB 7 1952

My dear Mr. Clubb:

On January 18, 1952 the Secretary designated Mr.
Nathaniel P. Davis to consider your appeal, requested
by your letter of January 4, 1952, from the decision of
the Loyalty Security Board of the Department of State
that you be separated from employment in the Foreign
Service as constituting a security risk to the Department
of State under the security standard and principles provided in Section 393 of Departmental Regulations and
Procedures.

On February 1, 1952 you, accompanied by counsel,
were duly heard before Mr. Davis. After consideration
of all the evidence, including that adduced at the appeal
hearing, Mr. Davis has found that no reasonable doubt
exists as to your security risk to the Department of
State and that therefore your removal from employment
in the Foreign Service is not necessary or advisable
in the interest of national security.

The Secretary has reviewed and concurred in Mr.
Davis' findings.

The Secretary's decision on the question of your
security is conclusive and final; however, the favorable
determination by the Loyalty Security Board on the question of your loyalty is subject to a post-audit review
by the Loyalty Review Board.

Under the authority of Public Law 733, 81st Congress,
you were suspended from active duty effective June 27,
1951, close of business. In view of the favorable determination in your case, and under authority of Public
Law 733, 81st Congress, you are hereby restored to active
duty and assigned to the Division of Historical Research,
effective February 8, 1952.

Sincerely yours,

For the Secretary of State:

Carlisle H. Humelsine
Deputy Under Secretary

Mr. Oliver Edmund Clubb,
1635 Madison Street, N.W.,
Washington, D. C.

CONFIDENTIAL

Letter of official clearance, February 7, 1952

new age of suspicion a Foreign Service officer who had been dragged publicly through the loyalty-security process found it extraordinarily difficult to redeem his reputation for loyalty and integrity. Such officer's position and career remained ever after in multiple jeopardy.

Those things had been uppermost in our minds since June 27, when I told my State Department chief, Assistant Secretary of State for Far Eastern Affairs Dean Rusk, that any publicity attending the LSB's action would surely destroy my usefulness. After the Department made the matter public on July 12, and Congressional committees had warmed up to the task, I knew that it would be impossible for me to recover my former standing. That the Department's administrative authorities were not insensitive to the changes their process had wrought was shown unmistakably by the last sentence of Humelsine's letter conveying Secretary of State Acheson's clearance: "In view of the favorable determination of your case, . . . you are hereby restored to active duty and assigned to the Division of Historical Research, effective February 8, 1952." I had been found innocent, but was put on the shelf, damaged goods, to be out of the way. I would now presumably be permitted to lend a hand at compiling the State Department's historical records, but I was no longer to participate in the making of history.

I could have dragged miserably on in the Service, "cleared" but not rehabilitated, subject to the buffetings of members of Congress and always open to new harassment by the LSB on the same or other grounds at any time an enemy might plant a malicious report with the FBI. Actually, given the LSB's disregard for chronological differences affecting orthodoxy and heterodoxy, it was entirely conceivable that at some time in the years ahead when the official line might have changed, the Board might charge me (or anyone else) with having attitudes exactly the opposite of those I was charged with harboring in the 1930s. It could with equal facility charge in the altered domestic circumstances of some uncertain future that I had been at some time or other "unfriendly toward the Soviet Union," had spoken "in favor of Chiang Kai-shek" in the early 1920s, or had had "close and habitual association" with a variety of *conservative* personalities solemnly described in the charge, let us say as hypothesis, as having opposed the rapprochement of the United States with Communist China. Under existing conditions, any optimistic view of my future in the U.S. Foreign Service would have been gross self-delusion.

There was one further consideration. In a full year of interrogatory and formal hearings, my feelings had been badly bruised. I felt that the Government of which I had long been a part had been disloyal *to me*. The State Department had not lived up to the spirit of the President's commission to repose "special trust and confidence" in my "Integrity, Prudence and Ability"; rather, through its Loyalty Security Board, in blatant disregard of my record of faithful and fruitful service, it had viewed me with inordinate suspicion. One admittedly could not claim the privileges of due legal process under the loyalty-security system, but the Board had violated even the procedures laid down in the Department's own regulations. So I saw good reason in principle, too, for leaving the U.S. Foreign Service.

Thus principle joined with practical considerations to determine the choice facing Mariann and me. Hard as it was to give up a career that we had selected for a lifetime, we were agreed on the final decision. In a letter of February 11 to the Secretary of State, I took due note of my clearance in respect to security, and loyalty, and my restoration to active duty under assignment to the Division of Historical Research. And I said:

> I invite attention to the circumstance that, even given the aforementioned verification of my loyalty and security, my Foreign Service career prospects have indubitably been seriously damaged by the loyalty-security process itself. I therefore having reference to my eligibility for retirement . . . respectfully request your consent to my retirement from the Foreign Service, . . . effective as from tomorrow, February 12, 1952. . . .

I thought that the selection of Lincoln's Birthday as the date for beginning my retirement was singularly fitting.

My request for retirement was granted the same day, and the Department issued a chary official pronouncement regarding the matter. There were no bouquets handed out for faithful service, and no regrets expressed at my departure. The announcement made no reference to the LSB's initial adverse finding in respect to my security, and I naturally followed that lead in my own subsequent statement of February 11 to the press. My friends, and newspapermen who knew the circumstances respected my position that any fuller explanation should come from the State Department. They breached no confidence. The next information from the State Department, however, seems to have come in the common manner of a leak to Congress. On February 26, while the McCarran Committee was grilling Owen Lattimore, Senator Ferguson asked the witness if he knew that Secretary of State Acheson had "set aside the ruling of the board and freed [sic] Mr. Clubb."

CLUBB IS CLEARED BUT THEN RETIRES

State Department Loyalty Unit Absolves Ex-China Chief — He Sees Career Crippled

By FELIX BELAIR Jr.
Special to THE NEW YORK TIMES.

WASHINGTON, Feb. 11—Oliver Edmund Clubb, formerly head of the State Department's Office of Chinese Affairs, was cleared today by the agency's Loyalty and Security Board of charges that led to his suspension by Secretary Dean Acheson last June 27.

In his statement following the department's announcement of his resignation today, Mr. Clubb said:

"As announced, I have been cleared by State Department processes of the charges laid against me on June 27, 1951, by the Department's Loyalty Security Board and was restored to active duty effective Feb. 8, 1952.

Recalls History of Case

"Traditional American principles clearly give me the right, and as a citizen and public official I feel that I have a certain obligation, to make a brief statement at this juncture.

"Having now been cleared, there would seem to be little point in reviewing the course of the matter in detail. I would simply say that in main I relied upon the voluminous written record of my work and service, and the testimony of persons who had known me for years, to combat the charges.

That positive evidence has evidently sufficed for the purpose.

"I and my family have been sustained in good part, in this process which has consumed so much of my time and energy during the thirteen months of its duration, by the confidence and sympathy of our friends, but at best the process has been tedious and trying.

"It is moreover clear from precedents that the present clearance does not automatically restore me to my previous career standing and protect me from future jeopardy on the same or similar grounds.

Says Usefulness Is Impaired

"I am compelled reluctantly to recognize that the circumstances attendant upon the very process which resulted in my clearance have actually combined to render it most difficult for me to continue to contribute in full measure from my experience and trained capacities to the work of the State Department as a foreign service officer, have in short impaired my present usefulness.

"I face the unavoidable conclusion, at last, that the same loyalty-security process, while resulting in my vindication, has seriously damaged my future career prospects in the Foreign Service. As it was succinctly put by the August, 1951, Foreign Service Journal editorial, 'The Cost Is Too High': 'The person so besmirched [by a loyalty process] can never obtain full retribution, nor can the Government regain the full value of his services.'

"It is with deepest regret that I therefore have adopted the only appropriate course which apparently remained to me, and have exercised the option which is mine by reason of my age and years of service, and with the consent of the Secretary of State have retired from the American Foreign Service. I retire proud of my record of twenty-three years in that service, and confident that that record will stand by itself."

Extracts from a **New York Times** news story, February 12, 1952

This was the signal for the leveling of a new barrage against the luckless State Department, and a number of Senators and Congressmen immediately leaped into the fray. There were new charges impugning the integrity of Secretary Acheson, and Senators McCarran and Ferguson joined forces to demand that a Congressional committee should look into the case. Representative Lawrence A. Smith of Wisconsin called for Acheson's dismissal. None discussed any charges against me. For the critics this apparently was no issue. It seemed to be assumed that, being a "China expert" in the targeted State Department, I must naturally be guilty. It was even suggested that my modest pension ought to be cut off. At this point, Mariann acidly remarked that "They will be wanting your skin for lampshades next."

The matter was now between the Senators and the State Department, which in effect had been charged with malfeasance. The Secretary stood his ground, and was backed up by the President, who on April 3 rebuffed the final move of the Senate troublemakers by instructing Secretary Acheson to withhold from a Senate Appropriations subcommittee (headed by Senator McCarran with Senators Ferguson and McCarthy both members) the Department files it had requested on loyalty and security investigations of employees. The result of compliance with such request, said the President's letter, would be to wreck the Federal employees' loyalty program. "In the process," the President wrote, "the reputations of hundreds of loyal employes would be pilloried and the entire Civil Service would be seriously demoralized." The validity of his statement was confirmed by the record of what had happened after the State Department initially gave publicity to Davies' and my cases.

Certain interpretations that appeared in the columns of the current press merit recording. The *Minneapolis Tribune* of March 9, referring to the Congressional demands for an investigation of my case, observed in passing that "it was learned . . . that Clubb's associations with several of the 'Americans and foreign nationals' mentioned above [in my February 11 press release] had continued after his return from China in June 1950, and that these associations formed the main basis for the board determination that he was a 'security risk.' " It *had* been easy to infer from the LSB's grilling respecting my "associations" that it demanded of me that compliance given by Balak to Balaam: "I wot that he whom thou blessest is blessed, and he whom thou cursest is cursed." And I had refused that obeisance.

Columnist David Lawrence had hinted at the upcoming news prior to Ferguson's posing of his leading question. Writing February 24 on "Loyalty Board of State Department Found to Have Puzzling Rules," Lawrence made reference to "an individual who was ordered dismissed by the State Department Loyalty and Security Board," and remarked in regard to the case that "there are rumors that some persons inside the department held a grudge against him." I had reached the same conclusion.

Given the mounting fury of the postwar attacks on the Government's "China Policy," and the strange coincidence that the major "loyalty-security" storms affecting senior Foreign Service Officers had centered in the China area—affecting officers like Service, Vincent, Davies and myself—the editorial comment of the *Washington Post* of March 7, 1952 was of especial interest: "The China Lobby has now succeeded in wrecking Mr. Clubb's career as a Foreign Service officer and in staining his reputation. This is punishment enough for his having dared to report events as he saw them during his 23 years of devoted service in the Far East."

Senator McCarthy had not been quite agile enough to catch the bus when my case became public knowledge in July 1951, and had admitted that he had not demanded an investigation of me. He was now to undertake to adopt me ex post facto. In an interview-type article published under his name in the May 1952 *Cosmopolitan* magazine, in response to the question "Can you give the names of some of those who have been removed from Government service as a result of your proof?" McCarthy stoutly answered "Yes"—and included my name along with those of other claimed victims. He said that I had been "cleared by both the Tydings Committee and the State Department," then had been ruled against by the LSB, whereupon "Dean Acheson overruled his Loyalty Board and gave Clubb a clean bill of health," and I had immediately "resigned." He did not cite his "proof," or note where and how it was brought forth.

In his *McCarthyism: The Fight for America*,[1] McCarthy gave the matter further adornment. He set up another question for himself: "All of those you named before the Tydings Committee were cleared by that committee. Since then have any of them been removed from government on the grounds that they were either disloyal or bad security risks?" (p. 13). McCarthy gave essentially the same answer as before; but he eliminated "the State Department," which left me cleared only by the Tydings Committee, and he added a footnote: "While I gave the Tydings Com-

[1] New York: Devin-Adair, 1952.

mittee information on Clubb, he was not one of the 81 cases." Later in the book, citing it as one item in Secretary of State Acheson's record, McCarthy expanded on his footnote:

Evidence on Clubb was given to the Tydings Committee, but he was not called to testify, nor was any part of the evidence checked by the Committee. He was part of the group given a blanket clearance by the Tydings Committee. He was later called before both the McCarran Committee and the House Committee on Un-American Activities. (pp. 29–30)

The fact of the matter is that the transcript of the hearings of the Tydings Committee (created by the Senate Foreign Relations Committee in February 1950 to determine whether disloyal personnel were or had been employed in the State Department) contains no record of mention of me by McCarthy (or by anyone else, as far as that goes) and, since I was admittedly not one of the "81 cases" and was not included among the specific cases considered by the Committee, the question naturally arises: when and in what manner did McCarthy give information regarding me to the Tydings Committee, and what was the nature of that information—which he was quoted on July 12, 1951 as saying did not merit his demanding an investigation?

No answer is available. But, the flimsiness of his materials notwithstanding, McCarthy continued to build. Speaking at the University of Minnesota, my own alma mater, on March 8, 1952, the Senator dealt extensively with our "suicidal foreign policy." He lamented that 600,000 "friendly troops" on Formosa were being prevented by the U.S. 7th Fleet from attacking the mainland, fought again his battles with (absent) Owen Lattimore and

others in the State Department and out, and all the time
hinted at treason. In view of the current publicity attending my name, some of the audience took the opportunity
offered by the question-and-answer period to get the Senator's opinion on the matter, and there ensued an exchange
along substantially the following lines:

Q. Just what was Clubb guilty of besides predicting that the
Communists would win in China, reporting things as he saw
them, and walking into a Communist magazine office?
A. Clubb was guilty of about the same thing that Service and
Jessup and all those who have been promoted by Acheson were
guilty of, guilty of helping to plan the sell-out of China. At no
time did Clubb raise his voice. . . . About three years ago Clubb
did come back and for a while it appeared that he was objecting
to a sell-out. . . . He was part of a group that planned every step
leading up to the Korean war, did part of the planning. Clubb
wasn't high in that group. If he had been he would have been
protected. He wouldn't have been kicked out. He was part of the
group which in effect signed the death warrant of every American boy who died in Korea since the 26th of June.
Q. Do you consider him a traitor?
A. It is a question of what your definition of a traitor is . . .
[reference to Acheson] All I know is that they shouldn't be there.
. . . Which of these men are in the class that take thirty pieces of
silver and which think Communism is the answer to the world's
problems, I don't know.

It was easy to see, from the Senator's last reply, that he
had suddenly felt the need for some Congressional immunity for what he was saying. But men before and after
Goebbels have known that calumny and lies, once
launched, go a long way. And they often grow with the
telling.

Jay David Whittaker Chambers remained near Washington, available to Senators and loyalty-security boards for

the evoking of new specters of Communism. His book *Witness* was published in 1952, and was accorded a mixed reception. Two reviews seem worthy of note. Senator Richard M. Nixon, who had been a member of the House Un-American Activities Committee when it dealt with the Hiss case, found the book good for the lesson it bore— "that men become Communists out of the best of motives and some of them cease to be Communists for the same motives when they learn that those who accept the pernicious doctrine of the end justifying the means will inevitably find that the means become the end." Looking at the author, he raised the question: "How can one have any respect for a man who admits that he didn't tell the whole story the first time he appeared before the [Un-American Activities] Committee? He gave his answer, "not . . . in justification but in extenuation": "Is it not better to tell the whole truth in the end than to refuse as Hiss to tell the truth at all?" [2]

Another critic in the same issue of the *Saturday Review* was of a different mind. Professor Charles Alan Wright [3] held that Chambers had depicted himself "too-well-scrubbed," expressed the conviction that *Witness* was "one of the longest works of fiction of the year," and suggested that the author would "do well to study the Ninth Commandment: 'Thou shalt not bear false witness. . . .'" And he pointed up what he considered a fundamental problem in the Hiss case in which Chambers had played so large a part: "for all of our fine legal doctrine to the con-

[2] Richard M. Nixon, "Plea for an Anti-Communist Faith," *Saturday Review*, May 24, 1952, pp. 12–13.

[3] In 1973, Charles Alan Wright was President Richard M. Nixon's legal counsel in the Watergate affair.

trary, in fact the burden of proof was on Hiss to prove his innocence, rather than on the Government to prove him guilty." [4]

So things went for Chambers, the ex-Communist. I, who had for some two decades reported to the U.S. Government on living developments in the same general field of revolution, but with relation to the Far East, packed my bags. On April 14, almost exactly two years since we had left Peking, Mariann and I departed from Washington into retirement, to count the cost and to endeavor to reorient the lives that we had constructed in a pattern fitting the career promised by the American Foreign Service back in 1928. And on my back I bore "a mark like a cross."

---

[4] Charles Alan Wright, " 'A Long Work of Fiction,' " *ibid.*, pp. 11–12.

XI

The Oligarchical Complex
and Foreign Policy

This conjunction of an immense military establishment
and a large arms industry is new in the American
experience. The total influence—economic, political,
even spiritual—is felt in every city, every State House,
every office of the Federal Government. We recognize
the imperative need for this development. Yet we must
not fail to comprehend its grave implications. Our toil,
resources, and livelihood are all involved; so is the very
structure of our society.

In the councils of government, we must guard against
the acquisition of unwarranted influence, whether
sought or unsought, by the military-industrial complex.
The potential for the disastrous rise of misplaced power
exists and will persist. We must never let the weight of
this combination endanger our liberties or democratic
processes.

—PRESIDENT DWIGHT D. EISENHOWER, farewell address
to the American people, January 17, 1961.

In the quarter century since the Cold War began,
since the government inaugurated its loyalty-security program, and since partisan demagoguery loosed its furies on
the government's decision-making process, there has been
an inexorable trend toward oversimplification in strate-

gic thinking—and thus toward fundamental error. Mc-
Carthyism was characterized by the total absence of scru-
ples, sense of justice, and common honesty; mendacity
was its very essence. The loyalty-security program dead-
ened initiative, and fostered conformism, in the career
Foreign Service charged with reporting and interpreting
events in the foreign field. The history of the Cold War
period discloses with startling clarity the devastating effect
of those forces upon the bureaucracy of the State Department, on the Asia policy of the United States, on the nation's world position—and finally upon the nation itself.

By February 1952, when I left the U.S. Foreign Service,
the State Department had handled 604 loyalty-security
cases, and had given clearance in nearly one-half of the
cases without submitting interrogatories or preferring
charges; 54 hearings had actually been held, with eleven
employees separated as security risks, but in no case thus
far had a man been judged disloyal. The danger to the
Republic had evidently been appreciably less than depicted by the demagogues. By that time, however, the
loyalty-security process, together with appurtenant threats
and fears, had become a permanent part of the machinery
of government.

In the Presidential campaign of that year, the Republicans predictably exploited the "China Question" and
forced upon their Democratic opponents the issue set forth
in the McCarthyite charge of "Communism in government." Republican candidate Dwight D. Eisenhower won.
With the inauguration of the new Administration, John
Foster Dulles began his career as Secretary of State by
calling for the "positive loyalty" of State Department
and Foreign Service officers for policies fixed by the Con-

gress and the Administration. The career bureaucrats could readily perceive that dissent would thereafter be viewed as tantamount to *dis*loyalty. Such linking of dissent to the loyalty factor would tend naturally to discourage any impulse to disagree with estimates—or with proposals respecting policy. That urge toward conformity would be strengthened by the growing practice within and between departments of the mushrooming Executive structure of striving to arrive at a "consensus" on questions of policy. Given the Cold War commitment to resort to the ultimate, nuclear force if need be to protect elements of the "free world," the consensus increasingly reflected the military element. Those several factors combined to reinforce dangerously the inherent bureaucratic tendency not to challenge a policy that had been adopted by the decision of the government's highest officials, even when it was demonstrably wrong.

The new Administration refined (if that is the word) the loyalty-security program, and applied it in a spirit that resulted in a further corruption of the policy-making process. Dulles's top security officer, former FBI man R. W. Scott McLeod, told an American Legion meeting in Topeka that the State Department was endeavoring to replace employees "whose viewpoint does not coincide with that of the Republican Party." And in fact Dulles ruthlessly cast more Foreign Service martyrs to the McCarthyite lions: loyal officers were struck down for their past reporting and political analyses, however accurate, apparently their unwelcome opinions. John Paton Davies, Jr., cleared by the LSB in 1951, was in 1954 dismissed from the Foreign Service as a security risk. Dulles explained the action by saying that Davies' performance was "not in accordance

with the standard required of Foreign Service officers."
He used effectively the same rationale to force the retirement of veteran China Service officer John Carter Vincent, with three decades of service to his credit. The loss
of skilled, experienced personnel seemingly did not trouble the Republican Secretary of State: he made it abun-
dantly clear at the start that he proposed to formulate the
nation's foreign policy himself, without reference to "area
experts."

If dissenting opinions and judgments were to be viewed
as prima facie evidence of disloyalty or security risk, how
was the government to obtain candid, objective views from
its officers regarding the Soviet Union, China, Southeast
Asia—or indeed any area where the official enemy, "Communism," might be present? The potential of the situation
was duly pointed up by five distinguished retired American diplomats, who expressed their concern in a letter of
January 1954 to the *New York Times:*

. . . a Foreign Service Officer who reports on persons and events
to the very best of his ability, and who makes recommendations
which at the time he conscientiously believes to be in the interest of the United States, may subsequently find his loyalty and
integrity challenged and may even be forced out of the service
and discredited forever as a private citizen after many years of
distinguished service. A premium therefore has been put upon
reporting and upon recommendations which are ambiguously
stated or so cautiously set forth as to be deceiving.

When any such tendency begins its insidious work, it is not
long before accuracy and initiative have been sacrificed to ac-
ceptability and conformity. The ultimate result is a threat to national security.[1]

[1] Letter to the Editor from Ambassadors Norman Armour, Robert Woods
Bliss, Joseph C. Grew, and William Phillips, and sometime Chief of the
Division of Foreign Service Personnel and Assistant Secretary of State G.
Howland Shaw, *New York Times,* Jan. 17, 1954.

This analysis was supported by the Secretary of State's Public Committee on Personnel, comprising eight outstanding personalities (most of whom had served in high positions in the Department of State). It found for one thing that "The morale of that [Foreign] Service today stands in need of repair." Why? The Committee referred briefly in passing to various pertinent elements and then came to the crux of the matter by observing that another factor had been at work, "one that until the recent past has been generally unknown to the experience of Government servants, namely, the Government's security program." [2]

Writing with the benefit of hindsight, the author of the loyalty-security program, ex-President Truaman, in due course gave indirect support to the Committee's analysis with his description of the consequent corruption of the policy-making process:

In such circumstances, key government employees tend to become mentally paralyzed. They are afraid to express honest judgments, as it is their duty to do, because later, *under a changed atmosphere and different circumstances, they may be charged with disloyalty by those who disagree with them.* Our nation cannot afford or permit such a mental blackout. [3] [Emphasis supplied]

The Public Committee on Personnel, in summing up, had issued a basic warning:

If the security program is to achieve its true purpose of protecting the Government and the American way of life, it must be so ad-

[2] *Toward a Stronger Foreign Service, Report of the Secretary of State's Public Committee on Personnel June 1954*, Dept. of State Publication 5458, Department and Foreign Service Series 36, released June 1954, Division of Publications, Dept. of State, p. 3.

[3] Harry S. Truman, *Memoirs*, 2 vols. (New York: Doubleday, 1956), vol. II, *Years of Trial and Hope*, p. 285.

ministered that it does not impair the things it is designed to preserve. And among the things that must be protected for the Foreign Service is the tradition of frank and objective reporting that long has constituted one of the State Department's most enduring sources of strength.[4]

Ex-President Truman, experienced American diplomats, and the State Department's own study group were thus in agreement that the loyalty-security program was having a deleterious effect on the U.S. Foreign Service in particular. Despite the warnings, the malady persisted. This was confirmed by a Senate Foreign Relations Committee study of U.S. foreign policy made five years after the State Department committee's report. The Senate Committee's investigators had invited a selected group of retired U.S. Foreign Service officers, not identified, to submit their views on American foreign policy. The answers were naturally far-ranging. But one of the strongest criticisms had reference to the impact of the loyalty-security program on the Foreign Service:

Until recent years diplomatic and consular officers of all ranks in the field were encouraged to report objectively and to make recommendations in accordance with their best judgment. . . . Now all that is changed. It is common knowledge in the Department of State and in the Foreign Service that Foreign Service officers have been reprimanded and even heavily penalized for making reports or recommendations unpalatable to certain persons in the Department and that they have been ordered not to repeat the offense. Foreign Service officers have been known to state that under present conditions it is unwise to the point of foolishness to send in dispatches which, because of the inclusion of unwelcome facts or unwelcome recommendations, will be displeasing to officers of the Department.[5]

[4] *Public Committee Report*, p. 5.

[5] *Study of United States Foreign Policy, Summary of Views of Retired Foreign Service Officers Prepared for the Committee on Foreign Rela-*

Another correspondent gave a graphic picture of the physical surveillance of officials that was a part of the day-by-day operation of the security system:

The exaggeration beyond all reasonable limits of the attempt to achieve security in Government personnel is one of the greatest misfortunes of our times. The Department of State and the Foreign Service of the United States have been among the principal victims. . . . it must not be forgotten that the security program has become institutionalized. There is a large organized body of men in the Department of State—I have no knowledge of their present number but they were several hundreds a few years ago—whose sole business is to spy upon and report upon their colleagues and associates. It can hardly be supposed that these men, many of whom have little capacity for anything else, have ceased the practices which they were originally organized to perform. I know that desks were periodically searched, that private correspondence, even while going through the mails, was opened and read, that telephones were tapped, that servants were asked to spy upon their employers, that secretaries were asked to report on the men for whom they worked, and that Foreign Service Officers were asked to make a practice of spying upon and reporting anonymously upon their colleagues. I do not know whether it is true or not but it is very generally supposed that listening devices were installed far and wide in offices and presumably also in private homes. It must be emphasized that these activities were directed not against persons individually suspected of disloyalty but were directed at the generality of officers and employees in the Foreign Service and in the Department of State. It was widely believed, and I think correctly, that much of the information collected by these nefarious means was used for purposes that had no relation to the loyalty and security program. . . . That such a system is susceptible of abuse and that outrageous abuses have actually occurred cannot be denied.[6]

---

tions, United States Senate, Pursuant to the provisions of S. Res. 31, 86th Cong. 1st sess., June 15, 1959 (Washington, U.S. Government Printing Office, 1959), p. 41.

[6] *Ibid.,* p. 51.

In sum, the U.S. Government had come to the point of demanding that its foreign-affairs officers should not disagree with the established policy line or present unpalatable reports, and it had established a degrading system of surveillance over its officials to make sure that there was in fact no circulation of unorthodox views.

That was the loyalty-security situation as it existed in 1959. John Foster Dulles died that year; Senator Joseph R. McCarthy had died two years earlier. The conclusive judgment with respect to McCarthy's campaign against "Communists in government" was bluntly voiced by a special Senate subcommittee, which investigated his activities and concluded that his conduct had been "contemptuous, contumacious, denunciatory, unworthy, inexcusable, and reprehensible." Vice President Richard M. Nixon acted to get the Senate as a body to omit the word "censure" from its condemnation of the reprehensible Senator, but Joe McCarthy died disgraced. Dulles contrariwise died honored. But there was no restoration, under the Eisenhower Administration, of departmental and Foreign Service morale and performance to the status quo ante McCarthyism and the loyalty-security program.

In the meantime, its internal critics largely silenced, the U.S. Government had continued unchecked along its mistaken course in foreign affairs. John Foster Dulles, motivated by an evangelical anti-Communism, had early consolidated the American position in its Cold War stance. In a broadcast statement of January 27, 1953, Dulles voiced the nation's peaceful intent; but he said something else notably more on the national-mission line: "To all those suffering under Communist slavery, to the timid and intimidated peoples of the world, let us say this, you can count

upon us." Here was clear promise of expanded commitments. Dulles proposed to bring salvation to the world.

The Korean War was indeed brought to a close, as Candidate Dwight D. Eisenhower had pledged during the
election campaign; however, before the year was out the
United States had reached an agreement to extend additional aid to France for "intensified prosecution" of the
war against the Vietminh. When, contrary to the expectations of the Administration, the Indochina situation wors-
ened for the French, Dulles in early 1954 evolved his
"massive retaliation" doctrine. In an address before the
Overseas Press Club in New York, he warned the Communist adversaries:

Under the conditions of today the imposition on Southeast Asia
of the political system of Communist Russia and its Chinese
Communist ally, by whatever means, would be a grave threat to
the whole free community. The United States feels that that possibility should not be passively accepted, but should be met by
united action. This might have serious risks, but these risks are
far less than would face us a few years from now if we dare not
be resolute today.[7]

A Vietminh victory in Indochina, Dulles held, would
result in Communist domination of all Asia. The "domino
principle" had been conceived. In a press conference a
week later, President Eisenhower gave explicit expression
to that concept, and warned of the "incalculable" consequences to the "free world" that would follow upon the
"loss" of Indochina.

The sounding of the tocsin did not arouse the "free
world." Dulles did not succeed in mobilizing "united"

[7] *New York Times,* March 30, 1954.

military intervention to save the French in their extremity at Dienbienphu, and the Geneva settlement of 1954 brought the military withdrawal of the French, and peace to Indochina. The colony had been "lost"—to the Vietnamese, Laotians, and Cambodians. Nevertheless, the American grand strategy aimed at the containment of Asian revolution by the erection of military ramparts had been consolidated, and governmental institutions developed accordingly. The "national security" bureaucracy was expanded, and became further entrenched. "Contingency planning," which customarily envisages the theoretically worst possible eventuality, was now taking precedence over analyses looking to simple probabilities. A weakening diplomacy languished; military judgments had priority.

In the American political arena, a parallel development contributed substantially toward the freezing of our Asia policy in the mold of a barren anti-Communism; Congress was effectively mobilized and "committed" to the cause of the defeated Chinese Nationalists. The China Lobby had taken on structural form with the organization, in October 1953, of The Committee for One Million (one million signatures to keep "Red China" out of the United Nations). Some nine months later, the organization claimed the projected number of signatures, and became The Committee *of* One Million. Its small steering committee was made up of Members of Congress and former government officials. In the forefront of the moving spirits was Congressman Walter H. Judd, member of the House Foreign Affairs Commission—and ex-medical missionary to China—who zealously crusaded for the Nationalists. Ex-Communist Marvin Liebman became the Committee's very active secretary.

The Committee came to count among its supporters a large number of Members of Congress, including both Republicans and Democrats; the two parties had arrived at the same safe "anti-Communist" position on "The China Question." Thus the nation's China policy was ossified, and it continued unchanged for nearly two decades. The U.S. Congress constituted no forum for protesting the policy of enmity toward the People's Republic of China.

The Cold War mentality had corrupted the very nature of our foreign relationships. By the evidence, the Cold War strategists lacked a realistic appreciation of the hazards attendant upon a great power's becoming so intimately "committed" to the fortunes of third-rate countries that it is subject to manipulation in power struggles in violation of its own interests. Oddly enough, Washington implicitly extended official acceptance to the essence of Whittaker Chambers' idea (and it was Mao Tse-tung's idea as well) that there could be no middle ground between the revolutionary and counterrevolutionary positions. Dulles condemned neutralism in the postulated world struggle as "immoral." There were those who were prepared to be partisan; and in service of its Asia strategy in particular the United States was led to enter into numerous bilateral and multilateral military alliances. It already had agreements permitting it to maintain military bases in the Japanese home islands, South Korea, and the Philippines. In 1954, under Dulles' guidance, it constructed the Southeast Asia Treaty Organization (SEATO), thereby linking itself to seven more states (of which only two could be strictly considered to be in the Southeast Asian area), and then went on to sign a treaty of mutual assistance with the refugee Nationalist "Republic of China" on Taiwan.

Our Asian "commitments" now extended in a vast arc

reaching from South Korea to Thailand and Pakistan, embracing the eastern and southern frontiers of China. Given the particular power aims of various petty Asian autocrats with whom we aligned ourselves, some of our treaty engagements were predestined to become true "entangling alliances." The United States, which had rushed to the salvation of Syngman Rhee in 1950, in 1973—twenty years after the Korean War had ended—still had troops stationed in South Korea to uphold the oppressive rule of Park Chung Hee. Our opposition to the nationalistic (but Communist) Vietminh in the twilight of French colonial days in Indochina led us almost automatically to become an ally of Ngo Dinh Diem, who opposed everything basic in the American political tradition; we remain bound to the support of autocrat Nguyen Van Thieu still, with danger-laden longterm potential for the American destiny in Asia. And the treaty commitment to Chiang Kai-shek's refugee Nationalists froze the United States into a legal position in which it was effectively blocked from formal recognition of the new "People's Republic of China" until it might repudiate the "Republic of China" by painful denunciation of the 1954 alliance.

The United States now stood bound in many areas by both formal and informal "commitments" (the count was 42 in Dulles' day), often to calculating Asian autocrats who had quickly learned how to manipulate in service of their own power aims the visceral "anti-Communism" of American policy-makers. Under Dulles' guidance, the United States was avowedly ready to go to "the brink." And each new "crisis," such as the Sino-Indian border conflict of 1959, led the U.S. Government to consolidate and enlarge upon existing pledges, usually by "Executive agreement" without reference to the Congress, but upon occasion with that body's blank-check blessing, as was extended in the Formosa Strait resolution of 1955.

The United States, it was assumed, would remain pure of heart and clean of hands for all of its entering into liaisons with despots and wrestling in the mire with "the enemy." Nevertheless, the adoption of the principle that "the end justifies the means" in adversary relationships led all too naturally to the employment by the United States of means and tactics that it purported to abhor as authoritarian deviations from the rules of civilized international behavior. The normal procedures, and the usual institutions, for friendly intercourse between nations were subordinated in critical respects to the machinery and devices of espionage, subversion, deception, and violence. Military capability, rather than international law and the values of the principle of peaceful coexistence, came to govern. Where considerations of the "national security," no matter how fragile, might be involved, what "the world's greatest power" could do, it would do.

Thus it was that, shortly after the disastrous—and unprincipled—Bay of Pigs intervention in Cuba, the slipping of the Ngo Dinh Diem regime to the brink of collapse led to the Kennedy Administration's military intervention in South Vietnam. In the course of fighting its own colonial Indochina War, the United States evolved more rationalizations than the White Knight of *Alice in Wonderland* had inventions. By the one critical standard, law, they were all false. The American military intervention and aggression over the years from 1961 onward in Vietnam, Cambodia, and Laos were in violation of the 1928 Kellogg-Briand Pact of Paris, of the principles of international behavior established (largely by American initiative) in the Nuremburg trials of Nazi war criminals, and of its obligations under the UN Charter to avoid aggression and keep the peace.

In his Nobel Lecture of 1970, Alexander Solzhenitsyn made a profound observation: "Whoever has once announced violence as his METHOD must inevitably choose lying as his PRINCIPLE." The adoption of lawless means and the exercise of violence in pursuit of its power aims led the American Executive to resort consecutively to deviousness, deception, and blatant falsehood. A series of Republican and Democratic Administrations alike denied the bald facts of their recourse to illegal and violent methods, as with respect to the abortive U–2 spy-plane mission over the USSR in 1960, American participation in the Bay of Pigs operation in 1961, and the circumstances attending our military intervention in the Dominican Republic in 1965; and, as the *Pentagon Papers* establish beyond challenge, the U.S. Government from the beginning of the military intervention in Indochina deliberately engaged in gross falsehoods over the years, before both the world and the American nation.

It was typical of American misrepresentations that on April 30, 1970, after the United States had been secretly bombing Cambodia for a full year, President Nixon in announcing a decision to send ground forces into that unfortunate country should state that, given the provision in the 1954 Geneva Agreement for Cambodia's neutrality, "American policy since then has been to respect scrupulously the neutrality of the Cambodian people." If that statement was for public consumption, the truth had fared no better when Secretary of State William P. Rogers testified secretly before the Senate Foreign Relations Committee on April 2, 1970, that "Cambodia is one country where we can say with complete assurance that our hands are clean and our hearts are pure." As of that date, some 100,000 tons of American bombs had been dropped on the Cambodians.

By treaties signed and engagements solemnly undertaken, our Indochina War formally ended in January 1973 after eleven long years, and the bombing of luckless Cambodia was actually terminated by Congressional action the following August. That adventure in imperialism had turned out disastrously for the United States: its costs will long be counted. But one feature of the affair is noteworthy: there have been no charges by Congressional committees, political lobbyists, or the press that the nation was led into that tragically mistaken enterprise by career members of the U.S. Foreign Service. For it is entirely evident that, from 1953 to 1973, the China policy and our Asia policy were not by any stretch of the imagination to be viewed as the handiwork of career Asian experts; those policies were the creation of officials at the top of the governmental hierarchy charged with service of the "national security"—men who pursued, with a singular unreality, what they fancied to be *realpolitik*, which the United States was thought called upon to practice by reason of a manifest destiny. The Foreign Service, and the State Department too, were largely bypassed in the policy-making process.

Formulation of the nation's grand strategy had come to be concentrated almost exclusively at the top level of the Administration, where the Chairman of the Joint Chiefs of Staff, the Secretaries of Defense and of State, the President, and the President's appointed advisers, had their abode. That area of government was immune from the "security checks" being exercised so liberally against the career bureaucrats. It was also effectively barred from routine surveillance and criticism of the professional area experts. Those involved in the process were accountable only to the President, and his own accountability to the nation showed every sign of shrinking. Under such conditions, error was perpetuated and compounded. Duplicity received official sanction: the Government argued that it possessed the inherent right to lie for reasons of "national security"—a sanction that was elastic enough to cover a host of misrepresentations. "To confuse the enemy," deviousness and deception had been institutionalized in the field of foreign affairs—and at home. The result was inevitable: practicing deceit, our rulers became the victims of self-deception, and led the nation into gross error.

The President finally came to wage war, with the advice and consent of the Pentagon, and of the Secretary of State as a captive of the National Security Council, as a virtual oligarch. The U.S. Constitution still provided, for those who would read, that the right to declare war resides with the Congress; in fact, Presidents Kennedy, Johnson, and Nixon all waged war without more than passing reference (usually, with respect to the military budget) to Congress, and over the years the trend toward an oligarchical administration of foreign affairs was measurably strengthened.

There was little outward evidence of dissent within the U.S. Government, *at any level,* to either the nation's Asia policy in general, the China policy of 1953–71, or the Indochina War. As regards the war, there was naturally some recurrent Congressional restlessness, but remarkably little perceptible dissent within the Executive branch. The hierarchical "loyalty" demanded variously by Hurley and Dulles had been firmly installed; there was usually uncritical loyalty even to the most flagrant error. A James Reston column of March 1969 in *The New York Times* testified to the existence of an intellectual malaise with respect to the Vietnam War on the part of some who had served under President Johnson. He remarked that there were many high officials in the Administration—and he named some of them—who disagreed with President Johnson on his Vietnam policy, but that despite their opposition to the war they "didn't quite speak their minds to the President, let alone to the public." They gave their loyalty to the President, said Reston, rather than to their country, and some "are now wondering in private life whether this was in the national interest," and were troubled.[8]

Quite apart from the occasional moves to correct the malfunctioning loyalty-security system, there had been periodical efforts since shortly after the end of World War II to make the State Department into a more "effective" organ, and in its first term the Nixon Administration likewise made fitful efforts nominally directed toward rejuvenation of the Department and of the Foreign Service. The new Secretary of State, William P. Rogers, in a speech of January 22, 1969 (sixteen years after John Foster Dulles had demanded "positive loyalty" to established policies), said that "I hope to lead a receptive and open establishment, where men speak their minds and are listened to on merit, and where divergent views are fully and promptly

[8] "The Doubts and Regrets of the Johnson Dissenters," *New York Times*, March 9, 1969.

passed on for decision." The omens seemed encouraging. In May, Rogers designated Under Secretary Elliot L. Richardson to be chairman of the somnolent Board of the Foreign Service, and Richardson promised that the views of the so-called Young Turks of the American Foreign Service Association, which had long been urging modernization upon the Department, would be given consideration in the "major and comprehensive review" that was projected.

In due course, thirteen task forces under the overall direction of Deputy Under Secretary of State William B. Macomber addressed themselves to the matter at hand, and in December 1970 the State Department published the fruits of their labors, a 600-page report entitled "Diplomacy for the Seventies." Over 500 reforms were proposed, but the general concept was that there should be created "a new breed of diplomat-manager" to function in a bureaucratic environment envisaging in main (1) greater creativity, and receptivity to fresh ideas; (2) more flexible personnel policies; and (3) improved administration of the departmental and national foreign-policy resources.

However, the report itself cited previous reform proposals that were "still largely unacted on"—those of the Hoover Commission (1949), the Wriston Commission (1954), the Herter Committee (1962), and the American Foreign Service Association (1968)—and remarked in passing that one of the Department's principal weaknesses had been its failure to overcome "strong pressures toward conformity" that had "dulled the creative impulse" and brought addiction to the continuity of outdated policies. The task force concerned with creativity remarked:

If the decisionmaker is to escape from entanglement in outmoded policies, or avoid entanglement in new but erroneous ones, he must have creative subordinates operating in an environment which encourages creativity. No Secretary of State has understood this more clearly than Dean Acheson. "The springs of policy" he has written, "bubble up; they do not trickle down."

And there was the warning: "An organization which cannot equip itself to adapt to change will increasingly find its role being preempted by others. This has been the bitter experience of the Department of State in the last two decades."

In considering barriers to creativity, that task force had something pertinent to say under the euphemistic heading "Outside Factors":

If the lackluster performance of the Department of State and the Foreign Service as creative institutions was in part their own fault, some of the blame can be placed on outside factors, particularly the security investigations of the fifties. The national pillorying of Foreign Service officers for unorthodox views has been the single most important inhibitor of creativity in the Department during the past 25 years. The loyalty investigations were products of their time and a body politic that was frightened, defensive, and concerned by Soviet postwar advances. What the Department, bound by the constraints of the midfifties, could have done to reverse the trend will long be a subject of debate. But urgings of "positive loyalty" and failure to defend officers against the attacks of Senator McCarthy created pressures for conformity that were to stay with the Department for years. . . .

Changes in both personnel and public climate during the 1960's have softened the effect of McCarthyism on Departmental thinking. Some of the bitter taste lingers on, however, and still inhibits to some degree the expression of unorthodox views.[9]

[9] *Diplomacy for the 70's, A Program of Management Reform for the Department of State.* Department of State Publication 8551, Department and Foreign Service Series 143 (Washington, December 1970), pp. 302, 303, 306–7.

The direct relationship between the demand for ideological orthodoxy and the State Department's sterility thus was recognized once more—nearly a quarter century after the government had instituted a loyalty-security program that penalized the country's professional diplomats for unorthodox—or unwelcome—views.

Doubtless some of the 500-odd recommendations of the Macomber group were acted upon. However, political forces making for a *fundamental* enhancement of the State Department's position in the governmental structure were absent, whereas forces tending to vitiate the Department and the Foreign Service remained in being, and were active. In May 1970, over 250 State Department and Foreign Service officers had sent a joint letter to Secretary of State Rogers protesting against the American invasion of Cambodia; the fifty Foreign Service officers associated with the action were warned by Under Secretary of State U. Alexis Johnson that, while in the diplomatic service, they were called upon to support the President and his Administration. This was a clear reaffirmation of the Dulles dictum. And the methods of enforcing the "loyalty" rules provided no respect for the ego. In September 1971 Attorney General John N. Mitchell directed the FBI to question State Department officials in connection with leaks to the press—and Secretary Rogers in a press conference did not deny reports that the FBI agents had subjected officials to lie-detector tests. In November, the Department instructed chiefs of mission and other principal diplomatic officers overseas that thereafter expressions of dissent within the Service should be restricted to official State Department channels. And in 1973 it would become known that, on President Nixon's authority, the telephones of three high-ranking State Department officials had been tapped. (Regular denizens of State must have been surprised that the number had been limited to three.) No one was trusted—not in the State Department.

The hard, inescapable fact was that the top-level policy-making functions in the field of foreign affairs had been concentrated in the White House, with Dr. Henry A. Kissinger in prime charge and the N.S.C. exercising a critical influence—as at the height of the Cold War. In 1971–72, there were major developments in the relations of the United States with Japan, the People's Republic of China, the Soviet Union, *and* Indochina; and it was manifest that the State Department had had very little to say with respect to any one of the matters. In December 1972, as Mr. Nixon's second term loomed up ahead, the White House again let it be known that the President desired to "vitalize" the State Department and the Foreign Service. But the policy-making and decision-making authority still quite evidently remained concentrated in the White House itself. For all of the exhortations to Department and Foreign Service personnel that they should take the initiative, and be fecund of thought, the explicit positions of the Secretary and the political appointees immediately under him were antipathetic to anything that smacked of dissent from the Chief Executive's line. Kissinger's succession to Rogers as Secretary of State in September 1973 could not logically be expected to work fundamental institutional change and bring about revitalization of the State Department bureaucracy. Something more was needed.

At the end of the road taken by the oligarchs lay the complex of antidemocratic procedures and actions encompassed by the generic term "Watergate." That malodorous

Watergate Hotel, Washington, D.C., the scene of an "unofficial" visit of June 1972

affair was a logical end of the process that began a quarter century earlier, when public servants were put on the dock for straightforward reporting and honest estimates, and their careers wrecked, in the service of calculated demagoguery and political chicanery. When the reporting of revolutionary achievement renders the reporter suspect of being a "security risk," when disagreement in political judgments is taken as tantamount to disloyalty, and when there is adopted the working principle that the end justifies any means within *or beyond* the law, institutions based upon democratic concepts are threatened with destruction.

"We become what we hate." The adoption of totalitarian methods against hated foreign "adversaries" led inexorably to the use of unlawful means against "enemies" in the domestic field. It took time, but the anti-Communist, anti-enemy, anti-"adversary" paranoia that infected the Government's decision-making process in domestic affairs from 1947 onward reached its logical outcome during the Nixon Administration. In the beginning, in the 1950s, the Executive branch and Congressional committees prospected for "traitors" and "security risks" among the country's China experts, but by Nixon's time the Executive branch had come to suspect that dissidents, the disloyal, and "enemies," were everywhere, among the citizenry as well as in government.

The FBI, the CIA, and the U.S. Army spread a web of surveillance over war protesters, radical students, political figures, and a variety of other people. As it warred against revolution abroad, the Government deployed against dissent at home the instrumentalities of counterinsurgency—subversion, sabotage, "black propaganda," and *agents pro-*

vocateurs. "Dirty tricks" pervaded the Watergate period. To qualify for the Administration's "enemies list," or at least for one of the intelligence community's extensive dossiers, one had only to differ politically. There was to be recalled Sidney Hook's comment in his own review of Chambers' *Witness:* "When heresy is identified with the enemy, we shall have seen the end of democracy." [10]

Disregard of Constitutional safeguards had finally become commonplace. From 1969 onward the Nixon machine undertook to effectively destroy political opponents by recourse to illegal methods that could only be described as authoritarian. The Watergate affair thus came as the natural end-result of the long chain of events that had begun with the embarking upon the Cold War, the unprincipled attacks on the State Department and the Foreign Service for the "loss of China," the abandonment of accepted principle and law, and the embracing of the ways of the "enemy" totalitarianism. There had been a pronounced thrust toward the establishment of oligarchical rule—all in the name of "national security."

But in 1973 the United States manifestly enjoyed less genuine national security than it had twenty-five years before. Coincident with, and partly as a consequence of, the institutional deterioration, the country's foreign relations had gone into a steep decline; its chosen strategy and tactics had borne bitter fruits, and the American world position, in terms of prestige and political influence, had been seriously weakened. The United States had succeeded in becoming a *military* power that could destroy the world; but it had failed lamentably in the political field, in which

[10] Sidney Hook, "The Faiths of Whittaker Chambers," *The New York Times Book Review*, May 25, 1952, pp. 1 et seq.

diplomats function; there it had plunged so deeply into error that it had not only been forced to cede contests to "enemies," but it had alienated friends and allies.

Fulfillment of the human destiny requires, in the present era, a convergence of political and economic structures based upon the realization that the fate of one sector of mankind promises to be the fate of all; the parts are inextricably linked, for good or ill. To give expression to that commonality, it is requisite that there be added emphasis on international morality, world law and supranational organization, and generous measures of economic equity and collaboration. In those circumstances, proper service of national security could come only through intelligent diplomacy and a large measure of economic collaboration in a world facing both rising nationalism and depletion of essential industrial raw materials. The United States thought to substitute military power for adept diplomacy against international rivals, and finally came to place "allies" as well as "enemies" in the "adversary" category, in the political and economic arenas if not in the military field. We were left with few friends.

The staggering cost of strategic error is seen with striking clarity in Asia. There, counting from Pearl Harbor Day, the United States fought its own Thirty Years War. That prolonged belligerency included the Pacific War, the Korean War, support for the French Indochina War, two Formosa Strait "crises," and finally our own Indochina War, with its tremendous cost for our economy and society—and the even greater cost for Indochina. In the end, it is discovered that the Communist regime in China, far from having "passed" as envisaged by John Foster Dulles, now entertains President Nixon's emissaries in Peking;

that the Soviet Union, far from being "contained," has substantially improved its relative power position during the
decades when the United States was squandering its resources in the vain effort to hold back, Canute-like, the rising tides of Asian revolution; and that, in fact, the United
States has actually advanced the cause of revolution in
Southeast Asia by contributing directly to a vast increase
of popular misery. As far as American influence is concerned, the dominoes are already falling in Asia. The magnitude of the disaster attending our Asia policy exceeds
anything that a conspiratorial band of Communist
underground agents, whether like Whittaker Chambers
and the other ex-Communists who enthralled Congressional committees in the 1950s or Moscow's or Peking's
best, could have hoped in their wildest dreams to achieve.

In the very week that Richard M. Nixon was elected to
his first term as President, there appeared an article by
Henry Steele Commager in which the historian observed
that the United States had "embraced an ideological approach to the great problems of international politics and
sought to imprison in ideological straightjacket the turbu-
lent tides of history." [11] We have failed to imprison history. By the combined efforts of demagogues, hag-ridden
Cold Warriors, and an Executive become oligarchical, the
United States Government truly got itself into an ideological straightjacket; and the nation that Henry R. Luce
would have had dominate the world in an "American Century" was brought to the brink of disaster, with imperium
lost. The security-obsessed simplifiers in American society
turned out to be the true "security risks" of our times.

[11] Henry Steele Commager, "1918–1968: Is the World Safer for Anything?" *Saturday Review*, Nov. 9, 1968, pp. 21–24.

Selected Bibliography

Andrews, Bert. *Washington Witch Hunt*. Toronto: Random House, 1948.

Biddle, Francis. *The Fear of Freedom*. With Introduction by Harold L. Ickes. Garden City: Doubleday & Co., 1951.

Bontecou, Eleanor. *The Federal Loyalty-Security Program*. Ithaca: Cornell University Press, 1953.

Chambers, Whittaker. *Witness*. New York: Random House, 1952.

Freeland, Richard M. *The Truman Doctrine and the Origins of McCarthyism. Foreign Policy, Domestic Politics, and Internal Security, 1946–1948*. New York: Alfred A. Knopf, 1972.

Jowitt, William Allen, 1st Earl. *The Strange Case of Alger Hiss*. London: Hodder and Stoughton, 1953.

Koen, Ross Y. *The China Lobby in American Politics*. Edited and with an Introduction by Richard C. Kagan. New York: Harper and Row, 1974.

Latham, Earl. *The Communist Controversy in Washington, From the New Deal to McCarthy*. Cambridge: Harvard University Press, 1966.

McWilliams, Carey. *Witch Hunt, The Revival of Heresy*. Boston: Little, Brown and Co., 1950.

Orwell, George. *Nineteen Eighty-Four*. New York: Harcourt Brace, 1949.

Rorty, James, and Moshe Decter. *McCarthy and the Communists*. Boston: Beacon Press, 1954.

Zeligs, Meyer A., M.D. *Friendship and Fratricide: An Analysis of Whittaker Chambers and Alger Hiss*. New York: Viking Press, 1967.

Index